Robert Pickus, Pacifist Warrior

Robert Pickus, Pacifist Warrior

Advocate of Representative Democracy, Developer of a Strategy of Peace

Robert Woito

Hamilton Books

Lanham • Boulder • New York • Toronto • London

Published by Hamilton Books
An imprint of The Rowman & Littlefield Publishing Group, Inc.
4501 Forbes Boulevard, Suite 200, Lanham, Maryland 20706
Hamilton Books Acquisitions Department (301) 459-3366

6 Tinworth Street, London SE11 5AL, United Kingdom

British Library Cataloguing in Publication Information Available

Library of Congress Control Number: 2020945511

ISBN 978-0-7618-7194-1 (pbk.)
ISBN 978-0-7618-7195-8 (electronic)

Dedicated to the memory of Robert Pickus (1923–2016)

Robert Pickus challenged us all to create a peace movement "worthy of the name," capable of turning this country's engagement in world politics toward achieving "the conditions essential to a world without war."

Contents

Preface

I believe Robert Pickus was not only a critic of some self-defined peace and justice movements in American and world politics but offered a defense of representative democracy in domestic politics and nonmilitary strategies to challenge and change military adversaries of the United States and its allies in world politics. The full documentation of Robert Pickus's career is available at the Hoover Institution "in perpetuity," which Hoover promised when they sought the archival record. It contains alternatives to war at the individual, societal and governmental decision-making levels.

I was assigned the task by Pick (as he was universally known) of ordering the archives and submitting them to Hoover. I did so from 2005 to 2013 with others' help: providing indexes, a conceptually ordered framework, as well as an Overview document listing colleagues, all publications and the start and end dates of different organizations as well as program and chronological files. The latter are divided into: 1) Organization, 2) Perspective, 3) Programs with specific dates and places, and 4) Research. There are nearly 500 boxes of materials at Hoover documenting Robert Pickus's and the national and Northern California regional offices' work. The Seattle regional office archives are both at the University of Washington and Hoover. The Chicago regional office archives are at the Swarthmore Peace Collection as are those of Turn Toward Peace and the Center for War/Peace Studies. The James Madison Foundation archives are at the Hoover Institution and George Weigel's papers at the Library of Congress. This work has been provided to each depository. George Weigel became the Council's primary national spokesperson with the continuous publication of *American Purpose* (1987–1996), 76 issues in all, and is available at each depository. After decades of working regionally, the Council's voice became available inside the Beltway through *American Purpose*'s commentary on the war, peace, and security agenda as focused by public policy questions before decision-makers in Washington, DC.

I understand that my own reputation and career with the Council are at stake in revisiting Robert Pickus's sense of mission and steady work. I began work with Turn Toward Peace in 1964. I am a coauthor of *To End War*, updating the book with Tim Zimmer in 1975, and as my own in 1982 (Pilgrim Press) and revising it into *Extending the Democratic Peace* in 2003. I revived the Council publications program in the 1960s, publishing Vietnam Peace Proposals, the first two editions of *To End War*, and the Modern Classics of Peace series (Camus, Gandhi, Clark, and Sohn). I also published Allan Blackman's *Face to Face With Your Draft Board*; T. K. Mahedvan (ed.), *Gandhi, His Relevance for Our Times*; Lucy Dougall's *War/Peace Film Guide* and her *War and Peace in Literature*; Anne Stadler et al., *World Without War Game*; Gene Sharp, *The Abolition of War*; and Lincoln Bloomfield's retitled *The Power to Keep Peace*.

I have been helped in national Council endeavors by many people in addition to Robert Pickus and George Weigel. Among them are: Allan Blackman, Lucy Dougall, Lowell Livezey, Holt Ruffin, Nancy Starr, and Kale Williams. This report has benefited from comments by Allan Blackman, Eric Blantz, Sr. Marion Cotty, and Philip Siegelman. Walter Naegle has edited the entire manuscript. Sister Marion Cotty has edited and provided encouragement. Holt Ruffin improved the manuscript in many ways. Andrea Murray orchestrated the end game masterfully. I am grateful for all the help I have received. All errors of fact and interpretation are mine alone.

Robert Woito
Madison, WI
2020

Editors note:

Regrettably, Robert Woito passed away shortly before this book went to press. We, his daughters, would like to thank the many wonderful World Without War Council colleagues who supported Dad throughout this project, and for their many kind words upon his passing.

Andrea Woito Murray and Katrina Severin

Chapter One

Developing a Sense of Mission

INTRODUCTION

Robert Pickus (1923–2016) worked from 1951 to 2016 as a leader of peace organizations seeking "a disarmed world under law, safe for free societies."[1] He worked intelligently and with intensity. In mid-career (1985) he asserted that there were two national organizations with a capacity to provide an overview of the world affairs field and improve competencies within it: the Carnegie Endowment for International Peace and the World Without War Council. The former focused on elite decision-makers, ultimately those in government, had 150 paid staff in Washington, an endowment, a magazine (*Foreign Policy*), a funded publications program, and public visibility. The World Without War Council had no one paid entry level wages, no funds on the first to meet obligations on the 30th, did not have a presence in Washington the first 30 years and (Robert Pickus) explained the lack by saying the country is like a cash register in that the transaction takes place elsewhere but is rung-up in Washington. The details of his consultancies, programs, regional associates, publications, and colleagues in other organizations explains how possibly his case might be plausible.[2]

Robert Pickus's career was rooted at the juncture where the pacifist and just war traditions met in developing and advocating alternatives to war.[3] He was profoundly influenced by his roots in Judaism and became acutely aware of the risks of pacifist thinking made personal by his life-long friendships with Midge Dexter, Max Kampelman, Norman Podhoretz, Philip Siegelman, Al Vorspan, Hugh Schwartzberg, and other leaders in the Jewish community.[4] But he believed the organized mass violence of war could be made illegitimate and unnecessary based on a nonviolent strategy of peace that would successfully replace war's legitimate functions. His appreciation of pacifist witness was mixed, fearing "that some forms are so confused they are worse than lies."[5] He added:

> In the shadow of Hiroshima, we had in America a clear goal and a moral commitment to sustain it. The goal was to end war. The moral commitment was the refusal to legitimize murder. "Not" as Camus put it "a world where murder no longer exists (we are not so crazy as that!), but rather one in which it is no longer legitimate."[6]

War would become illegitimate if a "rightly ordered world community"[7] was brought into being through leadership by one country that gained the cooperation of allies and the reciprocation of adversaries. "By definition," he insisted, a movement to end war "must concern itself with the use of military power by all states and political movements."[8] A peace movement worthy of the name could turn a great power to the task:

> We live in a country distinguished from many others by its wealth, size, diversity, technological capability, and, most of all, by the ideas that formed it. The idea that the people shall rule because of the innate dignity of every person has been progressively realized in our experience of building and sustaining our political community. Such a political community must address the problem of war. Such a country has a significant, perhaps the key, role to play in progress toward peace.[9]

He defended the institutions and understandings that constitute representative democracy, acknowledging that the gap between the ideals and the realities existed and work to close that gap is needed but neither creating parallel institutions nor preaching alienation is helpful. He believed that civil disobedience could be justified as an aid to democratic decision-making but rejected insurrectionary violence and revolutionary posturing.[10] He also believed that by addressing all coherent points on the political spectrum, and responding to each perspective's criticism, a democratic consensus could be formed. A reformulated consensus was needed before a democratic great power could act. The new perspective was potentially better because it had listened to, responded to and incorporated elements of truth from the others.[11]

As an undergraduate, Robert Pickus worked with Mortimer Adler and University of Chicago President Robert Maynard Hutchins's great books program. The War and Peace selection in the Great Books of the Western World (1952) summarized 2,500 years of Western thought on war and peace with over 1,500 citations and was prefaced with this claim: "the twentieth century may go down in history as the century of war and peace—the first in which world wars were fought, the first in which men [and women] established world peace . . . "[12] Robert Pickus's most audacious claim was that the conditions essential to a world without war were known, and further, that "A stable peace [is] possible within 40 years." He repaired to safer ground with the recognition that "the problem is how to bring them into being." He would state the conditions and describe how to get there in 1961.

It was Robert Pickus's mission in life to establish world peace based on world political institutions hinted at in the *Atlantic Charter* (1941), the United Nations Charter (1945), Robert Maynard Hutchins's et al. *A Constitution for the World* (1948), and Grenville Clark and Louis Sohn's *World Peace Through World Law* (1948). The Model World Orders Project of the Institute for World Order (1961–present) was an attempt to develop African, Latin American, Middle Eastern, and Asian models possibly in preparation for a World Constitutional Convention to which Robert Pickus ran as a delegate in 1968.

DEFINING THE MISSION: THE FIRST 35 YEARS

Robert Pickus was born Sidney Robert Pickus on October 31, 1923, in Sioux City, Iowa. He was the fourth child of Nathan and Annalece Pickus, emigrants from Gomel, Belarus, in 1905 and 1906. His brothers Morrie (1901–1995) and Louie (1903–1995) emigrated one year after Nathan with their mother. Iowa was chosen over London and Palestine (which Nathan visited in 1904) because a brother, Joe, lived there. Dorothy was born in Sioux City, Iowa, in 1907 (d. 1986). Nathan Pikus (Russian spelling) was a "steerage class alien" passenger arriving at Ellis Island from Liverpool. His first occupation was as a tinker selling dry goods in rural Iowa out of the back of a horse drawn wagon. He soon rented a store then built a brick one in Sioux City. The family moved to Waukegan, Illinois, where Nathan and Louie started Pickus and Sons Construction Company in 1926. It was still a family owned business in 2011.

When Robert Pickus was 20 months old, his mother died. His sister dropped out of college to replace the mother he did not remember. To Dorothy, brother Sidney was always Bobby. In 1931 Dorothy married Fred Gordon and moved to Indianapolis and Nathan married Rose the same year. Robert Pickus lived with Rose and Nathan, but Nathan became ill soon after the second marriage and remained so until his death in 1936.[13] The 8–18 year-old period is described by Robert Pickus as contributing to his tendentiousness as his third overstressed mother dealt with her husband's ill health and a precocious young man. Rose did write letters to Robert while in the Army but Dorothy remained his mother figure.[14]

Robert Pickus had impressive academic credentials and experience on which to base a career in public life open to challenge by all comers. In high school he ran for a school office, joined a Jewish youth organization (Aleph

Zadik Aleph) and devoted part of his social energies to addressing racial discrimination, poverty and anti-Semitism. The family physician was African American. He was also focused on the problem of war. Even at Senn High School, Chicago he wrote an essay entitled "An End to War?" (1940) and won a Chicago Tribune essay contest explaining "Why I am proud to be an American."[15]

In September 1941 he entered Robert Hutchins's University of Chicago,[16] took courses with Quincy Wright (A Study of War) and Hans Morgenthau (Politics Among Nations), and was a research assistant to Mortimer Adler's Great Books of the Western World program. Robert Pickus's classmates left to go to war in 1942 but wrote over 100 letters a year to Pickus. They have a tone of high seriousness, common dismissal of military discipline, and the expectation that they would do great things after the war as well as personal concerns. The scholars rejected World War II joining Winston Churchill in arguing that the war was unnecessary and could have been avoided if France and England had taken Churchill's advice to challenge Hitler and rearm early on. Robert Pickus's high school essay "An End to War?" made the case that the war could have been avoided if the democracies had united in the 1930s.

Pickus and his University of Chicago classmates debated whether the Soviet Union was led by an economic development scientist named Joseph Stalin, or by a totalitarian dictator who had murdered by state decree three million people in the Ukraine in one year (1933). Robert Pickus recommended Arthur Koestler's *Darkness at Noon* (1941)—an allegorical novel depicting the 1930s show trials in the Soviet Union in which old Bolsheviks justify their own execution since the science of history dictated that the Dictatorship of the Proletariat was necessary, scientific, and would achieve the classless society Marxists considered possible if not inevitable.[17]

Robert Pickus enlisted in the Army in 1942 and was called to active duty in April 1943. He both enjoyed the preparation of thousands of men for great deeds, and resented the mendacity of military discipline. He found ways to humiliate a sergeant after the sergeant made racist comments during a race riot near Camp Maxey, Texas, where Robert Pickus did basic training. He received stern warnings from his brother Morrie to accept military discipline and to recognize that millions of Jewish lives in Europe were in jeopardy.[18] Robert Pickus learned Swedish and Scandinavian Culture at the University of Minnesota in the Army's Special Training Program for which he also got college credit.[19] He reflected in 1944 in Minneapolis that "It hurts to be on the winning side when you know the stupidity of the basis for winning the game and when you know the pain involved for the losers."[20] He experienced the devastation of war in London and the disillusionment of refugees in Stockholm. He gave lectures in Swedish to Cooperative and Labor Organizations while on active duty in Sweden. Whatever intelligence assignments he undertook for the Office of Strategic Services (OSS), there is no reference in his letters despite family requests. He did not experience the noise, the smell, and a life expectancy in seconds on Omaha Beach where the waves of disciplined soldiers kept coming. He concluded that "you go where war takes you"[21] which included the fire-bombing of Dresden and other German cities and the first use of nuclear weapons at Hiroshima and Nagasaki.

After the war he returned to the University of Chicago. He summarized his year succinctly: "Returned to U. of C. Jan. '46. Received 4 year B.A. in Political Science Dec.'46. Honor scholar in the College; Phi Beta Kappa on graduation. Research assistant on Encyclopedia Britannica Great Books Index project."[22]

He also subscribed to a little magazine *Pacifica* published in California which he confided was influential in forming his pacifist convictions in 1945–1947. University of Chicago President, Robert Hutchins and others published *A Constitution for the World* (1948)[23] but Robert Pickus was drawn to labor politics by his University of Chicago friends, David Brazelon and Bill Dodd.[24] During the war Robert Pickus requested that Dodd set up a filing system on labor, labor politics, and nuts and bolts with four pages of instructions on both the Congress of Industrial Organizations (CIO) and United Automobile Workers (UAW).[25]

This came to fruition in his first career as an urban cooperative organizer sponsored by the UAW (1947–1949). In 1949–1950 he did independent study with Harold Laski and Karl Popper at the London School of Economics as a Fulbright Fellow. He noted in his journal that he preferred the intellectual atmosphere of the University of Chicago.[26] Then he traveled for a year "without a companion or money." During his travel year he wrote in Paris "A Dialogue on War" between a believer in Hans Morgenthau's six principles of national interest diplomacy as stated in *Politics Among Nations,* and a voice that saw this as a truce between wars, next time with nuclear weapons. He visited France, Italy, Israel, Pakistan, Iran, and India. He wrote cautiously glowing reports of the Kibbutz movement in Israel, based on the voluntary cooperation of men and women in a common enterprise whose purpose was both spiritual and material. He traveled from there to Tehran, Iran where he witnessed the 10 of Moukarran 1370 (Muslim calendar) religious expression which he described as:

> A few days ago the processions of flagellants began—great crowds of men bearing red and green banners that surge down the streets chanting and beating themselves with steel rods and since then the air has grown more and more charged. The peak ceremonies of truly sadistic frenzy are due today.[27]

Within 20 days he had written a four-page proposal for a reverse Fulbright program to bring Iranians to the United States.[28] He visited Quaker Centre in New Delhi, sharing his Dialogue on War with Charles Freeman and began his interest in the potentially reconciling means of conducting conflict via Gandhi's satyagraha.[29]

He was well prepared in 1951 to begin work with the American Friends Service Committee. He could probably have passed the Department of State's (DOS) entrance examination while criticizing the DOS's lack of knowledge of the Great Book's section on war and peace. He defined his mission as educating the society to change government's direction, not, himself, becoming Secretary of Defense.

Robert Pickus married his classmate from the London School of Economics, Sara Greenberg, on April 20, 1952. Sara was also a principled actor applying truth to power by refusing to sign a loyalty oath in 1951 affirming the intellectual integrity and primacy of conscience against State intrusion at the price of not being paid.[30] They had two children, Joshua Wolfe Rambam Pickus (1961) and Noah Max Jedidiah Pickus (1964). Pick and Sara had four grandchildren as of 2011.

SPEAKING TRUTH TO POWER

A Pacifist Base: The American Friends Service Committee 1955–1956

Robert Pickus began his 60-year career in 1951 working for the Quaker pacifist organization, the American Friends Service Committee. His now personal commitment to pacifism remained steadfast. The goals in world politics he sought—world law, sustained by a sense of world community, disarmament security strategies, world economic development, and the advance of international human rights—were to be pursued by nonviolent means. He was clear both in his pacifist conviction and his concern not to give a military advantage to an adversary.

Pickus's first program assignment with the AFSC created the first challenge. The AFSC had produced a film *A Time for Greatness* for use in peace advocacy, a critique of American militarism during the Korean War. In a memo to Steve Cary, Clerk of the Philadelphia Meeting, Robert Pickus, the AFSC Peace Secretary in Chicago, offered three major comments:

> First, [*A Time for Greatness*] criticisms of American militarism without a countervailing analysis of Soviet policy results in a distorted picture of the present crisis and leaves the AFSC open to exploitation by Stalinist groups seeking to use the film to advance their own political objectives.
> Second, its presentation of negotiation as "the other answer," with only a passing nod in the direction of the other 3 points in "Steps to Peace," vitiates the effective buildup of the first half of the film. The average, thoughtful audience is pounding its fist on the table halfway through the film, asking belligerently, All right, but what's your alternative program! Our answer,

"negotiate" [is important] but just not adequate in itself and does not speak to
the American (or the Soviet) condition.

Third, the 4 points in "Step to Peace" come closer, but, there too, the essential
question we must speak to is not met. Good will, the attempt to negotiate,
[President Truman's] Point Four program, the UN, etc. are all good political
points but, fundamentally, the argument comes down to one central question:
what methods, other than those of violence and war, are available to meet that
which seems to us evil? This question is not adequately treated. [31]

Steve Cary's response to these criticisms was to form a working party to
develop a Quaker alternative to violence in international conflict. Cary wrote
the first draft but incorporated changes from the working party, which included Robert Gilmore, Robert Pickus, and Bayard Rustin. [32] They produced
an 87-page pamphlet entitled *Speak Truth to Power: A Quaker Search for an
Alternative to Violence*. Both Robert Hutchins and Hans Morgenthau provided promotional blurbs. Robert Pickus was asked to summarize its truths in
a symposium published by *The Progressive* magazine, October 1955. Robert
Pickus's summary begins:

> The truth in *Speak Truth to Power* (hereafter STTP) is an ancient one: that love
> endures and overcomes; that hatred destroys; that the duty of a human being is
> to diminish hatred and promote love. But the study deliberately avoids focus-
> ing on a prophetic exposition of the pacifist position. It attempts not to preach
> religious truth, but to show how it is possible and why it is reasonable to give
> practical expression to it in the great conflict that now divides the world.

STTP asks not to be judged as witness for an impossible ideal. Instead, it will
show "how it is possible" [not likely but possible] to apply pacifism to an
ideologically justified, great power conflict. Both the Soviet Union and the
United States were building weapons of mass destruction, both had nuclear
weapons and the means to deliver them to each other's territory.

STTP challenges the assumptions that (1) it is possible in the twentieth
century for military power to be applied rationally, and a constructive program for peace [to be] carried on simultaneously with a program for military
preparations; (2) Soviet Communism is the source of our problems and that
by achieving its disintegration or even its containment we would move toward a peaceful world; and (3) military power is the essential "realistic"
means of dealing with international problems.

STTP maintains that a military response to Communist expansion has
been ineffective, and is inconsistent with the principles for which the United
States stands, makes us less secure, and debases our moral standards. There
is wide recognition of the inadequacy of:

> . . . the American response to its world responsibilities, there is considerable
> agreement on the positive requirements for peace (e.g., disarmament, develop-

ing world organization, fundamental attacks on poverty, an end to colonialism), [but] we do not act on these constructive policies.

We do not act for two reasons. First, our military commitment—in its nature
an open-ended rather than a limited endeavor—renders us economically,
politically, psychologically, and spiritually unable to give effect to the policies that so many agree are necessary if peace is to be won. And second,
many Americans recognize the self-defeating nature of a reliance on violence
but still cling to it because they see no alternative.

The "Section on Alternatives" acknowledges that a nonviolent strategy of
peace is in development and quotes Gandhi on the incompatibility of democracy with organization for modern war. These moral truths support the idea
that unilateral disarmament is a practical objective and that at worst, organized nonviolent training and coordination could overcome even foreign occupation. Dramatic changes are possible in history, as in the treatment of
criminals and the mentally ill. The institution of slavery has been effectively
abolished, although many patterns of abuse continue.

Robert Pickus conceded that, "many cogent and important questions may
be raised with regard to the application of nonviolent methods in group or
international conflict." That is why the study had been circulated prior to
publication to Robert Hutchins, Erich Fromm, and Hans Morgenthau, among
others. Morgenthau thought the study "ought to be considered widely and
associated himself with the importance of the intellectual effort" but indicated that he was "not in agreement with all the practical conclusions." Hutchins's promotion blurb stated, "[It] merits the most serious public discussion."

Robert Pickus broke into national prominence with his summary of
STTP. The summary opened a symposium with responses by Norman Thomas, George F. Kennan, Dwight MacDonald, Karl Menninger and Reinhold
Niebuhr. With nuclear testing in the atmosphere, and brinkmanship threatening nuclear war, the AFSC's working party was eager for a cost/benefit risk
assessment of their proposals. Pickus's summary concluded: "[STTP]
presents . . . a fundamental indictment of American foreign policy and a
reasoned case for believing that military power in today's world is incompatible with freedom, incapable of providing security and ineffective in dealing
with evil." The critics were appreciative of the quality of the statement (and
echoed the criticism Pickus had himself offered within AFSC circles). But
some were devastating.[33] Among friends, the cogent criticisms were not
considered devastating, and Pickus initially sided with them. But over a six
year period, developed what he considered to be adequate responses.

Five Cogent Criticisms and Two Important Questions

Norman Thomas: First Achieve a Consensus

I cannot accept the basic contention of the pamphlet that a constructive program for peace cannot be carried on "simultaneously with a program for military defense." As [STTP] says "it is manifestly impossible for a democratic state to change its standard of values until a substantial number of its people first change theirs. The government of the United States could not now begin to practice peace in the revolutionary terms of this pamphlet, for there is not the substantial support among the American people that would be required to support it. So great a change in American foreign policy requires a consensus within American society so informed and committed as to make whoever is in power to act.

George F. Kennan: Soviet Intentions Are Clearly Stated

The Friends [Society of Friends] appear to believe that the Soviet American conflict came into existence in 1945, and that it was occasioned by mutual "suspicions." One gathers that they regard these suspicions as unwarranted . . . Soviet-American differences, in other words, were only the product of misunderstanding . . . Do the Friends hold that never do people hold intentions dangerous and really unacceptable to other people? It is not conceivable that there should sometimes exist genuine conflicts of power and interest—no less tragic for the fact that they are real and not imagined . . . But in the era of Lenin and Stalin this was not even seriously pretended. The Russian Communist of that earlier period never concealed their conviction that people like the authors of the Friends pamphlet, and their readers, and myself, were really very bad and undesirable people, from which no good can come. In their book we were incapable of being right or useful. Our strivings could bring only misfortune and suffering to others. We were, therefore, to be controlled, disarmed, and rendered helpless by whatever means were at hand and whenever real power was in the hands of right thinking Communists, this meant imprisonment or death. They were not only suspected of holding such views and intentions; they held them. They said so on innumerable occasions.

Dwight MacDonald: There Is No Strategy of Peace

First,[34] it fails to give a convincing answer to the question: what should the individual pacifist do, here and now? And second, connected with this, while pacifism is attractive to men of good will as a long-run proposition--that is, the day on which its general values were realized in the actual workings of society would be a glad one--it is not clear how we get from Here to There . . . some pacifists, including several of the authors, have acted as individuals, by refusing to pay income taxes because most of the money goes for war preparations, by refusing to cooperate in air-raid drills and getting themselves jailed in consequence, and so on. These actions don't seem to me politically significant,

but they are actions. This pamphlet doesn't mention them, nor does it suggest
any other actions.

Norman Thomas: Multilateral, Not Unilateral Disarmament

> But unless the American government can so act as to make World War III
> impossible or increasingly unlikely within the next few years, we are lost . . .
> unless disarmament is made universal.

Author's note: Much passion and mutual recriminations was occasioned by
the distinction between unilateral and general and complete disarmament.
Must the goal be the disarmament of all States or the more seemingly achievable disarmament of one State, the United States? Pickus above claimed
"military power is incompatible with freedom, incapable of providing security and ineffective in dealing with evil" and his first organization, Acts for
Peace, published Erich Fromm's "The Case for Unilateral Disarmament"
(1958). So why the change?

First, there was no consensus Strategy of Peace stated in *Speak Truth to
Power* and it took Pickus 30 years to complete Phase I of the initiatives
project with George Weigel's and other's critical help. Second, the strategy
counted on incremental steps which created trust based on verifiable inspection and legalistic enforcement under a strengthened sense of world community which itself could take another 30 to 100 years to develop. In retrospect,
Norman Thomas's claim that the process from Here to There could take as
long as 40 years is conservative given the need to build a consensus, develop
a nonmilitary strategy of peace, test it on crises to build credibility, resolve
specific issues like nuclear proliferation, and implement the transformative
strategy to change an "eliminator" adversary into a co-creator of a "disarmed
world, safe for free societies." These achievements were not possible in a "7
minutes to midnight" approach. Finally, an adversary might misread unilateral disarmament by an enemy as admission by that enemy of the justice of
being "liberated" on behalf of humankind. Pickus preferred unilateral initiatives in which the adversary's intention was clarified by their reciprocation,
not a liberating invasion. This still had an air of unreality to the 1,300 foreign
service officers with responsibility for national security and whose options
were limited by the military threats they must acknowledge.

Despite this, charges of "in coalition with the Pentagon" and "United
fronting with the enemy" filled the air and produced much bitterness. Pickus
never yielded to the intellectual hostility and moral outrage of those convinced they knew how to achieve a stable peace. He would after 1985 express the desire to "make haste slowly" and "in a journey of 1,000 miles, it is
important that the first steps be in the right direction" without giving up the
urgency to act now. He recognized a host of people and organizations whose

act of sacrificial love on behalf of a sense of world community thereby help achieve it.

Dwight Macdonald: Representative Democracies Are Handicapped

> An[35] electorate of fifty million cannot decide anything: it cannot debate, argue. or consider: it can only react to grossly simplified and dramatized slogans . . . .[STTP] says . . . that the Communists are no worse than we are (or were), that unilateral disarmament by a pacifist America plus other policies that would naturally flow from such a radical change over here, would touch the hearts of the Communist peoples and force their leaders to reply with similar good will, and that, even if this falls, a pacifist America could make it impossible by nonviolent resistance, for the Soviets to subjugate us by force.[36]
> I disagree on all three points.

Reinhold Niebuhr and Karl Menninger also participated in the Progressive Symposium, but rejected the premise of STTP. Niebuhr insisted: "Force remains legitimate in the arsenal of power and justice; it is not a problem that can be solved." And according to Menninger, "Hate is the enemy; love is the answer."

SAFETY THE TWIN BROTHER OF ANNIHILATION?

The Progressive symposium concludes with Cary and Pickus responding that the critics have not addressed their argument, that the war system, not Communism is the enemy and participation in it is self-defeating. It concedes that, "A major examination of the possible limitations of the applicability of Gandhi's method is needed" but points out that 18 Russian soldiers were court martialed for refusing to fire on nonviolent German strikers. They conclude by reasserting that a person can say no.[37] The power of love combined with acts that embodied it could elicit the response Gandhi had achieved and the critics had not done the risk/benefit analysis.[38] [39]

We have argued here in terms of "time," yet confess a prior attachment to "eternity," to those experiences of the spirit which are primary. We have tried to be intelligent. Intelligence is not enough. When a society reaches the kind of impasse in which ours finds itself today—when it talks about "safety as the twin brother of annihilation" and would betrays its values in order to promote them—salvation is not gained by more calculation of expedience, but by rebirth.[40]

Pickus's response was to return to the University of Chicago and apply for a Ford Foundation fellowship to enable him to study the impact of Gandhi's thought on American civil rights and pacifist leaders and how to transpose satyagraha from domestic to world politics, from producing nonviolent

change within nation-states, to conducting nonviolent conflict between nation-states. His career was his dissertation, answering the "Cogent and Important Questions."

A PRIDE OF PACIFIST LIONS, THE WAR RESISTERS
LEAGUE, 1955–1957

In 1955–1956 most of the leading pacifists in the US gathered at the War
Resisters League, 5 Beekman Street, in New York. The nominating list for
the Board is a who's who of American Pacifists including David Dellinger,
Barbara Deming, Ralph DiGia, Alfred Hassler, David McReynolds, A. J.
Muste, Robert Pickus, Bayard Rustin, Gene Sharp, and Oliver Stone.[41]

Alfred Hassler, Robert Pickus, Bayard Rustin, and Gene Sharp remained
committed to the institutions and understandings that constitute representative democracy. David Dellinger and Barbara Deming were the dominant
voices seeking to humanize the revolution they thought inevitable.[42]

Barbara Deming, an advocate of nonviolent revolution, would broaden
the feminist currents that gained traction in the 1960s.[43] David Dellinger
became editor of Liberation magazine and would gain fame in the late sixties
as one of "the Chicago Seven."[44]

Robert Pickus, Bayard Rustin, and Gene Sharp's vocational commitment
includes the understanding that representative democracies have vital, important, nonviolent conflict resolution institutions to work through. They were
committed to civil disobedience as an aid when conscience is impinged by
policy but rejected insurrectionary violence.[45] Pickus, alone among these
pacifist lions, would devote his career to developing a strategy of peace
capable of being adopted by a government and designed to enable that
government to conduct interstate conflict without the organized mass violence of war. It was not intended to avoid conflict or deny its importance, or
to resist an occupier's will or surrender to an adversary, but to conduct
conflict between states without violence. He would call it "a developed peace
strategy."[46]

Robert Pickus wrote a memo to the Pride of Lions gathered at the War
Resisters League seeking to establish a West Coast office.[47] In response to
the cogent criticisms, he argued, it was self-defeating to have all the peace
organizations in the country housed at 5 Beekman Street, New York. He
proposed that the War Resisters League sponsor a West Coast office called
Acts for Peace which would become a clearing house for many peace organizations. Based on World War II conscientious objectors such as Roy Kepler,
Stan Gould, and Gerald Rubin, Acts for Peace would assist organizations
engaged in civil disobedience protesting United States nuclear testing and
supporting the San Francisco-to-Moscow Walk for Disarmament. The walk-

ers demonstrated at the Pentagon in Washington, were thrown out of France, and conducted the first successful nonviolent demonstration in Moscow's Red Square, protesting testing East and West.[48] Acts for Peace would publish Erich Fromm's "The Case for Unilateral Disarmament" and Jerome Frank's *Sanity and Survival*, the latter making the case for civilian defense. But neither Robert Pickus nor the Pride of Pacifist Lions who gathered at the War Resisters League in 1956 could state the conditions essential to peace nor describe the nonviolent means that would take the United States, the Soviet Union, and all others toward a world without war.

The Pacifist Lions agreed on two projects: the establishment of *Liberation* magazine and the acceptance of Robert Pickus's proposal to establish a West Coast organization to be named Acts for Peace.[49]

AN EPIPHANY IN 1961

This was prologue, the epiphany occurred in August 1961 after a train ride with Homer Jack, who was just back from Moscow, proposing an exchange of peace leaders from the provinces as well as Leningrad and Washington. The epiphany produced the first statement of the conditions essential to a world without war. Further, a Strategy of Peace Initiative Acts was to be developed to show how to get there from here.

In 1961 the Berlin Crisis threatened to conclude the risk/benefit analysis argument. The Soviet Union and the United States were prepared to go to nuclear war over access to Berlin within the agreed-to Soviet-occupied region. The superpowers were eyeball to eyeball with their arsenals ready to deliver within 30 minutes. Both countries responded: the United States responded by defending free access to Berlin's divided sectors and the Soviet Union by building the Berlin Wall. In response to the crises, Turn Toward Peace was organized based in the New York Friends Group and Sane (Committee for a Sane Nuclear Policy). Robert Pickus was asked to join Sandy Gottlieb in developing "the plans for a national campaign." Pick's goal was both to respond to the crises but also to "achieve a better relation between the different strands of thought in the non-Soviet-apologist peace movement" and to develop "continuing relationship among the major peace organizations as they approach local communities and the different regions of this country." In a letter to Homer Jack, Pick wrote:

> we will, of course, want to get agreement on the immediate issues, but there will be a campaign document along the lines of the Turn Toward Peace program I outlined for you on the train. This document would stand behind each of the specific issues we work on and would set the tone and provide the context for the effort.
> The outline is distinctive in that:

a. It does not assume agreement among cooperating organizations. It posits a direction which we share in common but is explicit in stating that different organizations are interested in different parts of this road away from war.
b. The document would lay great emphasis on the need for something more than offers to negotiate, rather on the need for American action undertaken without prior Soviet Agreement but designed to evoke the most favorable Soviet response.

Per our discussion, the acts called for would be acts in the areas of international law, international organization, reduction of political tension, disarmament, response to problems of world community and world development, and the nonviolent defense of values. We would be setting forth a developed understanding and policy for a country interested in fulfilling the values of a free society and achieving a just peace in a world under law. [50]

These goals—law, community, development, disarmament, leadership by the US to evoke a favorable Soviet response, nonviolence—constitute the minimum conditions essential to a world without war. They are modestly reformulated and affirming root values as the motivation to work beyond national interest diplomacy was added, but here is the first statement of the Turn Toward Peace policy framework, Seven Roads to a World Without War, and the Conditions Essential to a World Without War; in short what became the canon of the World Without War Council.

NOTES

1. A disarmed world under law, safe for free societies was adopted as the goal by Turn Toward Peace in 1961. The Turn Toward Peace policy framework added five other conditions to law and disarmament. The 50 plus organizations who agreed to the policy framework thereby also agreed to address all the belligerents in a war. Some formulations of the goal added "and democratic values" after "safe for free societies." The World Without War Council Inc. was formed in 1967 and dissolved 1/9/2014. Robert Pickus was its only Executive Director, Kale Williams the only President of the Board of Directors.

2. See Overview, World Without War Council Inc. archives, Hoover Institution for complete details. The Council-developed typology of Mainstream & World Affairs Organizations lists the Carnegie Endowment as the overview organization.

3. George Weigel, author of *Tranquillitas Ordinis* and *Witness to Hope* identified himself as committed to the Just War tradition. Weigel and Pickus worked together from 1979 to 1995 committed, as each tradition is, to developing, advocating, and seeking to apply alternatives to war.

4. See Judaism and War Kit, compiled first in 1958 for Acts for Peace, frequently updated throughout.

5. Preface to Albert Camus's *Neither Victims nor Executioners* (Berkeley: World Without War Publications, 1967).

6. Ibid, Preface.

7. The TTP Policy Framework affirmed world law, *To End War* (1971) offered five different routes: (1) create functional regional international institutions, (2) by nations changing their approach to the present United Nations, (3) through UN Charter revision, (4) by creating under treaty a new world organization In cooperation with the UN, and (5) through a world constitutional convention. *To End War* (1982) offered 11 and the Good Global Governance project

(1995) offered 12 different approaches to global governance; *Extending the Democratic Peace* (2002) identified five antinomies blocking the path.

8. Ibid, Camus preface.

9. "New Approaches to Peace," Chapter 9 in *Approaches to Peace: An Intellectual Map*, pp 228–232 (Washington: US Institute of Peace 1991).

10. "Civil Disobedience but not Insurrectionary Violence," Dissent, 1965. *To End War* (1982) offered six characteristics of representative democracy based on David Spitz's *Patterns of Anti-Democratic Thought*. In a representative democracy: (1) each individual has a right to be represented in governmental decision-making bodies; (2) the majority has the right to make and carry out policy provided it does not violate the inherent rights of the citizens or the constitution; (3) the minority has the right to contest for power and, if successful, to form a new government as the majority; and (4) there are periodic elections in which the consent of the governed is ascertained. To make this meaningful there must be: the right to form political parties, the free conflict of ideas throughout the electorate, the right to publish and disseminate ideas, to peacefully assembly, to petition, etc., and a safeguarded election process which accurately records and reports election results. There is also a distinction between the society and the State—the society includes nongovernmental organizations (religious, commercial, labor, educational, cultural, civic, and other organizations) and individuals and there is a definition of inalienable human rights protected by an independent judiciary. See also John Stuart Mill's *On Liberty* and *On Representative Government* and Lord Acton's "The History of Freedom in Antiquity" and "The History of Freedom Under Christianity." The World Without War Council published a series of "Democracy Defended" pamphlets and "The Law and Political Protest" in the 1960s.

11. See especially Robert Pickus's Summary of *Speak Truth to Power* in *The Progressive*, October 1955 and the responses of Dwight MacDonald, Reinhold Niebuhr, Karl Menninger, Norman Thomas, and George Kennan and "Contending Context," and "A Developed Peace Position" in *To End War*, 1971. See also Gandhi's Autobiography subtitled, "The Story of My Experiments With Truth."

12. Great Books, 1952, Great Ideas, Vol. II., p. 1010.

13. Dorothy Pickus Gordon wrote a six-page letter to family describing the origins of the Pickus family in Gomel, Belarus, and details of the family history probably written in 1947.

14. Letters of stepmother Rose to Robert Pickus, 9/8/1943 and 11/20/1944, World Without War Collection, Hoover Institution.

15. "An End To War?" Sociology Class 1944, and *Why I am Proud to be an American*, Chicago Tribune, June 1940. Both are included in the Hoover Institution's holdings.

16. One-page autobiography written in 1951. The course syllabuses for the Wright, Morgenthau, and other courses, as well as a journal kept while at the London School of Economics are in the Hoover Institution.

17. Letters David Brazelon, 7/5/1943; Jerry Zeigler, 2/5/1944; and R. S. Ginger, 2/21/1944.

18. Letters of Morrie Pickus to Robert, August to September 1943 with reply.

19. Letters to and from Robert Pickus, 1942–1945, Robert Pickus Collection, Hoover Institution.

20. Letter of Robert Pickus to family, March 23, 1944.

21. "You go where war takes you" appears frequently in his verbal communications.

22. One page autobiographical note, written in late 1950 or early 1951. World Without War Collection, Hoover.

23. *A Constitution for the World*, first published in 1948, drafted by a Committee headed by Robert Hutchins, with Rexford Tugwell, Stringfellow Barr, Mortimer Alder, Elizabeth Mann Borgese and others, and republished in 1965 by the Center for the Study of Democratic Institutions.

24. See personal letters of Bill Dodds of 2/17/1943, 1/7/1944, 9/16/1945 and 1/20/1946, the last urging Pickus to work with unions to "plant the seeds that will bear fruit in five to ten years" and David Brazelon steady stream of letters, 1941–1946, Hoover Institution Archives.

25. July 1944, letter of Robert Pickus to Bill Dodds, World Without War Council Archives, Hoover Institution.

26. Journal of Robert Pickus, 1950, Hoover Institution.

27. Letter from Robert Pickus to Sara Greenberg from, Tehran, Iran, October 20, 1950.

28. Letter of Robert Pickus to Vic (no further identification), from Lahore, Pakistan, November 6, 1950.

29. Letter of Charles Freeman, Quaker Centre, New Delhi, India after Robert Pickus's visit, 12/4/1950.

30. See AFSC 1951–1956, Hoover Institution. See also AFSC records at the Swarthmore Peace College.

31. Memo of Robert Pickus, Chicago Peace Secretary, to Steve Cary, AFSC Philadelphia, 1/20/1953.

32. The STTP working party was chaired by Stephen G. Cary and its listed members were James E. Bristol, Amiya Chakravarty, A. Burns Chalmers, William B. Edgerton, Harrop A. Freeman, Robert Gilmore, Cecil E. Hinshaw, Milton Mayer, A. J. Muste, Clarence E. Pickett, Robert Pickus, and Norman J. Whitney. Bayard Rustin fully participated but asked that he not be listed because of the stigma associated with homosexuality at the time and pending sodomy charges in Los Angles, California, to which he had pleaded no contest. He has subsequently been recognized as a member of the Working Party.

33. These "Cogent and Important Questions" quotes are from *The Progressive*, October 1955

34. Gene Sharp would later develop his 198 Golden Nonviolent Means and author several books on Civilian Defense. His pamphlet *From Dictatorship to Democracy* was translated and would aid leaders of many such historical transitions.

35. In 2019 the Marxist/Leninist/Maoist alternative conceptualization remains but without the empirical foundation Marx and Engels gave it the bourgeoisie has become the immense majority, not the proletariat, which commends itself to many. But does anyone prefer North Korea to South, forget that the two zones of peace in the world. North America and the European Union countries are made up of private enterprise countries, or still deny the mass atrocities integral to the Communist project? See *The Black Book of Communism* (1997) and Timothy Snyder, *Bloodlands* (2010). R. J. Rummel, a leader in the Correlates of War Peace Research Project, was surprised to find that dictatorships killed more people in "peace" than died in war in the twentieth Century. See *Democide* (1992) and *Death by Government* (1997). Robert Conquest (1973), Alekandr Solzhenitsyn (1971), and Anne Applebaum (2004, 2006) researched the death toll. Where is the Victims of Communism Memorial?

36. These are actions but not destined to gain a consensus. Significant thought went into developing a civilian-based national defense by Gene Sharp and A. J. Muste. Speculation about casualties ranged from zero to 300,000, the latter assuming elimination intent by the occupying force and the failure of love to transform the hate into love of a dedicated sect with State power.

37. This ignores Kennan's claim that the adversary had stated their intention may times and omits Allah from the list of prophets. St. Francis is a Catholic saint but he did not replace the Church's Just War convictions.

38. See Gene Sharp's 194 ways to say no to a government or other armed foe. See *The Progressive*, October 1955, also available at the World Without War Collection Hoover Institution and at the Swarthmore Peace Collection.

39. The Response was co-authored by Steve Cary who, according to H. Larry Ingle, "'Speak Truth to Power': A Thirty Years' Retrospective," *Christian Century* 102, pp. 383–385, 1985, wrote the first draft of the pamphlet. The Working Party then discussed and improved it.The cost-benefit analysis the Working Party requested came from Herman Kahn, whom Robert Pickus debated in 1962 in Topeka, Kansas. When Pickus stated his goal was "a disarmed world, under law, safe for free societies," Kahn replied, "There would still be two hands for every throat."

40. See *Speak Truth to Power*, Response to Critics by Stephen Cary and Robert Pickus.

41. Rustin organized the March on Washington, developed Martin Luther King Jr.'s appreciation of nonviolent strategies of change, and rejected Black Power ideologies in from "Protest to Politics." He alone among the Pacifist Lions made the cover of *Life Magazine*.

42. Gene Sharp joined Pickus and Rustin in supporting the institutions and understandings that constitute representative democracy. His list of "harsh facts which most peace workers rarely face" was adopted by Robert Pickus because it was both accurate and remarkably

succinct. It first appeared as a newsletter of the World Without War Council—Midwest and later won the Wallach Award of the World Policy Institute, formerly the Institute for World Order. *Making the Abolition of War a Realistic Goal*, Gene Sharp (Chicago: Word Without War Publications 1980). Sharp developed the idea of civilian defense as an alternative to military strategies.

43. Barbara Deming, "Revolution Equilibrium," *Liberation*, Feb. 1968.

44. See David Dellinger, from Yale to Jail, as well as the editorial stance of *Liberation*. The split with revolutionary posturing was expressed in Robert Pickus's "Political Integrity and Its Critics, Eleven Theses for Pacifist Thinking About United Front Peace Activity," *Liberation*, June/July 1965.

45. See Robert Pickus, "Civil Disobedience but Not Insurrectionary Violence," *Dissent*; Bayard Rustin, *From Protest to Politics*; and Gene Sharp's *The Politics of Nonviolent Action*, 3 Volumes. See document 10 in the appendix of this book.

46. *To End War* (New York: Harper and Row, 1970).

47. See Memo to the War Resisters League from Robert Pickus, 1956, Hoover Institution.

48. See *You Come With Naked Hands*, Brad Lyttle, Swarthmore Peace Collection. Support Czechoslovakia describes a War Resisters International demonstration in Prague, 1968 nonviolently resisting the Soviet Union's invasion, with for example, street signs pointing directions to Moscow, 900 miles away.

49. Acts for Peace, Archives, Hoover Institution.

50. Letter to Homer Jack, 8/6/1961 with copies to Jack Bollens, Steve Cary, Norman Cousins, Robert Gilmore, Sanford Gottlieb, Stewart Meacham, Larry Miller, Lou Schneider, Norman Thomas, George Willoughby, and Kale Williams.

Chapter Two

Steady Work

The first of the cogent criticisms of *Speak Truth to Power* was that government could not act unless and until a new consensus was formed in the society. From 1961 to 1982 Robert Pickus and the Council worked outside the beltway to develop that new consensus, finally opening a Washington, DC office in 1983 called the James Madison Foundation. Four strategies of change were implemented by Robert Pickus in the organizations in which he played a leadership role to enable the government of the United States to act toward the conditions essential to a world without war.

COMMUNITY PEACE CENTERS, 1958–1968

Acts for Peace was intended to prove that regional peace activity could be sustained; Acts for Peace engaged in demonstration activity,[1] supporting but not organizing other organizations' demonstrations;[2] initiated draft counseling, asking "Are You a Conscientious Objector to War?"; developed two kits, "Conscience and War" and "Judaism and War"; and offered realistic and specific answers to the question: But what can I do?

Acts for Peace organized 14 community peace centers (Diablo Valley, Marin, Peninsula, Sacramento . . .),[3] and acted as a clearing house for national peace organizations from the War Resisters League to the United Nations Association and World Federalists as well as organizations focused on human rights and world economic development. Acts for Peace protested nuclear testing in the atmosphere and published Erich Fromm's "The Case for Unilateral Disarmament." Acts for Peace used the movie "On the Beach," which demonstrated the consequences of nuclear war, as an organizational tool.[4]

VOLUNTARY ORGANIZATIONS AND A WORLD WITHOUT WAR, 1961–1985

Acts for Peace, Turn Toward Peace, and the World Without War Council engaged in deepening the engagement of organizations including the New York Friends Group, the Catholic Church, the United Church of Christ, the American Federation of Teachers, the A. Philip Randolph Institute, and the National Association of Evangelicals (NAE). This work gave direction to peace advocacy as described in Robert Pickus's *To End War* (New York: Harper Row 1971) and George Weigel's *Tranquillitas Ordinis: The Present Failure and Future Promise of American Catholic Thought on War and Peace* (New York: Oxford University Press 1987).

Turn Toward Peace (TTP) was composed of over 26 affiliated organizations in August 1962.[5] At its peak, a TTP spokesperson claimed 64 affiliated organizations. A series of conferences was begun in New York (1962) called Voluntary Organizations and a World Without War Conferences designed to involve business, religious (Protestant, Catholic, National Association of Evangelicals), peace researchers, academic organizations, ethnic, racial, and other nongovernmental organizations. This redefined the citizen peace effort to include every Nongovernmental Organization (NGO) from the Chamber of Commerce to the AFL-CIO, to the Catholic Church and the World Sports Federation. Follow-up Voluntary Organizations and World Without War Conferences were held in Chicago (1965), Seattle (1967), and San Francisco (1967).[6]

Each of these organizing conferences sought to engage the full range of opinions within the organization. "Standards of Responsibility for Voluntary Organizations wishing to help achieve a World Without War" were drafted, discussed, and recommended. The point was not to build a coalition of organizations, but rather to enable each organization to make its own distinctive contribution. Three organizations engaged all their members in thinking through guidelines and appointed staff capable of implementing them. They were the Episcopal Diocese of Northern California, Holt Ruffin staff, the Catholic Archdiocese of Oakland, with Sr.'s Helen Garvey and Marion Cotty, staff, and the Northern California Psychological Association, Robert Pickus, staff. In short, this strategy of change sought to move beyond fringe politics to the mainstream without losing the focus on nonmilitary alternatives to war.

The Council doctrine that a peace organization worthy of the name needed to address all military points of view was recorded in "Advices and Cautions" which urged those seeking peace to focus on developing and advocating alternatives to war, not competing military security strategies. The dominant military security strategy—deterrence—had great risks of an endless arms race, war by miscalculation, or unauthorized use. But as Robert

Pickus said, unless there is an alternative, realistic, nonmilitary strategy designed to ultimately replace deterrence, "Diplomats will do as they always have done, talk of peace but prepare for and wage war."

In developing military strategies for security contingencies, the President formulates his or her assessment of military threats that can be as various as the 2016 Russian attack on Crimea and the Ukraine; threats to Latvia, Estonia, and Lithuania that included nuclear war; China's creating military bases in the South China seas; Islamic Jihadist waging war in 18 countries; and Iran's stated intention to destroy Israel and the United States—to name only four. Then generals and defense intellectuals enter the discussion about how much military force is enough to meet these challenges. Robert Pickus wrote a complex assessment of the 18 ideas that may go into military force proposals but lamented that no strategies of peace ever, or very rarely, got into the discussion. Instead, the choices tended to be among military strategies: military parity however parity is defined; a second strike deterrence strategy based on what forces might survive a first strike by an aggressor; or a minimum deterrence strategy, for example, one submarine with 16 nuclear armed sub-launched ballistic missiles. The minimum deterrence strategy, Robert Pickus characterized as the most dangerous of the three military strategies because it meant "coming in second in an arms race." A realistic and developed nonmilitary strategy of peace was needed to enter the discussion.

A successful strategy of peace must meet the challenges of the military threat assessment. During the life of the World Without War Council three such strategies of peace were developed: Civilian Defense (Gene Sharp), Democratic Peace (Michael Doyle, Charles Lipson), and Robert Pickus and George Weigel's Strategy of American Peace Initiative Acts. Without some such nonmilitary strategy of peace, one had only a choice "with varying degrees of fraud" to claim to be for peace when at best there might be truces between the wars. But could such a strategy of peace be developed and realistically implemented?

Not in the Council's lifetime. When faced with enforcement of the genocide treaty, for example, it proved unenforceable when confronted with mass slaughter in Cambodia, Kosovo, and Rwanda—to name three instances. Iraq's invasion of Kuwait proved another challenge, in that an act of military aggression was, with the support of the United Nations Security Council, only met by military force, and only the United States had the military power, along with a "coalition of the willing," to repel Iraq's challenge.

This brief summary is inadequate to the many lines of thought that contribute to alternatives to war. Suffice it here to declare that the World Without War Council retained a belief that the United States was a part of the problem of war as an institution, but was a legitimate political community and had, perhaps the crucial role to play if a strategy of peace could be developed.

INTERNATIONAL CONFLICT AND AMERICAN
ORGANIZATIONS (ICAO), 1974–1981

Council initiated programs focused away from engaging NGOs to enabling constructive dialogue between engaged organizations and government. ICAO's first program was the State Department/Independent Sector series of programs. Department of State (DOS) representatives became a staple feature of Council programs in New York (1974), Chicago (1978), San Francisco (1976, 1978), and Seattle (1976). An ICAO consultative Group was formed, focused on what kinds of publications nongovernmental organizations needed from the DOS, with a request that they address "the road not taken" and why. In addition, the common challenges of NGOs for funding, media coverage, intern staff training, and organizational fragmentation were addressed.

One benefit of the ICAO programs was that governmental officials could explain why, for example, the US had ratified few International Human Rights Covenants and Conventions. One reason given was that international human rights treaties supersede domestic law. The Carter Administration finally submitted the Covenant on Civil and Political Rights to the Senate but with 52 reservations (these clauses do not apply to us) and understandings (e.g., the language of the Covenant that prohibits war propaganda does not limit freedom of speech). A more constructive dialogue on human rights would ensue.

Programs were also done with the National Council on Philanthropy based on the judgment that the impact of world politics on America was great and growing; the level of public understanding was low, with negative consequences. Donors were invited to explain why only one percent of foundation support went to the impact of world politics on domestic affairs. Among the answers: the world affairs field was fragmented, many organizations were vehicles for one personality, and the scale of the challenge facing organizations claiming to work for a world without war was not commensurate with their staff or budgets. A typology of organizations based on the functional tasks they perform, a joint intern program based on an agreed syllabus, and programs focused on providing feedback to media were adopted.[7]

Robert Pickus retained his focus on disarmament, working with Senator Patrick Moynihan whose position on SALT was to wonder how the process of negotiating arms control treaties actually was paralleled by the expansion of arms. For example, the SALT agreement limited nuclear delivery vehicles but technological innovation made Multiple Targeted Reentry Vehicles (MIRV's) possible, thus expanding the number of nuclear bombs targeted on Soviet or American cities. He spoke at the UN's Special Session on Disarmament (1978) NGO gathering, criticizing those who addressed only NATO weapons acquisition polices and not the Warsaw Pact's. The ICAO coalition authorized Pickus to seek areas in which realistic disarmament policies could be pursued with Eugene Rostow, head of the US Arms Control and Disarmament Agency (ACDA). This produced seven actionable proposals for ACDA.[8] These included requests for (1) regional conferences, (2) options considered, (3) ACDA statement of policies being developed and the opportunity for leaders of NGOs to be engaged in their development, and (4) reaffirmation of ACDA's enabling legislation.

IMPROVING AMERICAN COMPETENCE IN WORLD AFFAIRS, 1981–1991

The response to the five cogent criticisms of Robert Pickus's summary of *Speak Truth to Power* previously stated guided Council work from 1981–1991: (1) Form a consensus in the society, so that government can act; (2) Unilateral initiatives that gained multilateral responses were developed rather than unilateral disarmament or "less is best" military strategies that were considered more likely to start a war than end it. General and complete disarmament was the goal pacifists should seek and that peace requires, but this meant steps by one party toward disarmament must be reciprocated or unilateral actions would appear to be surrendering to an adversary's power; (3) Some conflicts in world politics are based on fundamental ideological, territorial, or cultural conflicts, not misperceptions; (4) The United States needs allies to contain the Soviet Union or other adversaries and for many other purposes essential to the global common good; and (5) A comprehensive strategy of peace was required which gained the reciprocation of allies and adversaries, and not just negotiations and United Nations "use it or reform it" proposals. Programs from 1981 to 1991 constituted Robert Pickus and the World Without War Council's responses to these cogent criticisms.

NOTES

1. Robert Pickus reported on his own and Acts for Peace protest of nuclear testing in "The NevadaProject," *Liberation*, 9/1957.

2. Among the demonstrations supported were the Golden Rule Voyage (2/1958); Vandenberg Air Force Base (12/26/1958); and the San Francisco to Moscow Walk for Disarmament (1959–12/1/1960).

3. "Handbook for Community Peace Centers," Joyce Mertz (Ed), Robert Pickus, Robert Gilmore Associate Editors, Homer Jack and Alfred Hassler, Turn Toward Peace, August 1962 is a 488 page, mimeographed collection of materials "based on the experience of Community Peace Centers in various parts of the country during the past few years." p. 3.

4. See "On the Beach, an Acts for Peace Appraisal," Acts for Peace documents, Hoover Institution.

5. In August 1962, the "Handbook for Community Peace Centers" working in cooperation with Turn Toward Peace listed 33 and distinguished them as cooperating (15), communicating (11), contributing (1), and regional affiliates (6) (see p. 417). Twenty-six organizations are listed as "affiliated" (pp. 473–474), including the American Friends Service Committee, Broth-

erhood of Sleeping Car Porters, Catholic Worker, Committee for Nonviolent Action, Committee for World Development and World Disarmament, Council for Correspondence, Fellowship of Reconciliation, Friends Committee on National Legislation, National Committee for a Sane Nuclear Policy, Post War World Council, Society for Social Responsibility in Science, Students for a Democratic Society, Student Peace Union, War Resisters League, Women's International League for Peace and Freedom, Amalgamated Clothing Workers of America, Amalgamated Meat-cutters and Butcher Workman, American Humanist Association, American Veterans Committee, Brethren Service Commission, Central Committee for Conscientious Objectors, Peace and Social Order Committee, Friends General Conference, International Union of Electrical, Radio and Machine Workers, United Automobile Workers, United Packinghouse, Food and Allied Workers, and Workers Education Local 189, American Federation of Teachers.

6. See World Without War Council–Midwest archives, Swarthmore Peace Collection, World Without War Council of Greater Seattle archives, University of Washington Library and Hoover Institution, and World Without War Council of Northern California archives, Hoover Institution.

7. See World Without War Council Inc. Overview, Hoover Institution, submitted with indexes of documents divided by organizational materials, perspective, strategy of change, and programs (with specific date and place).

8. Robert Pickus to Eugene V. Rostow, "A Thesis: An Analysis, and Seven Proposals for Action by the Arms Control and Disarmament Agency."

Chapter Three

Strategies of Peace

The Council's focus was always on developing and implementing a strategy of American Peace Initiative Acts. But there were three strategies of peace it lent credibility to, provided resources to and offered programs to implement.

INDIVIDUAL: IS UNIVERSAL CONSCIENTIOUS OBJECTION TO WAR A STRATEGY OF PEACE?

From the formation of Acts for Peace in 1958 until the draft was abolished, all draft eligible young men were asked by Selective Service: "Are you a conscientious objector to war?" The War Resisters League suggested a strategy of peace in its slogan, "Wars will Cease When Men Refuse to Fight." The American Friends Service Committee, as well as the Mennonite and Brethren religious communities, rejected military service as inconsistent with their interpretation of the New Testament and the commandment "Thou shalt not kill." Civil disobedience, as an act of conscience, placed the individual's conscience above the law. To help individual young men take seriously the Selective Service's question Acts for Peace published a "Conscience and War Kit." Turn Toward Peace added draft counseling service to its programs, and then formed the East Bay Draft Information and Counseling Service under Peter Shavitz and Steve Bischoff's leadership. Allan Blackman, himself a conscientious objector, wrote and the Council published *Face to Face With Your Draft Board: A Guide to the Personal Appearance*, which helped a draft-eligible young man get the "classification he wants and deserves." Sixty-three thousand copies of Allan Blackman's guide were published and distributed nationally—a work intended for young men whose initial request for a CO classification had been denied. Such books as Joan Bondurant's *Conquest of Violence*, Gene Sharp's *The Strategy of Non-Violent Conflict*, and M. K. Gandhi's *All Men Are Brothers* were integral to draft counseling and World Without War Council programming. *All Men Are Brothers* was published with the permission of the Navajivan Trust, secured by T. K. Mahadevan, whose anthology *Gandhi, His Relevance for Our Times* also became a Council publication as did Geoffrey Nuttal's *Christian Pacifism in History*. Nonviolence as a means of forcing needed change was one of Bob Pickus's and Turn Toward Peace's seven roads to a world without war. Individual acts of conscience could make a difference. Socially organized nonviolence gave acts of conscience the possibility of limiting the power of the state, forcing change without violence, aiding nonviolent transitions from dictatorships toward democracy, and providing an alternative, nonviolent means of national defense.

Among the pacifist lions, Gene Sharp identified 198 means of forcing change without violence. His *From Dictatorship to Democracy* was widely translated and used in the 20 transitions toward democracy between 1974 and 2003 in places as dispersed as the Philippines, Poland, and South Africa.[1] World Without War Council's Chicago office published Gene Sharp's *The Abolition of War* that asks its readers "to take into consideration some hard facts which most peace workers rarely face." These included the following:[2]

- Conflicts of some type will always exist within societies and between societies, requiring use of some type of power.
- "Human nature" need not, and most likely will not, be changed.
- People and governments will not sacrifice freedom or justice for the sake of peace.
- Mass conversions to pacifism are not going to occur.
- There is no break in the spiral of military technology within the context of military technology and military assumptions.
- Brutal dictatorships and oppressive systems exist, will continue, may become more serious, and may seek to expand.
- The abolition of capitalism does not produce the abolition of war.
- Negotiations are no substitute for the capacity to struggle and apply sanctions.
- Unilateral disarmament—abandonment of defense capacity—is no alternative to the war system and is not possible.
- Major multilateral disarmament is nearly as unlikely.
- National independence is not the origin of war.
- World government is either unrealizable, or if achieved would itself be likely to produce a world civil war, because tyrannical, and be used to impose or perpetuate injustice.

Within this framework, Gene Sharp offered a societally coordinated program of nonviolent resistance he called Civilian Defense, later providing a detailed development of the idea of how individual acts of conscience, combined into society-wide nonviolent resistance, could make a country unconquerable.[3]

Acts for Peace, Turn Toward Peace, and World Without War sought to incorporate seven roads to a world without war into one perspective, and defined a variety of roles for individuals in developing a strategy of peace. One of the first resources Acts for Peace developed was an answer to the sense of futility expressed in the question: But what can I do? The self-survey provided to every audience or drop-in to a community peace center asked for an individual's work preferences, interest in world politics, groups he/she wanted to work with, beliefs, talents, time, work experience, preferred work location, and preferred type of activity. Follow-up discussion could lead to work within an organization a person already belonged to in one of 29 program areas or to a career. Twenty-five careers were briefly summarized through existing professional employment opportunities.

CIVIL SOCIETY OR DEMOCRATIC PEACE

If it is a fact that democracies rarely war on each other, can a Strategy of Peace be implemented designed to make democracy universal? The idea that representative democracies do not war on each other was first expressed in Thomas Paine's *The Rights of Man* (1790) and developed by Immanuel Kant's *On Perpetual Peace* (1795). Robert Pickus's high school essay "An End to War?" maintained that World War II could have been avoided had the democracies united before the war. In Robert Pickus's career the "safe for free societies" makes civil society an asset in achieving a world without war. Michael Doyle in 1971 did a statistical study that established that democracies rarely war on each other—that nations with free societies had a separate peace. The European Union offered evidence for that proposition as membership is limited to democracies, with regulated market economies. They remained at peace with no weapons targeted upon each other and a zone of peace (1945–present) that is precarious yet still going. Charles Lipson's *Reliable Partners* believes the principal reason is that EU countries accept treaty enforcement between them and have independent judiciaries.

The Council conducted over 50 programs designed to defend representative democracy, aid in its implementation in other countries, or identify free and fair elections as essential to resolving a specific conflict with built-in safeguards to prevent the victor in elections from murdering their opposition. The Council succeeded in getting Conscientious Objections petitioned for recognition in Warsaw Pact countries, published a Democracy Defended Series as well as *The Law and Political Protest* in the 1960s, sought elections in Vietnam as part of the process of ending the war and enabling a transfer to a nonviolent conflict-resolution arena.

GOVERNMENT: AMERICAN STRATEGY OF PEACE
INITIATIVE ACTS

The key to any governmental strategy of peace is the reciprocation by a dedicated adversary. The initiatives idea found organizational expression in a leaflet titled "American Initiatives in a Turn Toward Peace" (1961), and was included in the Handbook for Community Peace Centers working in cooperation with Turn Toward Peace and in Peace and the American Community for Peace Interns, by Theodore Olsen.

The initiatives as a single act was embodied in John F. Kennedy's Strategy of Peace speech, June 1963, in which he initiated a unilateral halt of American testing in the atmosphere and promised not to resume testing as long as the Soviet Union refrained from testing. If they tested, the US would resume testing on a one-for-one basis, while working to negotiate a Comprehensive Test Ban Treaty. (Only a limited Test Ban Treaty was agreed to.)[4]

Beginning in 1964, Turn Toward Peace published a Goals and Next Steps statement enabling opinion leaders to endorse the minimum conditions essential to a world without war and develop next steps toward them set in a framework that sought Soviet reciprocation. These statements hinted at but were not themselves linked initiatives. Every four years from then until 1996 the Council published Strategy of Peace statements that embodied that framework. In 1972, under Lowell Livezey's leadership, the statement was called Peace and the Elections. In 1976 a Peace Ballot led to a Peace Platform that stated the conditions and allowed people to indicate which next steps they favored. The Seattle office added State of the World addresses in 2000. Ashoka Day was declared with an opportunity to reflect on the institutions of war and alternatives to it. President Bush's National Security Strategy was a focus with an essay, *How to Bring a Strategy of Peace Out of the War on Terrorism.* Robert Pickus claimed in 2004 that Condoleezza Rice's National Security Strategy statement for President Bush contained six out of seven of the Council's "Seven Roads to a World Without War." But all of these statements and claims were beside the point. It was getting there from here, the transformative vehicle that was the stated purpose of the American Initiatives Strategy.

By 1981 Robert Pickus and George Weigel had become national spokespersons and began work in Washington as well as in the regions. Through the American Initiatives Project (1981–1985) Pickus and Weigel attempted to develop the initiative idea into "A New Course for American Foreign Policy."[5] The need for such a strategy was crucial for the Council's claim that not only were the conditions known, but there was a strategy to get there from here. The Prospectus written in 1981 was addressed to a time when American engagement in world politics was in question, and if so, with what means to what ends. The Prospectus addressed the dilemma of re-engagement after Vietnam as follows:

> Who, on Monday, surveying the steady rise in Soviet war-making capabilities and the dangers in Soviet control over countries as widely separated as Cuba, Vietnam, Ethiopia, South Yemen and Afghanistan, does not see the logic of increased military expenditures? Yet, on Tuesday, after reviewing the massive figures of the arms race, acknowledging the tragedy of Third World nations outspending the great powers in the percentage of their national budgets devoted to arms, and noting the quadrupling of earth-destroying weapons that has proceeded in a decade of arms control, so often that same person concludes that the most important task is to somehow find alternatives to what is the armed road to disaster.
>
> But Monday's man acts—acts with the resources of a great nation available to serve his purpose of military readiness. Tuesday's man, in the absence of nonmilitary instruments that could change the intentions and policies of adversary nations, either deludes himself that the threat is not real, or stands by dispirited.
>
> We live in a world now dominated by preparation for war. Any American administration takes office in such a world with a commitment to organize national military power for the security of the nation and the defense of democratic values. The course of that commitment is not set by our choice alone, but primarily by the degree of threat posed by other nations' military programs. If one is involved in an arms race, no matter if the purpose is to keep the peace or to fight a war, preparing to come in second is not a reasonable course of action.
>
> It is so for all nations. Governments today will continue to talk peace and hope for peace. Fear, patience and skillful diplomacy may avert, for a time, the evil decree. But unless there is a major breakthrough, a serious start on a new course, governments will do as they have always done: prepare for and wage war.

Pickus and Weigel then claim "it is not utopian to act, without naivety, to change that system: to accelerate the growth of a nascent world political community while building those legal and political structures that are an alternative to war."

Pickus and Weigel next created an advisory Board of important public figures including Roger Fisher, Walter Laqueur, and Theodore Sorenson.[6] Then they sought 200 people with special expertise to develop initiatives which had to answer these questions:

1. What is the behavioral act? Who does it?
2. At whom is it aimed? How is it carried out?
3. What are the conditions for the act being halted, accelerated or taken back?
4. What form of reciprocation is expected?

5. How does the specific act fit into a general strategy?[7]

In sum, an initiative should be an act, not just a statement of intention; should be taken on behalf of an explicitly stated goal; should seek the reciprocation or response of others; should not seek to intimidate an adversary militarily, nor create the opportunity for increased military intimidation by any other party; and be capable of being combined with others into a peace initiatives strategy.

An initiative is a step toward one of the conditions. It is intended to achieve reciprocation. It can do so in two ways. An initiative can do 10% of anything, require a 10% response, and then do another 10% until both adversaries reach the goal. Alternately, an initiative can do something for a period of time, say three months, expecting reciprocation in that period. If it occurs, then the act is extended for another three months. In conducting a strategy of peace initiative acts, the 200 initiative ideas can be divided into intention-clarifying initiatives, force-reduction initiatives, and sanctioning or coercive initiatives. More than 20 initiative ideas were developed.

American Initiatives to Gain Arms Stabilization, Arms Reduction, and Disarmament Agreements

- Zonal disarmament: initiatives to create disarmed zones (Antarctic, the Sea Bed, Outer Space, and perhaps the Arctic [Lincoln Bloomfield]).
- Uniform military financial accounting: initiatives to develop systems capable of creating the base line for percentage reductions in all classes or arms (Daniel Gallick and Abe Becker were consulted, Joseph Slovenic authored it).
- Information arms control: using technological means of information gathering and sharing to monitor and protect secure borders; to lengthen the lead time of crises and to bind opponents to a common data base (David Bobrow and Stephen Hill).
- Swords into Shields: proposals for two joint US/USSR task groups to develop a needed technological capabilities research agenda for defense against nuclear missiles, to avoid unilateral deployment by establishing a joint timetable under which defense capabilities would be tied to offensive weapons reductions (Kenneth Largman, Mark Somers).
- Joint US/USSR crisis consultation center: developing a jointly manned institute at which senior US and Soviet officials would consult regularly to avoid war through miscalculation, computer malfunction, intelligence errors or other failures (Henry Jackson).
- Joint nuclear waste disposal research and model site development: tied to possible progress on verification and initial arms control data collection (George Pickering).

American Initiatives to Reform, Strengthen, and Expand International Legal and Political Institutions

- UN voting procedures (the binding triad): initiatives toward concurrent majority decision-making (Richard Hudson).
- UN charter reform: proposals to move the UN's peacekeeping function to the General Assembly and alter its voting procedures to more nearly reflect economic, population, and political realities (Louis Sohn).

American Initiatives to Strengthen World Political Community and to Help Catalyze Needed Changes in the Soviet Union

- Scholarly exchanges: Initiatives to replace current asymmetries within new programs of aid to open societies seeking to influence relatively closed ones; computer technologists, Jewish, and other dissidents (Philip Siegelman, Severo Ornstein); Youth Exchange Initiative (John Richardson, Edward Meador).
- Agenda setting: developing a common agenda for the world scientists, enabling joint work by institutions in adversary societies (Philip Siegelman).
- USIA: ethics and war—satellite broadcast events (George Weigel).

American Initiatives Toward Effective Economic and Desirable Political Development in the Third World

- Democracy defended: initiatives to strengthen democratic political parties, movements and civil society in developing countries (Alan Weinstein; William Douglas).
- Journalism: enhancing the technical and professional capacities of developing countries journalists in a democratic mode (Len Sussman).
- Department of State/nongovernmental organizations: to improve the dialogue in the international political arena; an ambassador to the NGO world (Robert Pickus).

American Initiatives to Secure the Defense of Basic Human Rights

- Court of man: initiatives to develop a nongovernmental arena for trying and designing effective sanctions against gross governmental violations of basic human rights (Gerald Gottlieb).
- Human rights in the UN: an initiative in the UN to clarify definitions and challenge hypocrisy (Raymond Gastil).

American Initiatives Toward Effective Regional Crisis Intervention and Mediation

• Namibia and South Africa: initiatives to secure and protect a democratic resolution of the conflict in Namibia (John Hutchinson); to advance human rights and end apartheid in South Africa (Fr. John Pawlikowski).
• Central America: interdicting revolutionary violence through social and economic reforms capable of enhancing democratic governance and negotiations over electoral processes (Roy Prosterman and Simon Williams).
• International satellite reconnaissance system: interdicting developing world crises through an internationally operated satellite reconnaissance system capable of detecting troop movements and threatening weapons deployments, thus removing any advantage of surprise to an aggressor (Adam Wasserman; Hans Mark).[8]

A full tracing out of the consequences of these ideas is out of place here. They were in every case the achievements of others and offered in a specific time-and-place framework. The democracy initiative idea was adopted by President Reagan and enacted with bipartisan support in the National Endowment for Democracy (NED). A US/USSR crisis consultation center was created—permitting direct communication in a crisis. There is an international space station permitting cooperation in space. There were over 20 nonviolent transitions from dictatorships toward democracy from 1974 to 2003, some with direct Council involvement (Poland, the Czech Republic, South Africa, Mexico), but also failures with Council involvement in China, Russia, and Vietnam.

The functional international organizations of the International Monetary Fund (IMF) and World Trade Organization (WTO) provide a mechanism for correcting currency imbalances in member countries and a dispute resolution mechanism in the WTO. The country by country enjoyment of civil and political rights increased from 1975 to 2005 largely through the successful transitions to democracy as measured by Freedom House's annual survey based on criteria developed by Raymond Gastil in consultation with Council staff. The idea of an ambassador to the NGO world is partially embodied in the US Institute of Peace and the Department of State's NGO window. But there are not regional offices of either organization. NED's work has been expanded by democracy promotion foundations in Canada, England, Germany, Taiwan, South Korea, all operating in 2019.

Robert Pickus challenged Senator Paul Simon (D-IL) to help make the then proposed US Institute of Peace capable of addressing intractable conflicts with nonviolent alternatives while supporting preventive diplomacy, mediation, and post-conflict reconciliation. President Reagan's Institute gained bipartisan support and has been taking on the Intern/fellows training role in 2012 advocated by the Council. The USIP had 15 programs in Afghanistan teaching how tribal laws could become compatible with national law. A strategy of American peace initiatives acts designed to bring into being a world order capable of resolving international disputes is not yet on the Institute's agenda.

The Global Governance program, 1991 to 1999, produced 11 different scenarios for "rightly ordered world political institutions" capable of achieving a "disarmed world under law, safe for free societies." The idea of combining 200 specific initiative acts into a Strategy of Peace capable of being implemented within the framework of national, military security strategies but designed, ultimately to replace it, was offered as an answer to the question "How Do You Get There From Here?"[9] but was never fully developed. The initiative idea retains promise as a response to specific crisis, to break conflict spirals, and as the entry ticket to global arms control and disarmament gatherings.

COUNTER CLAIMS

The consensus needed for a President to act intending to transfer a portion of sovereignty to an international body can never be achieved. It would require a higher level of public involvement in world politics than has ever been approached, a level of sophistication and a sense of jeopardy that even nuclear brinkmanship did not provide. Even if 200 initiative ideas were created, the problems of implementing a strategy of peace as stated, assumes that an adversary has similar flexibility in decision-making, and could concede the power to enforce international treaties to a third party. The history of the International Atomic Energy Agency is suggestive of both the intent and the limits of international enforcement. One of Robert Pickus's regional associates, Holt Ruffin, has left 11 specific criticisms of the Initiative Strategy as part of the archives pointing out that linkage between initiatives, the timing of them, the nearly universal consensus needed to sustain a strategy, rendered the initiative strategy idea dead in the water.

NOTES

1. See *Extending the Democratic Peace*, p. 84.
2. (Chicago: World Without War Publications 1980); Gene Sharp's essay won the Wallach Awards Competition of the World Policy Institute, formerly the Institute for World Order. Robert Pickus referred to this list as unusually succinct summary of lessons learned in his Chapter 9, "Approaches to Peace: An Intellectual Map," W. Scott Thompson Kenneth M. Jensen (eds.), (Washington: United States Institute of Peace 1990). Gene Sharp's *From Dictatorship to Democracy* aided the more than 20 countries that began transitions toward democracy from 1974 to 2004.

3. Gene Sharp, "Making Europe Unconquerable" (1986), *From Dictatorship to Democracy* (2003); Gene Sharp, *Waging Nonviolent Struggles: 20th Century Practice and 21st Century Potential* (2005).

4. See Amitai Etzioni, Columbia University Institute of War and Peace Studies, *The Kennedy Experiment* (*Western Political Science Quarterly*, June 1967); Theodore Sorenson's *Kennedy* (New York: Harper Row 1965), esp. Chapter 25; and Arthur M. Schlesinger, Jr., *A Thousand Days* (Boston: Houghton Mifflin 1965) esp. pp. 888–923. Richard M. Nixon's sending a ping-pong team to Mao's China, a country with whom we did not have diplomatic relationships, and Chou En Lai's willingness to accept them is another illustration of the initiatives approach. Khrushchev called it a policy of mutual example. But no comprehensive initiatives strategy was ever developed. First Jack Bollens, then Robert Pickus and George Weigel in 1981, sought to develop such a strategy. Robert Pickus and George Weigel published an American Initiatives Project Prospectus; recruited 15 nationally known advisers; printed a Memo to Initiative writers; and held discussions of the project and specific initiatives at the Woodrow Wilson Center (April 27, 1982). They also held a "Does America have a Peace Strategy?" conference with the US Arms Control and Disarmament Agency (San Francisco, June 4, 1982); formed a Bipartisan House Study Group on Developing a Peace Strategy for America with Joel Pritchard playing a leadership role; and held a conference at Northwestern University asking "Is there a Way Out?" and offering the initiatives strategy as a means. More than 20 initiatives were drafted, including Robert Pickus's on an international professional civil service, George Weigel on making the Strategic Defense Initiative mutual and, as in President Reagan's proposal, combined with offensive arms reduction. Uniform Military Accounting was offered by Joseph Slovenik after consulting with Dan Gallick of the US Arm Control and Disarmament Agency and William Douglas, as well as others, advocated what became the National Endowment for Democracy.

5. See the American Initiatives Project Prospectus, Memo to Initiatives Writers and complete documentation at the Hoover Institution.

6. The project advisers in 1981 were Seyom Brown, Herbert Ellison, Amitai Etzioni, Roger Fisher, Harold Guetzkow, Sidney Hook, Philip Klutznick, Walter Laqueur, Seymour Martin Lipset, Eugene Rostow, Bayard Rustin, Paul Seabury, J. David Singer, Louis Sohn, Theodore Sorenson, and Michael Walzer.

7. This is a summary of the four-page Memo to Initiative Writers.

8. The names above are people working through the American Initiatives Project in developing ideas in 1982. The ideas are listed to clarify that specific next steps were developed. Some of them have been acted upon; others remain ideas. The claim that a comprehensive American Initiatives Strategy was never fully developed remains a challenge in a very different set of circumstances. The Good Global Governments documents constitute one banker's box of materials at the Hoover Institution.

9. The American Initiatives Project, the Memo to writers, the list of initiatives, the 20 initiatives submitted for consideration, as well as related documents are duplicated at the Hoover Institution and the Swarthmore Peace Collection.

Chapter Four

To the Max

Council programs in this period were based on the judgment that an overview of the

world affairs field was needed. Work within any subdivision of the nongovernmental organizational world could best be described as undertaking the task of improving American competence in world affairs. Nonviolent conflict resolution then became one of a number of competencies needed. Robert Pickus stated it this way:

> [The World Without War Council] acted. . . . as a catalyst, coordinator, publisher, trainer, model program and curriculum developer [and engager of a major new constituency] to build a wiser, richer, better rooted and more effective American public effort for the nonviolent resolution of international conflict; one which serves the wellbeing of our own society and free societies everywhere. [1]

In the 1981–1991 period, Robert Pickus was joined by George Weigel in engaging civil society so government could act, and by Holt Ruffin and Lucy Dougall engaging global civil society while the Council opened an office in Washington engaging in dialogue with other national nongovernmental organizations and with elected representatives. Summarized here are 15 programs that involved conferences in five or more cities, engaged 100 to 500 leaders of nongovernmental organizations whose members numbered over 100 million, and which produced Guidelines for deepening engagement, educational resources, and contributed to the establishment of the United States Institute of Peace and the National Endowment for Democracy (NED). [2]

PROGRAM 1: STRATEGY OF PEACE STATEMENTS

Strategy of Peace statements were published every Presidential election year (1982, 1988, 1992, 1996).[3] These stated the conditions essential to a world without war and in summary form, suggested specific initiative acts to demonstrate intention to pursue them. If allies and adversaries reciprocated, new United States initiatives would continue progress.

Fifty or more opinion leaders endorsed the direction embodied in these Strategy of Peace statements with 15,000 to 50,000 copies published. Other organizations, student newspapers, and concerned citizens were encouraged to reprint these strategy of peace statements. The platform committees of the Democratic and Republican Parties were asked to incorporate the sense of direction.

PROGRAM 2: ADVOCACY OF THE US INSTITUTE OF PEACE AND A NATIONAL ENDOWMENT FOR DEMOCRACY

The United States Institute of Peace

The desire for a voice in government for peace ideas took many forms including the desire to form a cabinet level Department of Peace and the formation of a Peace Academy complete with a football team to rival West Point and the Naval Academy. Mary Liebman, a member of the National Strategy Forum, was also the head of the Council for a Department of Peace. She and Lowell Livezey, Midwest Director, 1969–1977,[4] took a leadership role in urging the Midwest office to circulate a Peace Ballot to gain visibility for the Peace Academy and other ideas circulating in self-defined peace circles.

The Midwest office circulated 50,000 copies of the Peace Ballot in cooperation with other organizations. In 1983 the Midwest office gained the cooperation of 50 Midwest organizations who agreed to the need for a Peace Institute of some kind and gathered 150 leaders of nongovernmental organizations with Paul Simon (D-IL) and Robert Pickus as the two resource people. Pickus clarified the need for an Institute that understood there were hard conflicts in world politics not based on misperceptions. The United States Institute of Peace charter was drafted in Congress and adopted by the Reagan Administration. The resulting United States Institute of Peace, established in 1984, gained bipartisan support for preventive diplomacy, conflict mediation and resolution, and post-conflict nation-building, but not for a nonmilitary strategy of peace.

Robert Pickus was asked by the United States Institute of Peace staff to contribute to *Approaches to Peace, an Intellectual Map*, W. Scott Thompson and Kenneth M. Jensen (eds.) (Washington: United States Institute of Peace

1991). Pickus's chapter, "New Approaches," summarized new ideas while clarifying that a sense of direction was essential and that Thucydides and Morgenthau should also be consulted. He offered the Berkeley office's fellows program as "the best thought through Fellows Program for young people seeking a year's training opportunity in preparation for a vocation of work for peace and freedom"[5] and counseled the United States Institute of Peace staff in 1991 on developing a similar National Fellows program.

National Endowment for Democracy

Roy Prosterman, Seattle Council Board member and Law Professor, University of Washington, was an advocate of land reform in developing countries both as a means to increase agricultural production and to create a middle class constituency for democracy when either military dictatorships that protected large land holdings or Communist collectivization of agriculture appeared to be the only alternatives.[6]

In the American Initiative project (1979–1987, 1991–2005) Robert Pickus and George Weigel encouraged William A. Douglas to develop the idea of United States support for strengthened civil society organizations in developing societies. Douglas book, *Developing Democracy* (Washington: Heldref Publications 1972) advocated the creation of a specific agency to encourage the participation of the private sector in democracy promotion abroad.[7] This idea was published as an initiative in *Freedom at Issue*. The Reagan Administration announced its intention to form such an agency in President Reagan's Westminster speech on June 8, 1982.

The NED was created in 1983 and has gained bipartisan support. NED has four component organizations: the AFL-CIO, the United States Chamber of Commerce, and the Republican and Democratic party Institutes. They provided a partially government funded base for the international promotion of democracy. The political party institutes create what European political parties and the Soviet Union already have, an international presence. NED through its four institutes developed an international capacity to strengthen civil society institutions in other countries with over 1,000 grants in 2005 to African countries NGOs alone.

At the initiative of democracy promotion advocates in India, NED became the Secretariat of the World Movement for Democracy (WMD) in 1999. The founding statement of the WMD indicates: "The idea of the World Movement for Democracy is to take advantage of the opportunities presented by advances in information technology and enhanced economic interdependence to build a global 'network of networks' focused on the promotion of democracy." The WMD holds bi-annual world conferences which address common problems, develop educational materials, and encourage support for civil society, human rights, and principled representative democracy organizations.

Since 1983, other countries have formed their own democracy promotion organizations including England (the Westminster Foundation), Canada (the Pearson Institute), Germany (the Schroder Foundation), South Korea's East Asia Institute, and Taiwan's Foundation for Democracy (2003).[8]

At the initiative of Madeleine Albright, United States Secretary of State, and Bronislaw Geremek, Polish Foreign Minister, an intergovernmental Community of Democracies (CD) was formed in 2000. As of 2014 the CD governing council had 29 member states, met bi-annually, drafted joint declarations and made specific policy recommendations. It acted as a caucus within the United Nations, expressing the "hope of the UN members that through democracy we can end the scourge of war." It also sponsored a World Forum for Democracy[9] that facilitates global civil society and nation-state interaction.

PROGRAM 3: THE HISTORIAN'S PROJECT (1980–1987) AND THE ASSESSMENT PROJECT (1983–1992)

The Historian's Project sought to engage historians in describing the goals, strategies of change, and perspectives on American history from the Peace Congress movement (1891–1914), through the American Peace Society (1928), the keep-America-out-of-war neutrality legislation (1919–1941), and the Vietnam War era (1964–1975). Thirty historians submitted essays to aid in the description of different themes of peace advocacy in each period alongside the events advocates were attempting to influence.[10]

The Historian's Project engaged 37 historians in describing the public effort for peace which then provided the basis for Assessing the Public Effort for Peace in America. The historians' essay focused on the 20th Century and offered interpretations of American Isolationist/engagement, pacifist advocacy/governmental security obligations, and anti-war vs. anti-American movements and currents of thought.

The project produced 17 "Advices and Cautions" for leaders of organizations that count work for peace as at least one of their endeavors and three essays published in the Wilson Quarterly, Spring 1986, which offered three interpretations of the 20th century peace movement's strengths and weaknesses.

The Assessment Project grew out of the Foundation International Group's efforts to increase the level of funding throughout the world affairs field. The charge to the foundation world was that the impact of the world on America was great and growing, the level of understanding of the impact in the public was embarrassingly low, and that there should be regional arenas in which, if obstacles could be overcome, foundations would increase their funding in world affairs from 1% to 2%. Regional programs (New York, Cleveland, Minneapolis, as well as San Francisco, Seattle, and Chicago where the Council had staffed offices) were sponsored by the National Council on Philanthropy and 30 to 50 foundations were represented in each meeting. Foundations explained that it was difficult to fund organizations in a fragmented field; the size of the organizations was out of proportion to their stated objectives; many organizations reflected the ideas of only one person; and keeping-up with the complexity of world politics was not on their agenda, much less dealing with challenges to established views of history and world affairs. In short, if you gave funds to one peace advocacy organization you made 30 others angry. You could fund established institutions but, the publicly visible ad hoc organizations got the media attention.

This led to the encouragement of Foundation funding to collaborative programs such as intern training, to programs that focused on the media's awareness of the full range of organizations as described in the Council's developed typology of organizations, and to the funding of forums in which areas of agreement and disagreement could be clarified and the possibility of a consensus approach to specific regions and policy choices explored. Want to form a new organization when there are thousands already organized? Check first if there is an organization you can work through.

Consequences: Standards of competence could be set within each subsection. Leadership could meet quarterly to assess common problems such as keeping up with world affairs, fund-raising, media relations, education of board, staff, fellows, interns, and their members. This avoided duplication of efforts and fragmentation. Directories of organizations were prepared by Council staff in Chicago (Karen Egerer, Madeline Goodman, Mary Tatro), Seattle (Steve Boyd, Lucy Dougall), and Berkeley (Margaret Pollack, David Keck). "A Guide to Doing a Guide" (Robert Woito, Foster Tucker) was offered to organizations in Pittsburgh, Kansas City, Milwaukee, and other cities. The temptation to start a new organization (endemic among peace seekers) was buffered by the realization that your work may duplicate another organization's work, your initial success may depend upon the media's interpretation of a crisis and you may not last a year without it, and rather than work on the problem, you will spend 80% of your time building a board, training a staff, and raising funds.

PROGRAM 4: PROJECT SOUTH AFRICA

Bayard Rustin and Robert Pickus were members of the Quaker working party that produced *Speak Truth to Power*. In the 1980s Rustin worked for the A. Philip Randolph Institute which became the lead organization in developing nonviolent methods to encourage a transition in South Africa from white minority to majority rule. Rustin, Walter Naegle, and Charlie Bloomstein went to South Africa, meeting with white and black societal leaders. Such leaders recommended that a program that related similar organizations in the United States to organizations in South Africa would strengthen civil society in South Africa and help provide a constituency for nonviolent protest and engagement with corporations to provide black employment opportunities and promotion possibilities. Humanitarian, educational, labor, and special interest organizations were engaged. Staff in South Africa obtained descriptions of 100 organizations and counterpart organizations in the United States would become linked organizations. Sister city relationships were also encouraged. Within Council circles staff was provided by Noah Pickus, Nancy Starr, and in Chicago, Axel Kolb, an intern from Germany.

Through the work of Kolb, 15 organizations in Chicago developed affiliations with 15 organizations in South Africa including the Roosevelt University student association, Near North Montessori School, the United Nations Association, and the Illinois Association for Multi-Cultural, Multi-Lingual Education.[11]

PROGRAM 5: AMERICAN INITIATIVES PROJECT (1979–1987)

The American Initiatives project sought to develop a comprehensive, nonmilitary strategy of peace. It would put paid to the cogent criticism that neither *Speak Truth to Power* nor the Pride of Pacifist Lions had such a strategy that governments could implement.

William Douglas's initiative on aiding democratic organizations abroad contributed to President Ronald Reagan's Westminster address, endorsing the idea and promising to develop and implement it. Weigel and Pickus concede that NED is the achievement of others but "we are happy to have had a role in promoting the idea and nurturing it along."[12]

Other initiatives submitted to the project included a uniform military financial accounting system as a "means of setting the baseline for across the board, percentage reductions in all classes of arms, the expansion and enhancement of student exchange programs as a means of strengthening links among the democracies" through the United States Information Agency (USIA), and a Joint US/Soviet Crisis Consultation Center. But the new, cogent criticisms were that these initiatives did not challenge the curve of Soviet expansionism; that, as containment strategy had suggested, change at the societal level within the Soviet bloc was perhaps a precondition to change at the governmental level.

PROGRAM 6: PLURALIZING THE SOVIET UNION

George Weigel, through his Congressman Joel Pritchard's office, organized a study group of congressmen to study ways to "pluralize" the Soviet Union. [13] This included identifying dissidents within Poland, then Czechoslovakia, now the Czech Republic and Slovakia, as well as the Soviet Union. It included support for the Helsinki Accords, and the follow-up review conferences which tied human rights improvements to lifting trade restrictions in place with the Soviet Union. Max Kampelman, a World War II conscientious objector and principal Reagan Administration arms control negotiator, was a colleague in this work. [14]

Philip Siegelman was a Council Board member and a colleague in another organization, the Center for Democracy in the USSR Projects that Siegelman conducted included gaining public visibility for dissidents such as Nathan Sharansky, Yuri Orlov, and Andrei Sakharov, the latter under house arrest at the time. Through S.O.S. (Skharov, Orlov, and Sharansky), Siegelman succeeded in organizing 8,000 scientists in 44 countries to defend Sakharov and other leading dissidents in the Soviet Union, and open possibilities of communication among scientists based on their scientific achievements and not the nations in which they worked. Robert Pickus was a Board member of the Center. [15]

The Berkeley office led in a VISA project, seeking to enable American citizens of Ukrainian origin to visit family freely in the Soviet Union and, vice versa, to enable Ukrainians resident in the USSR to obtain permission to visit their relatives in the United States. [16]

Exchange programs with the Soviet Union sought to base the selection of scientists coming to the United States on their academic credentials not their good standing with a repressive government. [17]

George Weigel led in drafting a declaration on Religious Liberty and sought public visibility for religious liberty on the Millennium of the introduction of Christianity into Kievan Rus. The petition gained over 500 signatures from religious opinion leaders in the United States and was presented to Ukrainian organizations in the United States and to Soviet officials through the Helsinki Review process. [18]

Kent Hill, a leader in the Evangelical Christian world and Council Board member, highlighted the plight of the Siberian Seven, seven Evangelical Christians who had taken refuge in the American Embassy fearing religious persecution. [19]

PROGRAM 7: A WASHINGTON OFFICE: THE JAMES MADISON
FOUNDATION, 1985–1994

The opening of a Washington office was a symbol that "work to change the
society so that government could act," was coming to fruition. As indicated
above, programs with Congressional representatives and the Initiatives project required frequent travel by Pickus and Weigel. Weigel was prepared to
move to Washington and broaden the programs to include governmental
decision-makers and leaders of national and international nongovernmental
organizations, including the Catholic Church.

The James Madison Foundation (JMF) was founded in 1985. It was described by its president and founder, George Weigel, as "an extension of the
work of the World Without War Council and an expression of the intention
of the American Peace Society."[20] As Weigel further explained,

> JMF was established . . . in the conviction that a marriage between the con-
> cepts of national interest and national purpose is essential today. In our name,
> we have chosen to honor the American Framer who thought best about the
> ways in which plurality and community could be combined in a society and
> polity fit for human beings. Because we take pride in, and are committed to,
> America as a watershed political community in human history, we would have
> our country serve large ends in its encounter with an often-hostile world.
> Peace, security, and freedom are, in our judgment, indivisible. American lead-
> ership toward a world that is peaceful, secure, and free is a matter of both
> national interest and national purpose.[21]

American Purpose began publishing in January 1987 and published continu-
ously through 1994, when Weigel became president of the Ethics and Public
Policy Center. Whether one agreed with Weigel or not, the clarity of his
prose, his ability to pull readers along, and his choice of subjects up for
governmental decision-making made this both a significant intellectual
achievement and a recognition that his voice was one to be reckoned with
internationally. His biography of Pope John II, *Witness to Hope* (2004), was
published in 27 languages, including Chinese. The words flowed from his
word processor like Niagara Falls from the time he was a Scholar-in-Resi-
dence in the Seattle office. The seventy-eight issues of *American Purpose*
provided a significant, erudite commentary and criticism of the national dialogue on questions of war and peace. His magnum opus with the Council
remains *Tranquillitas Ordinis: The Present Failure and Future Promise of
American Catholic Thought on War and Peace* (New York: Oxford University Press 1987).

PROGRAM 8: NATIONAL ASSOCIATION OF EVANGELICALS

The National Association of Evangelicals (NAE) "is the principal umbrella organization of Evangelical denominations, agencies and churches in the United States. The NAE is an association of over 50,000 churches from 72 denominations including 42 member denominations. Through its affiliates and subsidiaries, such as World Relief and National Religious Broadcasters, it serves a constituency of 10 to 15 million." Beginning in 1985, George Weigel, Robert Pickus and Kent Hill sought to engage the NAE and its various constituencies in reconciling "biblical responsibilities to be peacemakers" with a Christian "obligation to support the social structures of freedom, especially religious liberty." The first stage in engaging the NAE was the development of Guidelines that "provide the outlines for thoughtful obedience to both of those spheres of obligation."[22]

In the development of these guidelines "over 60 clergy and lay leaders, representing NAE member denominations, local churches, national organizations, colleges, and seminaries participated." Billy Melvin, Executive Director and Robert P. Dugan Jr., Director of the NAE Office of Public Affairs, recommend the Guidelines so that Evangelicals will "be active participants in the programs and debates that explore roads to peace, to the protection of democracy and international human rights, and to national security." The 48-page Guidelines include sections on the program's intentions, biblical foundations, political understandings and policy goals. "The purpose is clearly stated: The intention of this program is to develop within the Evangelical community leaders whose reflection on the theological, moral and political problems involved in the pursuit of peace and freedom in a fallen world will lead to realistic opportunities for an American contribution to a world safe for free societies, in which international conflict is resolved without war."[23]

The Guidelines include a section on "Other Voices" which include "Other views of how Evangelicals should relate to problems of peace, international human rights and national security, encountered in the writings of the Guidelines, together with a brief explanation of why the other voices were not incorporated into the Guidelines."

Brian F. O'Connell became the first Peace, Freedom and Security Studies Program Coordinator, working out of the NAE Washington office. Kent Hill became a colleague of Robert Pickus, working together to implement the Guidelines and developing a correspondence course to deepen understanding and extend implementation. Father Richard Neuhaus helped gain public visibility with the "new boy on the block"[24] of religious institutions engaged in peace education and action.

PROGRAM 9: *AMERICAN PURPOSE*, 1987–1995

American Purpose became the articulate house organ of the James Madison Foundation and the World Without War Council Inc. from January 1987 to 1995 (see program 7). George Weigel wrote the eight page newsletter with verve, erudition and significant insight into the "argument over America's very purpose in the world."[25]

Robert Pickus wrote the lead editorial for the April 1987 issue. Titled "Teaching the Young," it surveyed work in the pre-collegiate educational world. Precollegiate education became a focus of his programmatic work, much of it conducted through the Alliance for Education in Global International Studies (AEGIS) which he had help organize and drafted guidelines for in 1985. Throughout the 1981–1991 period, in addition to running national programs, Pickus maintained regional offices in Berkeley, Seattle, and Chicago, as well as the Washington office. National programs frequently had regional components that regional associates helped conceptualize, and for which they recruited an audience and provided logistical support and educational resources to help enter and continue the discussion.

American Purpose's focus on specific events, and executive and legislative branch decisions, encouraged a transition in Council thought. Its policy framework was not an organizational vehicle but the application of abstract concepts to specific policy choices. As the April 1987 issue explained:

> The James Madison Foundation has grown out of the complex history of the American peace movement. But we reject as dangerous misconceptions many of the non-regnant ideas guiding what is described as "work for peace" in America today [1987]. We reject grossly psychological concepts of international conflict. We are unapologetically anti-Communist. We seek the advance of human liberty. We know that there is a connection between Soviet brutishness at home and Soviet aggressiveness abroad. We believe that survivalism is morally degrading, and threatens the very peace it claims to serve.
>
> We affirm just law and democratic politics as instruments of peace and freedom. We believe that "interdependence" and "intervention" are two dimensions of the same contemporary reality. We are more interested in democratic forms of political community in and between nations than we are in micromanaging the evolution of the American weapons systems. We wish to contribute to a wise understanding of the relationship between moral principles and foreign policy choices.
>
> We believe, in short, that work for peace, freedom, and security can be an expression of the best instincts of the American experiment, rather than an attack on the experiment itself. . . . American Purpose will report and comment on the debate over the national interest and the national purpose in the opinion-shaping and values-teaching centers of American Public life.

George Weigel set out to articulate a new means to get there from here after the American Initiatives Project produced initiatives but no strategy. That new strategy was significantly different in that it accepted that general and complete disarmament—the declaratory goal of the Kennedy Administration—was not a realistic prospect in the current political system and perhaps would never be. The question *Speak Truth to Power* addressed was "Is there a means other than war to counter that which we consider evil." *American Purpose* in Weigel's capable hands would ask a different question: Is there a form of political community "in and between nations" that would yield freedom and security and would enforce international treaties that serve essential values—security, peace, and freedom?

But political community between representative democracies and dictatorships is a chimera. The nine cultures in the world were formed around religious belief and the deeply-rooted behavioral consequences of different religions produce a world of adversarial states for whom enforceable international treaties are rejected as intrusive. Good global governance means reforming the UN into an institution capable of enforcing world law. Neither were realistic possibilities in the period from 1985 to 2015. So what is realistic and what does a stable peace require?

Weigel in *American Purpose* explored answers to both what is realistic and what is needed. What follows are excerpts from *American Purpose* written by George Weigel but with Robert Pickus's enthusiastic support. Along with key staff, everyone including Weigel agreed that the previous answers in the Council's canon had failed and were not conceptually adequate to suggest how a stable peace could be obtained by 2050. *American Purpose* thus became an introduction to a world order models project that accepted international agencies like the International Monetary Fund and the World Trade Organizations and the International Atomic Energy Agency as functioning but improvable parts of the needed world order. The UN General Assembly is a forum not a legislative body. The Security Council is in need of reform but there is no acceptable reform formula likely to make it into an effective enforcer of international norms. You are invited to join the discussion, recognizing that nation states remain the dominant actors in world politics, and the security of 195 states is still sought through military security strategies and will continue to do so unless and until a strategy of peace emerges from the contemporary dialogue.

George Weigel summarized for eight years the decisions made inside the beltway and advocated specific solutions to them, with intelligence, verve, and erudition. Among the specific proposals discussed and advocated are:

- Good Global Governance: Proposal for an Association of Democracies.[26] After summarizing Charles Krauthammer's six reasons the United Nations has become marginally effective, Weigel agrees with Jeane Kirkpatrick,

US Ambassador to the United Nations, that reform is possible within, but he also argues for "the creation of an Association of Democracies," summarizing Morton Kaplan's detailed proposal which includes standards of what constitutes a democracy and therefore membership.

- Help for Conscientious Objectors. "A Warsaw-based independent pacifist movement, Freedom and Peace, had successfully pressed the case for conscientious objection to military service in Poland. . . . 400 East European intellectuals and dissidents, including 77 from the Soviet Union petitioning their governments to make legal claiming conscientious objector status."[27]

- Pacifist/Just War Roots: Just War After the Gulf War. Iraq's invasion of Kuwait produced a quandary for the pacifist/just war/national interest diplomacy make-up of the Council: In a rightly ordered political community, in which war was illegitimate, how would the community repel acts of military aggression? Weigel here applies the Just War criteria asking: "Was ours a just cause? What were our intentions? Who could authorize the resort to armed force? Did we have a reasonable chance of success? Was military action a last resort? Could we conduct military operations that respected the rights of innocent civilians?" He concludes the Gulf War met the criteria and finishes: The issue...is not whether the just war tradition is obsolete. One might as well ask whether politics—the organization of human life into purposeful political communities—is obsolete. Rather, the issue is how we can refine the moral logic of the just war tradition to take account of the new political and technological circumstances in which we find ourselves. The Gulf War and the world that has emerged from the Cold War have shown us just how urgent a task that is.

Weigel also became an advocate for Pope John II, summarizing religious pronouncements such as *Centesimus Annus,* an extraordinary statement of faith: faith in freedom; faith in man's capacity to order his public life properly; affirming free will and individual conscience expressed in legally recognized human rights.

> . . . And above all faith in God, who created man with intelligence and free will. It may well be the greatest of the social encyclicals, given the breadth of the issues it addresses, the depth at which questions are probed, and the empirical sensitivity John Paul II shows to the "signs of the times" as they illuminate freedom's cause today. . . . With Centesimus Annus, the "Pope of Freedom" has not only marked the centenary of a great tradition. He has brilliantly scouted the terrain for the next hundred years of humanity's struggle to embody in public life the truth that makes us free.[28]

ON SOCIALISM VS. CAPITALISM

Centesimus Annus is interpreted to endorse a free economy. If by capitalism is meant what the West at its best means by capitalism—a tripartite system in which democratic politics and a vibrant culture discipline and temper the free market—then that is the system the pope urges the new democracies and the Third World to adopt, because that is the system most likely to sustain a human freedom that is truly liberating.

Weigel also quotes *Centesimus Annus*:

> The fundamental error of socialism is anthropological in nature. Socialism considers the individual person simply as an element, a molecule within the social organism, so that the good of the individual is completely subordinated to the functioning of the socio-economic mechanism. Socialism likewise maintains that the good of the individual can be realized without reference to his free choice, to the unique and exclusive responsibility he exercises in the face of good or evil. Man is thus reduced to a series of social relationships, and the concept of the person as the . . . subject of moral decision disappears, the very subject whose decisions build the social order. From this mistaken conception of the person there arise both a distortion of law . . . and an opposition to private property. A person who is deprived of something he can call "his own," and of the possibility of earning a living through his own initiative, comes to depend on the social machine and on those who control it. This makes it much more difficult for him to recognize his dignity as a person, and hinders progress toward the building up of an authentic human community.

George Weigel also quoted Vladimir Bukovsky, a Russian dissident, that socialism was the slowest route to capitalism. Weigel accepted the range of regulated, market economies, governed by representative democracies from the United States to Sweden as capitalist. The signature goal of nationalizing major industries, as was accomplished by the Atlee government in England (1945–1951), was rejected because nationalized industries did not pay taxes, did little to improve workers' conditions, and polluted. This was not the view of many World Without War Council staff and Board members.

IS UNILATERAL DISARMAMENT OR MILITARY STRENGTH THE WAY TO WAR AS WELL AS PEACE?

In response to the argument that nobody won or that Gorbachev drove the policies of the 1980s, *American Purpose* takes on the hard argument from the Council's origins in the pacifist world: Are arms races inherently dangerous and ultimately destabilizing or does military strength deter aggression? *American Purpose* discusses this question through a review of Patrick Glynn's, Closing Pandora's Box: Arms Races, Arms Control, and the History of the Cold War.[29] Glynn concludes that arms control treaties are unenforceable and arms control negotiations are usually accompanied by the expansion of the weapons systems under negotiations, as with SALT II.

Weigel concludes: "Closing Pandora's Box is, in sum, a far more trustworthy guide to understanding the military-political dynamics of the Cold War than is Kissinger." but closing Pandora's box leaves out the role of "soft" power, the Helsinki final act and the subsequent eruption of human-rights monitoring organizations in Central and Eastern Europe—organizations that became the backbone of the democratic resistance to Communism in the 1980s. The cold war was won—and, yes, the correct verb is "won"—because of a complex of factors. Even after Alamogordo, military power is not a negligible aspect of the politics of nations. It made a great deal of difference indeed, in the endgame of the Cold War, that the "hardware" side of the strategic deterioration of the 1970s had been reversed.

Yes, the deepest values of the American people proved more resilient and more attractive than the debased and inhuman anti-morality of Marxism-Leninism. But that victory of the human spirit was made possible by the fact that containment—hardware, and hardball—had created circumstances in which an effective, nonviolent moral resistance could succeed.[30]

DO DEMOCRACIES HAVE A SEPARATE PEACE AMONG THEM?

Weigel argues that the cause of human rights has become one of the most powerful forces in contemporary world politics. The evidence for this is not only to be found in decent societies with a long record of protecting civil rights and political freedoms, or in the recent triumphs of human rights activists in Solidarity and Charter 77. Even more compelling proof lies in the tribute that vice pays to virtue: in the fact that virtually every tyranny in the world today tries to justify its repressions in the name of an "alternative understanding of human rights."[31]

Weigel goes on to trace the origins of civil and political rights embodied in the concept of citizenship which both sets limits to what governments should do, and establishes an area in public life where the individual, and the society, not the state, is sovereign: in the areas of "the right to vote, to organize a political opposition, to petition for redress of grievances and to be judged by a jury of one's peers." The claim that the "right to food" was being pursued by a regime that starved 3 million people to death in one year by state decree is abhorrent.[32]

An application of this interpretation of human rights in *American Purpose* was reported at the World Conference on Human Rights held in Vienna under UN auspices in mid-June, 1993. It demonstrated in painful detail just how the old rationalizations for tyranny were being justified as alternative interpretations of human rights and the priority of economic, social, and cultural rights. While Warren Christopher "nails the hypocrisy" of human rights declarations that use one set of rights to suppress civil and political rights, nonetheless the consensus procedures means endorsing the Vienna Declaration with "no clear articulation of the basic human rights of: "religious freedom, or freedom of association, or freedom of assembly, or freedom of the press. Which is to say, the Vienna Declaration is not serious business." It does not, in short, provide a basis for an individual to challenge a state tyranny.

There follows a paragraph by paragraph critique of the Vienna document and the action plan which turns over administration to the UN Bureaucracy. Weigel quotes approvingly Joshua Muravchik's tough strategy:

> The end of the Cold War has brought down many barriers, including, it seems, the barrier that used to divide communist and anti-communist tyrants. On the other side of the coin, advocates of human rights and democracy are united across the political spectrum as never before. Why shouldn't the democracies accept the challenge thrown down by dictators? Who needs false unanimity? Why not declare that the new dividing line in global politics is between those who honor and practice human rights and democracy and those who do not? Why not have a vote?

Weigel concludes:

> What the cause of human rights needs is an assertive United States, unashamed of its own human rights traditions, committed to the notion that civil and political freedoms are the basic building blocks of decent societies, and willing to challenge the shibboleths that have fouled international human rights discourse for two generations now. That is not, unfortunately, the United States that showed up at the World Conference on Human Rights. And the real losers were the victims of human rights abuse throughout the world. [33]

CRISIS AREAS, BOSNIA: TO INTERVENE OR NOT TO INTERVENE?

The Balkans are, to repeat, primarily Europe's problem. But "Europe" doesn't exist, as an effective instrument of policy. American leadership, in forging a pan-European policy, and then in helping to provide the diplomatic and perhaps military muscle to back it up, has been the key missing ingredient in the diplomatic mix for almost two years now. Bushbaker "realism" and its successor, Bill Clinton's imitation of Jimmy Carter, have left the United States in the ridiculous position of supplicant before people who can't even rouse themselves to restrain the neighborhood's hoodlums. [34]

Weigel then offers a set of criteria that frames the question of military intervention—whether by aerial means or "boots on the ground" invasion—to prevent genocidal slaughter and impose order. This implies a possible justification of military intervention, while former Chairman of the Joint Chiefs of Staff Colin Powell's criteria for intervention nearly precluded the possibility.[35]

American Purpose offers track II diplomacy (Track I is State-to-State diplomacy) as an alternative to military intervention:

> [The] Immediate start-up of round-the-clock Radio Free Europe broadcasts in Serbo-Croatian would make a lot of sense. So would identifying and financial- ly supporting democratic forces in those countries (and in Bosnia-Herzegovi- na), in order to help build an "opposition" that might someday be able to make real peace. Joint charitable and reconstructive activity by Catholic, Orthodox, and Muslim organizations in the West might provide both needed services and an important example in the ruins of Bosnia- Herzegovina. . . .

Finally: the argument above is not conservative-isolationist. In fact, there is a place elsewhere in the world where genocide is occurring right now; where the friends of the West are being slaughtered by the enemies of the West, and where Western military force could effectively impose a political solution, perhaps in the form of a trusteeship. That place is Sudan. The odds on a successful Western (and US) military intervention are much better there than in the mountains of Bosnia. Alas for the Sudanese Christians, CNN isn't paying attention. Why aren't the rest of us?

TERRORISM: AFTER THE [FIRST] TWIN TOWERS ATTACK

American Purpose addresses terrorism in Europe, Latin America, and the Middle East, states 11 mistaken understandings, criticizes four Levantine strategies, and then offers a policy outline for a potentially successful coun- ter-terrorism strategy.[36]

> International law and international conventions are of little use in confronting terrorism today. International law is primarily of interest to lawyers and to insurance companies; international anti-terrorism conventions provide little leverage in a situation in which Egypt cannot even get counter-terrorist coop- eration from its Islamic brethren in other countries. No, what counts is national policy and its effective implementation—sometimes, to be sure, in active col- laboration with friends and allies. . . . Deterrence is the crucial first goal of a successful counter-terrorist strategy. A terrorist attack thwarted is not a draw: it is a victory for the forces of order, for it saves lives and property while demonstrating (and strengthening) society's resistance capabilities... An en- hanced intelligence capability is indispensable to counterterrorist deterrence. It is essential that the US government understand the motivations, ideology,

capabilities, and vulnerabilities of those groups and individuals that are the likely sources of terrorist activity. . . . Strengthening our intelligence capabilities will require publicly acknowledged cooperation with friendly intelligence services in countries facing similar threats.

Deterrence of terrorism also requires a far more assertive nonproliferation effort against the spread of ballistic missiles and the technology needed to use them. Severe sanctions should be imposed on any Western company that provides missile technology or the computer equipment needed to support a missile capability to any state known or suspected to be involved in terrorism . . . ballistic missile defense: in a decade in which it seems probable, not just likely, that an outlaw state will acquire weapons of mass destruction and the capability to deliver them over long distances, ballistic missile defense—not the Astrodome, but the kind of effective defense we could mount in the next few years against smaller attacks—is a moral and strategic imperative. . . .

Finally, deterrence of a terrorist atrocity may, in special circumstances, require preemptive military action. Effective counter-terrorism will thus mean a creative extension of the just war tradition. The tendency in recent decades has been to narrow the "just cause" criterion to the point where many specialists argue that force is justifiable only in "response to an aggression already under way. . . . In the case of terrorists, the "aggression" is clearly "under way" before the action actually happens. No one has a right to use the instruments and processes of democracy as a means to destroy democracy. Abusing civil liberties in order to deny others their most fundamental civil liberty—their right to life—is the act of an enemy of freedom, and an enemy of the United States. There is no reason why we cannot hold fast to those propositions and to our fundamental moral and political values at the same time—even in the face of terrorism.

George Weigel repositioned the Council with Robert Pickus's approval. *American Purpose* was welcomed by key staff for its application of the Council's canon to specific decisions, declarations, and crises, but it was not a product of a consultative process. It entered the discussion through the just war lens, not pacifist convictions. Weigel faced the morally difficult questions of how to prevent aggression, genocide or terrorism without a choice of a nonviolent means. It was unapologetic in its interpretation of American civil and political rights history, joining Robert Pickus in the caveat that civil and political rights had been progressively realized here.

Coming at the conclusion of the American Peace Initiatives project, the idea of initiatives is noticeable by its absence. Instead, the basis of a democratic peace strategy is evident. That is, not only is there a dividing line between democracy and dictatorships, there is also substantial evidence[37] that democracies rarely war on each other. The Council programs that aided transitions from dictatorship toward democracy could be interpreted as extending in time the democratic peace that existing among European Union and North American democracies and geographically.

But this was George Weigel's answer to the failure to develop a comprehensive Strategy of American Peace Initiative acts. Pickus agreed with nonviolently aiding transitions to democracy but retained the conviction that a successfully developed initiative strategy at the global level could get us to stable peace in 40 more years (now 2005–2045). But a nonviolent strategy to secure government against domestic violence, prevent genocide, punish terrorism or military aggression would have to be improved to make good the claim. So also, the existing boundaries of states in the Middle East and Africa would have to be either accepted, or a nonviolent means of testing self-determination claims adopted.

PEACE AMONG DEMOCRACIES WHILE AIDING TRANSITIONS FROM DICTATORSHIPS TOWARD DEMOCRACY

The national World Without War Council received a grant from the National Endowment for Democracy in 1991 to "help strengthen independent sector development in Russia and other former USSR republics."[38] The Civil Society: US/USSR program built on the Project South Africa experience of linking nongovernmental organizations in one society with their counterpart organizations in another.

Kent Hill, a Council Board member and leader in the National Association of Evangelicals, advocated for and published about the Siberian Seven–Christians who had taken refuge in the American Embassy in Moscow.

The Seattle Office's Holt Ruffin led much of the work and provided the computer expertise that permitted internet-inspired detailed programs and publications. These included Lech Choroszucha (trans.), *Wolnosc I Pokoj (WIP): Documents From Poland's Freedom and Peace Movement* (1989); Lucy Dougall and Holt Ruffin, *Raising the Curtain: A Guide to Independent Organizations and Contacts in Eastern Europe* (1989); Lucy Dougall's "Report From Tashkent"; Holt Ruffin and Richard Upjohn, *Neformalniye: A Guide to Independent Organizations and Contacts in the Soviet Union* (1991); Holt Ruffin and Richard Upjohn, *The Post-Soviet Handbook: A Guide to Grassroots Organizations and Internet Resources in the New Independent States* (1991); and Holt Ruffin and Daniel Waugh, *Civil Society in Central Asia* (1999).

The Chicago office worked through ethnic organizations aiding transitions to democracy in their homelands. Leaders in the Chinese (Zhang Zin, Center for Democracy and Freedom in China), Polish (Polish American Congress), Mexican (Mexican-American Art Institute), Romanian (Gabriel Nicolescu, Romanian Freedom Forum), and Vietnamese (Ngoan Le, Vietnamese Community Center) communities were encouraged to contact nongovernmental leaders in their homeland, much as the Chicago office had done through Bayard Rustin and others in Project South Africa. Carl Gershman, President of the National Endowment for Democracy, engaged in a dialogue with leaders from these communities which was published in a Democracy Roundtable series, Democracy Transcendent: A Discussion of Universal Democratic Values.[39]

Gilbert Ghez, Council Board member and Roosevelt University professor of economics, formed a Scholars for Freedom program bringing Central European students to Chicago for a refresher course.

THE SOBERING

For pacifist witnesses to an impossible ideal, an evaluation of their career is based on their intention. In Robert Pickus's summary of *Speak Truth to Power* he set a difficult standard, thou shalt not kill is not only a commandment, it was more likely to sustain foreign policy goals against what was recognized as evil, requiring a new course for US foreign policy and it could be brought into history through American peace initiatives, reciprocated by adversaries and allies alike. The goal of the strategy of peace was building the institutions that could enforce treaties creating a disarmed world, under law, safe for free societies—began immediately but with 40 years needed to build incrementally the acceptance of an obligation to enforce treaties. The organizations he had led from 1958 to 1987 had progressed and survived, but the obstacles encountered required a new time frame.

> A different sense of time is moving through the imbroglio of organizations in the American public effort for peace. Even peace groups whose entire ethos is a contribution of eschatology have changed. Their sense that the end is near once moved them to urgent action and to the images and language of apocalypse. Now, even among such groups, there is a widespread recognition that, whatever the urgency, the obstacles to progress toward a world proof against the outrage of war will not yield to a two-minutes-to-midnight approach.
> Recent years have seen a move away from "mobilizations" and nuclear horror films that, while ostensibly presenting scientifically objective portrayals of the consequences of nuclear war, do in fact, through heightened fear, try to galvanize support for ill- conceived policy prescriptions. The politics here have not changed—only the painful recognition that there is no way out, now, of a world dominated by fear and the threat of war. The third or fourth year of passionate work leads to the realization that a way out will require changes measured by generations, not apocalyptic "campaigns."

This shift in time perspective led Robert Pickus to reflect on the state of pre-collegiate peace education. He cited Andre Ryerson's, "The Scandal of 'Peace Education,'" as accurately rejecting Educators for Social Responsibility and others that focus on the evils of America. Vietnam references abound, but nowhere in the pages of Dialogue or Perspectives will you find a paragraph on the war in Afghanistan. The crudest fabrications in Soviet propaganda are taken at face value. Ronald Reagan is the obstacle to peace. The sources of East/West conflict lie in the United States. The Hiss and Rosenberg trials are a "hoax on history."

Constructive work is going on, particularly on developing global education. The work of Michael Novak, Albert Shanker, Ruth Wattenberg, and Paul Gagnon in the American Federation of Teachers is cited as instrumental in developing "Education for Democracy" which addresses how to educate for peace and freedom in ways that apply, rather than debase, sound educational standards. The Education for Democracy curriculum has been translated into many languages and is aiding in the transitions to representative democracy underway. A new educational association was being formed, American Education for Global and International Education (AEGIS) which Robert Pickus committed to work with after 25 years of working with Global Perspectives in Education based in the New York Friends Group. AEGIS was to become a professional association with guidelines to keep them on track. Out of this refocus on international perspectives in schools could come a new generation of leaders committed to work toward world community and national well-being.

What was the sobering experience? The painful recognition that there is no way out reflects a sobering and a new time perspective. Among the possible explanations are: (1) a citizen peace effort that refused to address all the armies engaged in internal, regional, or global conflicts; (2) The failure of the American Initiatives Project to produce initiatives that met the criteria of the "memo"; (3) The insistence of the authors of each initiative that their idea become the focus of advocacy, not part of an overall strategy that had as its objective, creating a political community in which war is illegitimate; (4) An awareness that nuclear fear was being replaced by the contending doom at the heart of the global warming, now climate change movement; and (5) The fact that the recognized international organizations, specifically the United Nations, were perceived as "dangerous places" in the words of Daniel Moynihan, not stepping stones to "a disarmed world under law, safe for free societies."

In short, the Turn Toward Peace policy framework captured and incorporated the ideas of one peace-concerned generation, but Robert Pickus's "New Approaches to Peace"[40] recommended that whatever new approaches were developed, they would need to take into account that world politics was still driven by power as described in professor Hans Morgenthau's Politics among Nations. In this sobered condition, the withdrawal of one country from a conflict, does not lead to peace, it increased the power of another country. Hans Morgenthau, not Robert Hutchins, was the wiser of the two but they needed each other. Robert Pickus's synthesis of their and others' ideas required fresh thought on war, even with new concepts. But not from scratch.

NOTES

1. "But What Did You Do?" World Without War Council, Inc., December 1991, Hoover Institution Archives.

2. The Organizational support, Boards, Perspective Statements, Strategy of Change, and Programs with specific dates and places are archived at the Hoover Institution, as well as regional offices at the University of Washington, Seattle and Hoover and the Midwest Office at the Swarthmore Peace Collection. Overviews of the National Archives and the Midwest Archives are also available.

3. The 1996 version listed contending perspective, obstacles, means to overcome obstacles.

4. Lowell Livezey's Council career began as the Director of the Midwest office. His work in Chicago constituted a significant part of the Midwest Office's archives at the Swarthmore Peace Collection. His personal papers are also archived there. Swarthmore is Livezey's alma mater.

5. "But What Did You Do?" December 1991, Berkeley, Hoover Institution Archives.

6. See Roy L. Prosterman, "Vietnam: Politics, Land Reform and Development in the Countryside," *Asian Survey*, Vol. 10, No. 8, August 1970, pp. 752–758. The Land to the Tiller program of President Thieu, 3/26/1970 cut Viet Cong recruitment by 80% and increased rice production by 30%. Prosterman formed the Rural Development Institute, now Landesa, which worked for land reform in 40 countries, successfully establishing land ownership rights for 400,000,000 people. In 2010 Prosterman received the University of Chicago Public Service award. He graduated from the University of Chicago in 1954 and Harvard Law School in 1958.

7. William A. Douglas, *Freedom at Issue* (1982).

8. Taiwan's Foundation for Democracy website recommends "Taiwan's peaceful transition to democracy as not only a historical accomplishment for its twenty-three million people, but a landmark in the worldwide spread of democracy. Only after years of struggle and effort could this transformation take place." See also Sook Long Jee's, *The Experience of the East Asia Institute* (June 2013).

9. Timothy E. Wirth, United Nations Foundation, 2005; see also *Democracy Rising, Assessing the Global Challenges*, Heraldo Munoz, editor (Boulder: Lynne Rienner, 2005).

10. Three essays were published in the *Wilson Quarterly*, New Year's 1987 by Nurnberger, Woito, and Weigel.

11. See World Without War Council, Midwest newsletter, Project South Africa, May 1987.

12. Memo to American Initiative Project Advisors, November 1983, p. 4.

13. Work with Congressmen was summarized in *Exploring Soviet Realities: Problems in the Pursuit of Peace, Report of a Bipartisan Seminar in the US House of Representatives, 1983–1894*, George Weigel, editor.

14. See Max Kampelman correspondence file, World Without War Council archives, Hoover Institution.

15. See Center for Democracy in the USSR, organizational folder, Hoover Institution.

16. See Visa Project, Hoover Institution Archives.

17. See Exchange Initiative, American Initiatives Project, Hoover Institution.

18. The Helsinki Accords, signed by 35 nations on 8/1/1975, affirmed existing national boundaries and, in clause 7, affirmed international human rights. The Accords, and the Review Process required in their implementation, created a multilateral framework for the programs summarized in Program 4, Pluralizing the Soviet Union as well as many others, including the AFL-CIO's support for Solidarity and Charter 77 in Czechoslovakia.

19. See Kent Hill, Council Board Member, National Association of Evangelicals leader, *The Soviet Union on the Brink: An Inside Look at Christianity and Glasnost* (1991).

20. The American Peace Society was founded in 1828 and is considered the first, secular nongovernmental organization committed to peace between nations. Quakers, Mennonites, and Brethren religious orders have deeper roots, as does the Catholic Church.

21. George Weigel, *American Purpose*, Vol. 1, No. 1, January 1987. Weigel also produced a critically important pamphlet, *Human Rights, Democracy and US Foreign Policy, a Report of a Bipartisan Seminar in the US House of Representatives, 1985–1986*. James Madison Foundation, 1986. Weigel's papers are at the Library of Congress.

22. Guidelines, Peace, Freedom and Security Studies, 1987, 1989, p. 3.

23. Fr. Richard John Neuhaus, The Religion Society Report, March 1987.

24. First Things.

25. *American Purpose*, Vol. l, No. 1, January 1987, pp. 1–2.

26. *American Purpose*, Vol. 1, No. 5, November 1987, p. 67.

27. *American Purpose*, Vol. 2, No. 5, May/June 1988, p. 33; With the Vol. 3, No. 7, September 1989 issue of *American Purpose*, The Ethics and Public Policy Center became the Sponsoring Organization, George Weigel its President. Robert Pickus became president of the James Madison Foundation and the office was moved to Berkeley, California.

28. See also George Weigel's *Witness to Hope: The Biography of Pope John II* (New York and London: Oxford University Press 1999) and his *The Final Revolution. The Resistance Church and the Collapse of Communism* (New York and London: Oxford University Press 2003).

29. New York: Basic Books 1992.

30. *American Purpose*, Vol. 6, No. 10, December 1992. George Weigel became President of the Ethics and Public Policy Center in 1989; Robert Pickus, M. Holt Ruffin and Robert Woito ceased to be listed as contributing editors in 1992. Robert Pickus assumed the James Madison Foundation presidency in 1989.

31. *American Purpose*, Vol. 7, No. 6, July–August 1993.

32. See Timothy Snyder, *Bloodlands*, for a scholarly description of the terror famine in the Ukraine (1933) with documentation of the three million casualties, and *The Black Book of Communism* documenting how the "right to food" was perverted in both the Soviet Union and Mao's China. The "Great Leap Forward" is estimated to have caused 45 million deaths (1958–1962) (Yang, Jisheng, "The Fatal Politics of the PRC's [People's Republic of China] Great Leap Forward," *The Journal of Contemporary China*, 2010).

33. *American Purpose*, July–August 1993, "The New Human Rights Debate."

34. *American Purpose*, Vol. 7, No. 5, May–June 1993, p. 39 [each issue is 8 pages long, but pages are numbered consecutively].

35. See Colin Powell, *American Power and Intervention From Vietnam to Iraq* (2009).

36. *American Purpose*, Vol. 7, No. 4, April 1993, pp. 32–34.

37. See Michel Doyle (1971), Bruce Russett, *Grasping the Democratic Peace* (1994), Charles Lipson, *Reliable Partners: How Democracies Have Made a Separate Peace* (2005).

38. See But what did you do?, December 1991 program description, Hoover Institution Archives.

39. The Democracy Round Table series included round table discussions published as *The Transition to Democracy in Poland* and *Democracy in Vietnam?*

40. Ken Jensen (Ed.), *Approaches to Peace* (Washington: New Approaches to Peace 1991).

Chapter Five

The Learning Curve

Robert Pickus reflected in college on the question "Where did the idealism of the Russian Revolution go wrong?" He shared Arthur Koestler's *Darkness at Noon* analysis and expressed it in his break with the Pacifist Lions in "Political Integrity and Its Critics"[1] and in the Camus preface's assessment of the Vietnam era, misnamed, anti-war movement. There were many currents of thought, but the dominant one insisted that the US had misused its power in defending a South Vietnamese ally and denied (often implicitly) that North Vietnam was at least as murderous and indiscriminate in those it killed. Over a million Vietnamese fled Vietnam as "boat people" in small boats preferring the roughly 50% survival rate on the South China seas to life in "liberated" Vietnam. Pickus and Weigel's Advices and Cautions offer 17 specific recommendations for a peace movement to be "worthy of the name."

IMPROVING THE LEVEL OF PUBLIC DISCOURSE ABOUT WORLD POLITICS?

As Robert Pickus said, nearly everyone who seeks to organize a citizen peace effort has a speech in their vest pocket they will never give: In Praise of Public Apathy. The agreed-to facts are few, the intentions of adversaries as well as those of the United States are rarely transparent, and there are seven or more coherent contexts that suggest which facts you consider significant and which you ignore. Programming across lines of division had to be organized at colleges to learn from multiple perspectives and synthesize a better, more realistic, viewpoint around which a consensus needed for a country to lead could be formed. The appropriate role for citizens and nongovernmental organizations was in setting goals, considering appropriate means to achieve them, defending human rights . . . but not in discussing the internal politics of countries such as Iran—unless aided by a panel of experts with the requisite language skills and knowledge available to clarify the choices.

GENOCIDE—NEVER AGAIN?

The Universal Declaration of Human Rights, and the two Covenants that turn it into treaty obligations, suggests a developed sense of world community which neither existed nor could be quickly created. The Genocide Treaty, long delayed in ratification, did not produce the will to enforce it. Never again? We stood as silent witness to genocidal scale slaughter in Darfur or Rwanda.[2] Neither a nonviolent nor violent solution was ever recommended. Romeo Dallaire's attempt to stop the genocidal carnage in Rwanda, was never addressed by the Organizations of African Unity, the US, or the UN He was charged by Belgium for his heroic but unsuccessful efforts in which eight Belgian peacekeepers under his command died.

The Council had not succeeded in building a constituency that would have required the UN or the US to respond, whether with a nonviolent brigade or with trained military force. In short, genocide was outlawed by an international convention; but how would the pacifist, just war advocates enforce it? Mass slaughter provoked no coordinated potentially effective response in Cambodia, Bosnia, Kosovo, Rwanda, Somalia, Sudan, Iraq, Syria, and Burma.

THE MIDDLE EAST

The Middle East proved intractable. The Midwest Office gathered American Jewish leaders to dialogue with Americans of Palestinian origins prior to Anwar Sadat's breaking ranks and visiting Israel.[3]

The United States, the European Union, the Soviet Union, and the United Nations could agree on a road map to peace, but mediation by United States leaders (Jimmy Carter, Ronald Reagan, Dennis Sell, Bill Clinton, George Mitchell, John Kerry), produced little progress on the goal of a two-state solution indicated in the road map. Robert Pickus concluded in 2000[4] that one must recognize:

> No matter what Israel does, there will be no peace without steady but funda-
> mental change in the character of the Arab world and the disastrous impact
> that Palestinian nationalism has had on the world: encouraging Middle East
> Arab politics to focus on what they hate, instead of what is needed for more
> life, liberty and the pursuit of happiness in their nations, e.g., the one-eyed
> telling of who is responsible for the sad plight of Arab refugees over the last 50
> years. . . . In sum: without change in the Arab world's politics, economics, role

of women, press, attitude toward Israel, etc., there will be no peace. Whatever Israel gives, short of disappearing, won't help without such change.

Robert Pickus and the World Without War Council failed. A world without war remains the thing that is not. Robert Pickus accepted that he had failed, but added with emphasis that he was "an experienced failure." He left a legacy of organizational work and thought that answered these important questions: How do you define war? Mass violence? What are the conditions essential to a stable peace? What countries or alliance of countries are capable of the needed leadership? How can individuals in nongovernmental organizations contribute to help get there from here?

The Council also asked difficult questions: If you claim to be for peace, are you addressing all military powers in the conflict? If you are a referee and you hold one fighter's arms while the other pummels away, are you a mediator or an accomplice? What methods, other than those of violence and war, are available to address and change that which you consider evil?

DIFFICULT QUESTIONS

There are challenging quotes from the Bible and the classics that dismiss the possibility: "there will always be wars and rumors of war," and "only the dead have seen the end of war."[5] If war is inevitable, the Council was the worst kind attempting to form a consensus in the United States for something that can never be. That viewpoint deserves consideration but so does the likelihood of nuclear war if no alternative is found. The *Bulletin of Atomic Scientists* doomsday clock is at its most alarmist in 2017. But is a world without war impossible?

ANTINOMIES

A world without war in most renditions is a utopian fantasy incapable of comprehending that no matter what you have done or not done, somebody is organizing to kill you and yours.[6] The fantasy is more likely to produce appeasement of expansionist dictatorships, such as Nazi Germany or Stalinist Russia (or in some others' view, apologists for capitalist imperialism), than a stable peace. But utopian fantasy can be a motivating force encouraging us all, concerned by the loss of life, the waste and costs, if not the very future of the species, to try to do better. The antinomy is in the survival of the nation-state, and its capacity to resolve domestic conflict vs. its risk of capture by secular or religious ideologies claiming justification in the use of mass violence. In *Speak Truth to Power*, Robert Pickus accepted the idea that the organizational requirements of war, the institutional, behavioral, training, indoctrination, and mass hatred of the enemy, all block any constructive approach to world politics. George F. Kennan, advocate of the containment doctrine, maintained without some form of military deterrence whatever your strategy of peace, it will trade words for deeds. Sects that gain the control of nations and seek through mass violence to impose their ideology on others—Bolsheviks, Fascists, Baathist, Islamic Jihadists—want their enemies dead. They will negotiate the time, place, and manner of your execution, but not the rectitude of their goal of world domination or the use of mass violence to achieve it. Changing their minds is the hard problem. Denial produces appeasement, not peace.

As the coercive instruments of enforcement by international agencies increase, consent for their use declines. In discussions of how to abolish genocide, the accusation that Israel is committing genocide when it is responding to violent attack on a one-for-one basis, obfuscates any solution to genocide and reinforces the Palestinians' commitment to wage a war of annihilation.[7] If peacekeeping is by consent and is restricted to lightly armed soldiers, its prospects for challenging aggression are small. Is there a nonviolent brigade ready to intervene to stop genocide, terrorism, and aggression?

Patriotism and Cosmopolitanism ("familiarity with and at ease in different cultures and countries") could reinforce each other or undermine each other. For example, STTP advocated unilateral disarmament as a patriotic obligation, while Norman Thomas, Reinhold Niebuhr and George F. Kennan said the pacifist goal should be universal disarmament in the face of Bolshevism whose ideology was universalistic. The history and potential for conflict with mass violence can be embedded in "my country right or wrong, but my country" as well as with cosmopolitanism when bland pronouncements of universals collide with fundamental cultural differences. For example beliefs about gender, equality of opportunity, or same sex marriage can collide with cultures in which a single same sex act is punishable by capital punishment.

Inner peace, peace as the achievement of harmonious relationships, is a worthy goal; but peace in the killing fields of world politics requires the achievement of the minimum, essential conditions within which real conflicts over territory, ideology, and religion, to name but three factors, can be continued without mass violence.

A stable peace by 2043? Robert Pickus in 2003 would amend his earlier, "I am an experienced failure," concession:

> It was never our intention (or at least not mine) to establish a continuing organization. We intended a base for 40 years of steady work (the name of our first newsletter). We've had forty-five and will mark that fact on November 8th, 2003 in San Francisco. Trouble is, we picked the wrong 40 years. It's the next 40 years that will determine whether the possibility of rightly ordered

political community capable of sustaining stable peace and governance that reflects belief in the dignity of man comes into being. The alternative is the Tower of Babel story, repeated but with more horrendous consequences.[8]

To those who wish for no more wars, a world without war, a stable peace, the questions you need to ask are clear. He asked and answered them and acknowledged his failure. The challenge remains, as the Great Books forecast in 1952: "Even if world peace is not actually begun in our time, we may prove to be the first generation . . . who, under the impact of world wars, have made a firm attempt to draw a decisive conclusion from all the accumulated wisdom concerning war and peace."[9] The case statement that Robert Pickus made a "firm attempt to draw a decisive conclusion" is established.

> We live in a country distinguished from many others by its wealth, size, diversity, technological capability, and, most of all, by the idea that formed it. The idea that the people shall rule because of the innate dignity of every person has been progressively realized in our experience of building and sustaining our political community. Such a political community must address the problem of war. Such a country has a significant, perhaps the key, role to play in progress toward peace (1991).[10]

The Council insisted that the United States of America could be constructively engaged in world politics on behalf of the conditions essential to a stable peace.

ACHIEVEMENTS

The United States successfully negotiated significant reductions of nuclear weapons as well as precautionary measures to avoid nuclear war by accident. No nuclear war occurred in this period, but there were close calls. In the arms arena, the Council proposed that SDI be done jointly and combined with offensive arms reduction. Also, a uniform military financial accounting system was proposed that could facilitate meaningful multilateral arms reduction if "national technical means" of verification were available. Robert Pickus proposed an initiative toward an international civil service among others.

The Council rejected single villain approaches to the cold war but held fast to the principle of universal human rights as articulated in the Universal Declaration of Human Rights (1948) and accepted implementing the Covenant on Civil and Political Rights after the Carter Administration clarified that there were 52 "reservations and understandings" necessary to protect existing human rights provisions in the United States.

The Council supported nonviolent demonstrations in Washington and Moscow (1961) and engaged in or supported fifteen programs designed to support the Helsinki Accords and aid in pluralizing the Soviet Union (conscientious objection recognition among Warsaw pact countries, travel rights for Soviet citizens, restoring religious liberty in Poland, exchange programs based on expertise not ideology, public visibility for dissidents (Sakharov, Orloff, Sharansky, Sergei Grigoryants, the Moscow Trust Group, the Siberian Seven, and tying economic policies to the safe passage of Russian Jews to Israel—the Jackson-Vanik legislation). The change in the United States is in the leadership expected in the Strategy of American Peace Initiative Acts.

World economic development: although we are preoccupied with quarrels over the distribution of wealth and whether fossil fuels are essential to sustainable growth there is one obscured truth: between 1960 and 2010, world life expectancy increased from 52 to 69 years while the population increased from 3,039,000 in 1960 to over 7 billion in 2010. No other 50 year period of human history can claim to have increased life expectancy while populations more than doubled; the engines of production, improved nutrition, increased medical knowledge were all more widely distributed in 2010 than they were in 1960. But the overwhelming source of energy for 50 years of economic growth was fossil fuels.

The World Without War Council paid attention to individuals. That was apparent in draft counseling which sought to get individuals the classification someone wanted and deserved; in its intern training program; and in day by day programming. The founding judgment was to focus on individuals, not groups, societies, cultures, believing only volitional actions could alter what the big battalions defined into existence by sociology or political scientists.

NOTES

1. *Liberation Magazine*, Dave Dellinger, editor.
2. George Weigel recommended military intervention to stop genocide in Darfur and advocated that the UN create there a Trust Territory p. 45.
3. Karen Minnice, Co-Director of the Midwest Office 1979–1982, organized this with Rabbi Herman Schaalman and Ayub Talhami, helping to draft an agreed-to two-state solution after two years of dialogue.
4. Letter to Eddie Pickus and others on World Without War Letterhead, 10/16/2000.
5. This quote ostensibly from Plato is written in stone at the Imperial War Museum (London) but no classic scholar has found the source. It was used by Douglas MacArthur in his farewell address but is best attributed to George Santayana's "Soliloquies in England" (Scribner, 1924, p. 102), Soliloquy #25, "Tipperary." Santayana was countering Woodrow Wilson claim that WWI was the "War to End all Wars."
6. Contradictions between two beliefs or conclusions that are reasonable in themselves; a paradox, *Compact Oxford English Dictionary.*
7. Seth Mandel, *Commentary*, "The Cautionary Tale of Samantha Power," pp. 30–32, February 2017.
8. Memo to Board, 2003.
9. See *Great Books of the Western World, The Great Ideas II*, Robert Maynard Hutchins, editor in Chief, War and Peace selection, p. 1010.
10. Robert Pickus, *Approaches to Peace* (Washington: United States Institute of Peace 1991).

Chapter Six

In the Council's End, a New Beginning

This chapter builds on Robert Pickus's developed sense of mission (1923–1961) as presented in Chapter 1 and Chapter 2, Steady Work to fulfill that mission (1961–2016), and asks "Do the concepts and work have a second life?" While chapters 1 and 2 are based on documents at the Hoover Institution, this chapter applies lessons learned in a new time. But as Heraclitus said, time is like a river ever flowing: you cannot step into the same place twice.

CHANGE OF VOICE

I was often an outlier[1] in organizations committed to the pacifist premise that international conflict can and should be resolved without the organized mass violence of war. I had been an Air Force Information Officer (1960–1963) serving in Minot, N.D. and Istanbul, Turkey. One day the SAGE (Semi-Automatic Ground Environment, an early computer system that preceded the semiconductor) was showing 2,000 incoming ICBMs (Intercontinental Ballistic Missiles). The NORAD (North American Air Defense Command) scrambled jets to visually confirm and reported back a flock of banded geese were triggering the radar. To paraphrase a song at the time "The B-52's and ICBM's will scare Khrushchev, I hope he is half as scared as I." National security is a very deadly challenge. If it can be changed, we should surely try.

I came to the Council office at 1730 Grove Street asking to be engaged as a work-study student while focused on graduate school at UC (Berkeley). I made my case and was hired, accepting the moral commitment to develop realistic and credible nonmilitary alternatives to war. I was and am on the just war/national interest diplomacy side of the "terrible dividing line" between pacifist and those of us who say yes, but . . . I produced annotated bibliographies, one of them called *To End War* (1968) first published by the publication program I had enlarged.

I received my PhD in History (1975) and worked in the Chicago office (1973–2006) with Kale Williams, Lowell Livezey, Karen Egerer, and P. Wesley Kriebel, a retired foreign service officer, among others. I taught international relations courses at DePaul, College of DuPage, and University of St. Francis while directing the Council's Midwest Office (1982–2006). With help from the Berkeley staff, I prepared and indexed much of the Council archives (2005–2013) and have now offered an interpretation of Robert Pickus's sense of mission and the steady work done to fulfill it.

I believe the body of thought introduced in chapters one and two challenges all points of view, takes something from many, and melds the ideas into a new synthesis more adequate than any of the others. That is a tough act to follow. My own effort is here stated. I have asked twenty people to provide a written response, a *Commentary* magazine style symposium. Robert Pickus would not have offered so many vulnerable judgments, preferring the clear concepts involved in Seven Roads[2] and "context education." George Weigel applied the Council context with Robert Pickus's approval believing as I do, that a context only gains credibility if it can be applied to the present. I have summarized our achievements in the preface and attempt here to show it is a base to work from in this as well as other times and places. We all need to be aware of Heraclitus's caution that history is ever-flowing. This is not a bipolar or unipolar system of world politics.

This chapter takes up the challenge Robert Pickus left us: in 2005 he claimed, as he had in 1961, that a world without war was possible in 40 years. He died in 2016. I will maintain there are now two regional peaces: within the European Union and among NAFTA (North American Free Trade Association, now American Free Trade Association) countries. These precarious peaces have good prospects for lasting until 2045 and beyond. In addition, there are representative democracies that are allied with the United States in every region and culture. Israel and Turkey in the Middle East, Taiwan, Japan, South Korea, India and Australia in East Asia, most of Latin America, South Africa and Nigeria in Africa, and others.

My essay that follows addresses these primary questions: (1) Is war inevitable? (2) Can representative democracy survive "by all means necessary" advocacy? (3) Can terrorism be reduced to a police matter? (4) Is intervention to prevent genocide just? (5) Can the present wars be ended? And (6) Can agreements between nation states be reliably enforced, creating a world order safe for free societies? I offer illustrative peace initiatives which if reciprocated would renew progress toward a world of democratic states free from war. I conclude with summary suggestions for the North Korean crisis recommending nonmilitary acts, including programs supported by the National Endowment for Democracy.

ARE WE "ALMOST THERE?"

My preliminary pessimistic conclusion is that the world is no closer to making war illegitimate than when the Council began. This view is based on the prevalence of domestic violence from openly and routinely threatening the life of the President elect, to resistance rhetoric justified as if the country were occupied by a foreign State and dangerously difficult police law enforcement not always just. There are also mass shootings and Presidential rhetoric that does not help. So also the absence or ineffectiveness of institutions capable of responding to aggression leaves war and preparation for war the preferred strategy of peace of all states. Even when there is a response, as in Iraq's case in the Gulf War, the coalition forces were unable to act on the need for regime change. States sponsor and inspire terrorism with impunity, including suicide bombers, drone strikes and truck slaughters. Genocide, even when detected and known, did not and does not produce an effective response. There are challengers to this interpretation. Two scholarly books offer a big history approach (detecting trends from 10,000 BC to 2010) with the hope captured in one of the titles: *Winning the War on War*.[3]

The expectation is based on replacing Margaret Mead's view of communal cooperation prior to 10,000 B.C. with the statistically supported view that in 2010 the 7 billion people on earth had the least expectation of dying a violent death in war than in any previous period. Joshua S. Goldstein concludes *Winning the War on War* on an upbeat note: "Today, bit by bit, we are dragging our muddy, banged-up world out of the ditch of war. We have avoided nuclear wars, left behind world war, nearly extinguished interstate war, and reduced civil wars to fewer countries with fewer casualties. We are almost there."[4]

NOTHING IS PERMANENT BUT CHANGE (HERACLITUS)

A good historian can discern patterns of change in language that enable him or her to place a document within 10 years. The attempt here is to combine generalizations with instances to suggest that a world order, safe for free societies and particularly religious, business and labor organizations, possibly could be achieved in 40 years if the United States of America and its democratic allies undertake the task. An educated citizenry, wise diplomats, and a strategy of peace that gains the reciprocation of allies and adversaries alike is essential. Whether we regain a sense of direction depends upon persuading you that order is possible as well as chaos.

Yes, we are almost there if we can overcome six obstacles. Hypothesis: a world order (a world in which there are agreed laws, customs and rules regulating international behavior) is possible within 40 years. It could be a

Trotskyite dictatorship of the world proletariat or an Islamic Caliphate or a tyranny imposed by one state seeking world hegemony. The proposal here is that the United States and its democratic allies in every region seek a world order that enforces treaty obligations between states, cherishes religious liberty, and is "safe for free societies." In short, a stable peace is possible but it must overcome at least these six obstacles: the belief that war is inevitable; domestic violence and foolishness; the present wars; genocide; terrorism; and ineffective international institutions

To overcome these obstacles we need the following: a successor overview agency; agreement on a distinction between conflicts that require cultural change while containing violent, universally expansionists sects and those for which there are possible nonviolent solutions now; a strategy for getting from here to stable peace; and finally, crisis response with regime change: North Korea, Iran, and China.[5]

OBSTACLES TO PROGRESS TOWARD A WORLD ORDER

The Belief That War is Inevitable

Visit any elementary school playground or hospital emergency room; or contemplate the regularity with which states war on each other, and face the fact that violence is everywhere. On the contrary: first distinguish individual and small group violence from organized mass violence--that is war. The definition the Council used was an interstate conflict in which 1,000 or more people were killed in one year.[6] Mass violence results from decisions: armies are recruited, conscripted and trained, military strategies debated, funds appropriated, victories celebrated, defeats motivate revenge—all human choices. Violence among individuals and small groups is considered illegitimate within 195 places on earth called states. Those advocating a new form of justice (not equal opportunity for all, but equality of result, for example), or advocating civil or revolutionary war, expect to impose a different order they hope to control. Human nature is not the obstacle; perceived injustice from burning coal, to racism, to statistical differences in achievements between groups, to gender inequality can all motivate violence. But in the moment of victory expect the coalition of the victimized to turn on each other with rival claims as to what justice requires. Representative democracy provides a nonviolent means of resolving for a time conflicting claims to justice and can achieve social change. In any of the 195 states, if you engage in mass violence in domestic politics you will be considered a criminal and imprisoned if not executed.[7]

Conflict is ubiquitous. Cultural differences trace their origins to religious foundations. Anthropologists tell us it is difficult to identify universal customs or beliefs that all cultures share. All cultures accomplish certain tasks but in different ways. These include: maintenance of social order, external and internal; production and distribution of food, goods, and services; giving meaning or purpose to life; education; and reproduction.

Within and between cultures there are calls to arms to settle quarrels about how to accomplish these essential tasks. Different attitudes toward them, as well as about race, class, gender, and status become deeply rooted patterns of behavior. Conflict is inevitable but mass violence is not. States are now the essential building blocks of any world order. Centralized bureaucratic authority has survived the challenges of exclusionary nationalism, military drives for world hegemony and fragmentation. Each of the world's 195 states has a monopoly on the legitimate use of violence in enforcing domestic law and suppressing groups that go beyond advocacy to the stockpiling of weapons, formation of militias, revolutionary brigades, or street gangs—to name but four. Whether dictatorships or representative democracies have a better record in controlling the police and enabling them to do their essential function earning the trust put in them, would be clearer if dictatorships had a free press. Trust in the police is earned or lost daily; when it is lost, restoring trust requires many things, but obeying the law and contesting arrests in court and not on the streets, is the most important one.

Violence and Foolishness in the US

This analysis[8] depends on the survival of representative democracy in the United States. It is not assured. Who is responsible for this perilous state? The first step is to reject all "by any means necessary" advocates, who by threatening whoever they oppose, place themselves in jeopardy, given that self-defense is an honored tradition. Second, the preponderant political parties in academic institutions need to talk to opposing parties or points of view, clarifying where they agree and disagree. Third, the Revolution is not going to happen and even if it did succeed, it would promise decades of suppression because the country is too diverse, the institutions of representative democracy too deeply rooted, and the claims of vengeful justice would be too multiple. There is no other way to governmental legitimacy but through the electoral college or by a constitutional amendment that changes the national system to a simple majority vote that would weaken the regional and rural representation the current system provides.

There are two perennial arguments against representative democracy. First, it is wrong in theory. The common person, the theory goes, does not know his or her own self-interest, the problems are too complex, the homework required will not be done, thought-out alternatives to present policy will not be debated. Instead, if you want to be elected, reduce the opposition to one word: bigoted, crooked, racist, unpatriotic, un-American. Only a few people have the expertise; they should make the decisions: philosopher kings, enlightened dictators, the 2%, the ones who know the laws of history, or climate change, or the general will.[9] The self-appointed elites, the theory goes, know what the people need better than they themselves. And second, it does not work in practice. Instead, in the absence of democratic elections, there is an "iron law of oligarchy" which ensures that special knowledge or expertise will rise to the top and hopefully pursue wise policies.

Defenders of representative democracy claim the theoretical arguments fail to distinguish between direct and representative democracy. Policies will not be wise if the uninformed vote on every question. No one accepts open heart surgery by majority vote in the cardiologist's waiting room. Demagogues do pose challenges as does a poorly educated or uninterested public. Legislators play a useful intermediate role when they interact with their electorate, informing them as the electorate articulates its wisdom. In one form of representative democracy, with upper and lower legislative branches, both long and short term considerations have an institutionalized voice. The power of the purse is lodged in the lower house, thus giving representative democracy a powerful and democratic check on executive authority. Further with an independent judiciary, the executive and legislative branches are limited by legal precedents in exercising authority. There is a bill of rights specifying where the individual and not the state is sovereign. As for the second argument, if the oligarchs mess up in a representative democracy, they can at least be removed from office in favor of a contending elite.

These arguments apply to states. They rarely apply to corporations, unions, religious institutions, political parties and other nongovernmental organizations formed for a specific purpose. There are a multitude of organizational forms that comprise the society in a democracy, including labor unions, communes, co-operatives and corporations.[10]

Restoration of the ideals of representative democracy begins with the recognition of unprecedented change with minimal violence in 20th century America and the urgency of unprecedented challenges in this century: climate change, fossil fuel energy utilization, and national security, to take three. Ours remains the form of government best capable of processing change and resolving conflict between contending groups without violence. It is far preferable to the empowerment of one or 50 "just rulers" who all define justice the same way. That realist recognition is the first step toward world order in the 21st century. Success requires closing the gap between what is and what ought to be in our representative democracy without threatening assassinations, civil war, and revolutionary or other violence. Those who advocate violence but do not practice it should be aware that they can motivate other strong-willed people with weapons, as well as those whom they threaten, to do evil deeds. Is the staged assassination of a Trump look alike in a performance of Shakespeare's *Julius Caesar* in New York's Central Park just a clever shock element and expression of artistic freedom? Or was it a possible prod to a would-be John Wilkes Booth sitting in the audience and prepared to assassinate our 45th president with a heroic cry of "Death to Tyrants?"

With depressing regularity, violent, universalizing sects seek and sometimes gain state power—Bolsheviks, Trotskyites (Mensheviks), Tupamaros, Fascists, Nazis, Maoists, Baathists, various racial supremacists, Jihadists, as well as those who believe we have achieved a universal and precise view of science—and having consolidated their power, seek by mass violence to make their creeds obeyed and universally enforced. Religion too may inspire mass violence against the infidel. There are 20 monotheistic religions. Representative democracy is undermined whether the creed or ideology at the point of the spear is considered universal and scientifically derived from History (Marx),[11] climate change (Al Gore), brain chemistry (Timothy Leary), behavioral psychology (BF Skinner), or divine will. Representative democracy thrives on a loyal opposition able to move beyond ad hominem arguments to debate substance.

Representative democracy is polarized when the Democratic Party umbrella becomes the self-styled "resistance"—the name of the guerrilla force that fought Hitler in occupied France during WWII and that portion of the Vietnam antiwar movement that spelled America with a "K."

The Present Wars

President Obama left office with the United States waging war in six countries that have predominant Muslim populations—Syria, Iraq, Afghanistan, Iran, Libya, and Yemen—as well as in territory claimed by ISIS (Islamic State in Syria). In March 2016, ISIS was formally charged by John Kerry, Secretary of State, with genocide toward religious groups: Shiite Muslims, Bahais, Christians, Mandaeans, Yazidis, and Zoroastrians.[12] Islamic jihadists are waging war in the above countries and in 13 African countries and has successfully inspired terrorist attacks in Europe and the United States.

Robert Pickus et al. in *Speak Truth to Power* accepted the challenge to create nonviolent alternatives to war in 1955, recognizing that brinkmanship made peace the twin brother of annihilation. He also believed that the institutions and understandings essential to wage war were themselves an obstacle to peace. In 1961 Robert Pickus responded to George F. Kennan's "cogent criticism" that military containment of an expansionist dictatorship was a prerequisite to pursing any strategy capable of achieving a stable peace in 40 years. From 1961 to 1991 he insisted that steps toward disarmament must be reciprocated, leadership deeds followed by reciprocal deeds. Otherwise general and complete disarmament (GCD) was not achievable.

The debate about "How much military force is enough?" would then proceed among alternative military strategies but pacifists would have no distinct voice unless GCD was the goal. A national military security strategy had many voices; a nonmilitary strategy of peace had few. A great nation needs a consensus to act in world politics; it could not be built from those witnessing for an impossible ideal unless they were willing to require reciprocation to unilateral peace initiatives from legitimate threats to the security of the United States. But with such a nonmilitary strategy of peace cooperation could be built out of many organizations.

In 2003 Pickus, believing that the Oslo Accords (1993) were Israel's maximum concessions short of annihilation, clarified that peace in the Middle East was hostage to changes in the Muslim world. Those changes, specified earlier,[13] have not come about; instead a continuation of a centuries-old conflict is being waged within Islam, and with the Jewish state in the Middle East. All European and North American states are also targeted and attacked by terrorists allegedly inspired by the Koran. In the Gulf War, Robert Pickus remained a pacifist but said if he had governmental responsibilities he would respond to Iraq's aggression against Kuwait with the only means available. The UN Security Council approved the Gulf war with China's abstention.

George Weigel, carrying the Council's burden of advocacy, would apply just war criteria to the Gulf War: Is the cause just? What are our (the West's) intentions? Is there a reasonable chance of success? Have we exhausted the diplomatic and other nonmilitary alternatives? Will the conduct of the war distinguish combatants and noncombatants, a distinction complicated by the use of human shields mixed in with military targets? Weigel concluded the Gulf War met these criteria.

National interest diplomacy has difficulty defending a country with these criteria. When you are convinced it is either them or us, civilians may only sometimes be distinguished from combatants, through enhanced interrogation techniques from torture, and when under fire, the safety of any prisoners you may have is not your first concern. Saving your own life and achieving your military objectives are first.

But peace through expanding the United States military capability to defeat Islamic Jihadists before it metastasizes ignores the risks military power poses to those who use it, as well as those contained or destroyed by it. There are no ideal choices, and denial of the challenges is not a way out. But pacifists need not be part of a coalition of appeasement or be part of a less-is-best military coalition. Unless and until you have formed a consensus to sustain a nonmilitary strategy of peace capable of addressing and changing a heavily armed, expansionist ideology, you are either advocating a different military strategy or witnessing for an impossible ideal.

Genocide

The international human rights movement that arose following World War II had a goal: "Never Again."[14] The Holocaust would not be repeated. A convention outlawing genocide was signed in 1948 and ratified in 1988 by the United States (the United States was the 98th country to ratify the convention). Gregory H. Stanton of Genocide Watch has addressed the problem of detecting genocide in its early stages.[15] According to him, genocide occurs in ten phases: (1) classification, (2) symbolization, (3) discrimination, (4) dehumanization, (5) organization, (6) polarization, (7) preparation, (8) persecution, (9) extermination, and (10) denial. But there is insufficient will to intervene even at the extermination stage either with a nonviolent brigade or military force. George Weigel recognized the need and recommended military force when faced with genocidal slaughter in Darfur. Military strategies can also have many unpredicted consequences, including failure.[16]

In 2017 the Rohingya, a Muslim ethnic group in Burma, was facing "extermination," the ninth stage of genocide, according to a report of the International State Crime Initiative of Queen Mary University. Samantha Power, who described genocide as a "Problem from Hell," became the US Ambassador to the UN but ignored or rejected the report. It doesn't make sense. One reason could be, we are at war with radical jihadists inflicting genocidal scale mass violence apparently wherever they can. NATO provided motivation when it failed to intervene in Srebrenica to stop the slaughter of Muslims by Serbian Christians. Samantha Power did consider a multilateral and possible American force as part of an overall strategy of preventing genocide. If the UN-approved Gulf War with Iraq was based on humanitarian intervention (more than 20% of Iraq's citizens had been killed, primarily Kurds and Shiite "marsh Arabs"),[17] would there be a coalition offering support? The hard question is "is there a nonviolent interventionist force ready without military backup to respond to genocide?" Asked and answered. In the existing system of world order, genocide occurs again and again.

The UN's timorous response to the looming crisis in Rwanda in 1994, and its failure to support the small force of peacekeepers already there, has been documented by General Romeo Dalbaire, force commander of the UN Assistance Mission for Rwanda (UNAMIR) and others. The Community of Democracies, if authorized or self-authorized, will need to make a choice between the loss of legitimacy by either intervening or also standing as silent witness to genocide. There is neither a sense of world community that makes intervention to prevent genocide a foregone conclusion[18] nor much likelihood that it will be created, as the "Responsibility to Protect" recommends.[19]

Terrorism

Terrorism is a form of preemptive aggression seeking territory or the reversal of a policy held by a sovereign State; Representative democracies have a nonviolent means to process such claims although they act on police powers when countering terrorists and are acting on the Just War doctrine when preemptively intervening as in the intervention in Pakistan to capture and kill Bin Laden. The force used was proportionate and fit the crime and is considered a police action, not a war.

George Weigel's offered in *American Purpose* a seven point plan in response to terrorism: National policy is the decisive agent, with the collaboration of friends and allies, not international law. Deterrence is the crucial first goal of a successful counterterrorism strategy. An enhanced intelligence capacity is indispensable. Intelligence must be shared with cooperative allies. Deterrence requires a far more assertive nonproliferation effort. Ballistic missile defense is needed against North Korea and Iran. Deterrence of a terrorist atrocity may, in special circumstances, require military action.[20]

Thus, in George Weigel's application of just war doctrine and in the absence of credible nonmilitary means, he is speaking for the James Madison Foundation, as well as I, in recommending "preemptive military action." Violence may be necessary for the survival of the State, itself essential to nonmilitary conflict resolution in domestic politics. Everyone prefers nonmilitary means and it could be argued that terrorism is a national or international police matter aided by State agencies. If terrorism is State-sponsored that adds to the challenge.[21]

Denial leads to appeasement, not to a stable peace.

Ineffective International Institutions

The United Nations was created to eliminate the "scourge of war"[22] by providing for a collective military response to aggression if approved by the Security Council's five permanent members (China, France, Great Britain, Russia, and the United States). When any one disagreed, the United Nations could not act. The Korean War was fought with the UN's blessing because the Soviet Union was boycotting the Security Council for an unrelated reason at the time of the vote. Many unarmed or lightly armed peacekeeping missions have been authorized to separate combatants while mediating disputes. They operate with the blessing of the host country,[23] as was the case when President of Egypt Gamal Abdel Nasser asked the UN to remove the Sinai Mission, provoking the Six Day War in 1971.

The United Nations is of limited effectiveness in civil wars and against terrorism. The Council and many others held conferences on UN reform, internal or civil wars, and self-determination as partial answers to terrorism.[24] But there are not now effective international institutions able to process self-determination claims or intervene by whatever means in civil wars, like that in Syria, or to prevent genocide in Burma or the Democratic Republic of the Congo.

PATHS TO WORLD LAW

Robert Pickus and I defined five paths to international institutions capable of enforcing international or world law:[25] by developing regional and functional international institutions, by nation-states changing their approach to the present United Nations, through United Nations Charter Revision, by creating under treaty a new world organization in cooperation with the UN, and through a world constitutional convention.[26] Twenty-five years later, Eric Blantz defined twelve "major perspectives which underlie arguments about global governance."[27] Secretary of State Madeline Albright led in creating a Community of Democracies to work as a caucus within the UN but capable of acting independently,[28] a thirteenth possibility then, partially fulfilled now. Condoleezza Rice has advocated a Commonwealth of Nations.

Learn from Five 20th Century Failed Attempts at World Order

The Versailles Treaty (1918) established a League of Nations which agreed to combine to prevent or repel wars of aggression. The League neither required European states to free their 19th century colonies nor created a sense of community through economic development, good global governance or the promotion of human rights. The League failed to respond when Italy invaded Ethiopia in 1931 and soon thereafter became marginal to world politics. The United States not only refused to join the League but did not answer mail received from the League.

The Russian Revolution was fueled by many currents of thought, among them the Socialist Revolutionaries (democratic socialists), the Bolsheviks, and the Mensheviks. The Mensheviks, led by Leon Trotsky, sought a new world order with the seizure of power in Russia, to be followed by working class revolutions in every industrial society, and the revolt of the masses in European colonies. Only then was it foreseen that government would become, in Marx's words, "the administration of things" with the withering away of the state to follow.

The Axis powers—Nazi Germany, fascist Italy, and imperial Japan— sought to subordinate rival states and achieve racial and national purity through mass murder. Rather than accept a conquered people's status, allied powers formed a military alliance and at great cost in lives and treasure won the war the Axis powers had started. But the allied democracies violated just war standards with the fire-bombing of Dresden and first use of atomic bombs on Hiroshima and Nagasaki.

The victors in WWII formed the United Nations, giving themselves the veto power in the Security Council, forming a General Assembly and an Economic and Social Council. In that world order a convention against genocide was adopted and ratified, as were other treaties. Enforcement was blocked by the veto power in a divided Security Council. The UN, like the League before it, became marginal to world politics when it failed to enforce the Genocide Convention, did not stop nuclear proliferation, and failed to reduce human rights violations when compared to numerous transitions to democracy between 1948 and 2003.[29]

An Islamic Caliphate entered the world stage with the first World Trade Center bombing giving new shape and energy to an old desire. It is possible to imagine a legitimate motive for the Caliphate in the failure to enforce the Genocide Convention and passive inaction when mass slaughters occurred at Srebrenica, Kosovo and later in Burma. This overview is too short to satisfy anyone and leaves out various interpretations of the United States' role. The attempt here is not to gain agreement about the past, only to claim that a new beginning is possible.[30] [31]

If US citizens are willing to extend their involvement from domestic to world politics they could take seriously *The Global Agenda*, published annually by the United Nations Association of the US in September each year when UN General Assembly meets.Tightening world communication patterns, economic interdependence with the exponential growth of world trade, rapid technological innovation, environmental strain, population growth—all make the world as well as the nation state the political community in which you should participate because your life and well-being are at stake. When universal religious traditions formed and supported in separate cultures are added to the mix, the attempt to impose one religion on others threatens everyone, and deepens the jeopardy of everyone. Religious liberty is the bedrock for any world order enjoying stable peace.

We live in a world in which some form of order exists. The results of millennials of history are in but not permanent. There exists in 2020 195 countries. Some of them have entered into alliances with other states; some become subordinate to powerful countries or are occupied. Five have veto powers in the Security Council of the United Nations. Most consider this unfair but cannot agree on the change. Most fully participate in other UN related bodies like the International Atomic Energy Agency. The World Trade Organization and the International Monetary Fund and there are private organizations like the Catholic Church, chamber of commerce and labor unions. Corporations and functional agencies like the International Monetary Funds and the World Trade Organizations fulfill important functions. There are many other private international and national nongovernmental agencies that form a global civil society.

Diplomats pretend they believe in the sovereign equality of state, but power intrudes throughout the existing order. Basic tasks like the enforcement of the Genocide Convention, preventing Nuclear Proliferation and suppressing terrorist do not get done. These and other shortcomings of the exiting order are succinctly explained away as State Centered Realism.

Eric Blatz, Good Global Governance Project stated:

> Formal global governance is a non-issue. Nation states are, and will remain, the primary actors in world politics. In a lawless environment states must defend and pursue their own national interest since no one else will do so. Conflict and violence among states is inevitable and cooperation is inherently unstable. Those who advocate ceding power to global institutions assume common ground that does not exist. Without such consensus, attempts to create world institutions are likely to undermine the national interests of democratic states. Moreover, moves toward global governance could by upsetting the balance of power that presently "governs" international relations, result not in a freer, more peaceful, or just world order, but in one decidedly less so. [32]

Beyond realism there are attempts to transform the State System which open a window to mass violence, without a way to close that window.

In 1985 the majority of States were Socialist, combining those States that called themselves "democratic socialist" and those that called themselves scientific socialist. Internal challenges from Margaret Thatcher, Prime Minister of England (1977–1990), Boris Yeltsin, Russian Leader (1991–1999), and Dang Yiaoping (China's head of State 1978–1997) plus the resistance of the United State labor movement broke the inevitability myth. Trade Unions are a vital part of representative democracies; in Russia, China, and other states that claim the mantel of scientific socialism for their dictatorships, the government decides what in in labor's self-interest.

The belief that Socialism is in the self-interest of the working class sustains the belief system and makes organized mass violence the norm when combined with Leon Trotsky's doctrine of permanent revolution: "Only that which prepares the complete and final overthrow of imperialist bestiality is moral, and nothing else, the welfare of the revolution—that in the supreme law." [33]

Islamic jihadists have sought to create a new State, or make Iran (Shia) or Saudi Arabia (Sunni), into the World caliphate imposing Shria law by terrorism and waging war. Motivation for waging permanent jihad is provided by the example of the prophet Mohammad, the belief that martyrs go directly to heaven and in some versions are rewarded with 70–100 female companions. The existing world order's power relationships have left many Muslims aware that events like the slaughter of Muslims at Srebrenica, Kosovo, and

Burma, and their imprisonment of hundreds of thousands in China, provide motivation that is not lessened by power brokers who claim "The weak suffer what they must, the strong take what they can."

The 20th Century experienced this danger to any world order in the fascist, Bolshevik, and Baathist sects. In the 21st Century racist, environmental alarmists ("12 years to catastrophe," "do what we say or the planet dies . . ."), gender separations and redefinition of the categories, robots, planet of the apes. . . . This is a catch-all category which expects new sects to arise and old ones to revive. The formula is the same: form a myth, repeat it endlessly, threaten violence at every turn but use it only when gaining absolute power can be an outcome. There are many nonmilitary based strategies to change the existing order.

In today's international system, global governance is most effectively realized within the UN. By ensuring the sovereignty of the many nation-states, providing a forum for the expression of national interest, allowing a veto for the most powerful nations, and creating functional organizations to pursue universally lauded goals. The present UN system is the only form of global governance that fits present realities. Our energies should go into learning to make this system work (by considering a range of proposals for improving the UN system) rather than diverting energies into utopian efforts that cannot.

The present UN, because it admits all nations as equals regardless of internal politics, is not acceptable as an institution on which to build desirable global governance. Alternative cooperative institutions which admit only democratic nations are therefore necessary. Such institutions will best enable member states to leverage positive change within nonmember states, i.e., adoption of democratic institutions which encourage the peaceful pursuit and resolution of political conflict. "Self-governance" among nation-states might be practical once all nations are genuinely democratic, or, alternatively, a democratic union might be a first step toward overarching, democratic, global structures.

While isolated nation-states are incapable of solving problems beyond their borders, neither can organizations like the UN, with so much diversity under one roof, achieve the level of consensus that is needed if they are to act as effective governance institutions. Shared values, greater cultural and ethnic homogeneity, and even history, make the "region" the appropriate level at which to solve problems and make progress toward needed governance. Regional cooperation might be limited to security and/or economic cooperation among sovereign states, or might aspire to full-blown integration along the lines of the European Union. Regional institutions might then be linked at the supraregional level to tackle issues that span regional boundaries.

In the absence of economic integration, which is the process most likely to support global governance, attempts to create such governance structures are doomed to failure. By opening markets across the globe we can achieve the level of economic integration and interdependence necessary to sustain global peace, security, and prosperity. Free trade regimes such as the GATI and NAFTA are more important in progress toward desirable global governance than are the highly politicized and ineffective bodies of the UN.[34]

21st Century Problems No State Can Solve Alone

Trade

World trade's volume passed 16 trillion in 2015 up from 1 trillion in 1977. Exports and imports combined equaled 18% of world GNP in 1977 and has risen to 52% of world GNP in 2008. In the same period, combined imports and exports tripled among Southern Hemisphere trading partners. These increases in trade are voluntary, in the self-interest of each nation in which there is a political process to decide terms and make crucial previously marginal decisions like who is on the governing body of the World Trade Organization. In August 2017 the United States trade deficit with the rest of the world was 42.4 billion (exports 195.3 billion, imports 237.7 billion). The importance of trade deficits "is closely linked with macro-economic facts like the relative growth rates of countries, the value of currency, the strength of the dollar as a global reserve currency and the global trends in savings and investment."[35]

There are significant implications for every person on earth from the price of grapes in your supermarket to the ability of cheese makers in Wisconsin to compete with Germany and France, the two largest cheese makers in the world. Wisconsin is third ahead of Italy and the Netherlands in volume. The world economy thus briefly described is based on the principle of comparative advantage succinctly summarized as "Do what you do best, import the rest." The world economy expanded in an unprecedented amount from 1960 to 2015 but not without secondary consequences such as the displacement of some domestic businesses and the elevation of others and the introduction of plants into environments where they have few natural enemies.

With the volume of trade exceeding 50% of world production international institutions such as the World Trade Organization and the International Monetary Fund become increasingly critical functioning agencies resolving conflicts and maintaining exchange rates between national currencies. The IMF exchange rate is based on the average of 16 democracies GNP thus preventing dictatorships from setting the official exchange rate at $1=1 ruble as Russia attempted to do during the Cold War. A perk of being among the largest economies (24 out of 25 of the largest economies are representative democracies, China's being the exception) is the means to determine the value of your currency in exchange. To be sure, there are other ways of establishing a means to exchange currencies essential to international trade but the current method is working and facilitates the growing volume of world trade. Domestic deficits pose a problem as well as 42 billion monthly trade deficits, but the expansion of the world's credit is necessary and inflation is resisted by paying interest on the debt $200 billion a year in 2018.

Global Environmentalism: Eliminate Pollution or Lose it All?

There are a set of interrelated propositions which would, if true, recommend a world order with control of every commercial, transportation-based, or private cause of pollution:

- "Greenhouse" gases resulting from burning any fossil fuel are trapped in the upper atmosphere and have been accumulating for a millennium.
- The effect of this entrapment is the heating of the atmosphere and sea.
- There is no limit to restricting pollution, only replacement with renewable energy sources can mitigate the damage already done and pending.
- In a state system of 195 states with more than half of each state's GNP tied to trade, if you regulate to the third decimal point (0.001) in one state, you must regulate to the same degree in all, otherwise no regulated state's producers can compete in the global market place.
- There is only one real choice: either a leviathan state with universal regulatory and enforcement powers or an environment unable to sustain human life. These propositions are questioned at every point.[36]
- There is not yet a science of climate change and may never be: "The climate system is extremely complex involving many different components and interacting processes, that even with the biggest, fastest computers, it is not possible to come close to representing them accurately."[37]
- The greenhouse gases are neither trapped nor accumulating. Upper atmospheric winds and the earth's movement disperse gases preventing either precise measurement or the recognition that existing figures are not correlated with temperature trends.
- Seven billion people's energy needs will not be met by renewable energy even after hundreds of billions of dollars have been spent on renewables development from 1970 to 2015.
- Population growth will not be reversed.
- International treaties are acceptable if they apply equally to each state; Accords that are only enforced in representative democracies are not.
- Regulations that reduce pollution .001% increase the costs of goods sold by billions thereby handicapping in world trade States that abide by them.
- Sustainable development using many kinds of energy is the route to a stable world's population with the lifestyle we either enjoy now or to which we most aspire.

• Renewable-energy-only states will need to negotiate their most favorable terms or surrender to intimidation from the remaining fossil fuel states.

The fossil fuel debate is far from resolved. There is a climate threat but the science of climate change "cannot predict the climate and its impact with precision."[38] By 2100 climate change scientists have offered predictions that the seas will rise 1 feet,18 inches, 3 feet, 8 feet, or 200 feet (the latter being Al Gore's prediction in 2005). Scientists at Massachusetts Institute of Technology (MIT) in 2017 "determine(d) that the worst case of more than 8 feet has only a one tenth of 1 percent chance of occurring by 2100 even under a business-as-usual with current emissions scenario; but a rise of more than 1.5 feet may occur with high emissions." The anomalies in the past data include the fact that the Pacific Ocean as measured at San Francisco actually sank between 2005 and 2015 (Discovery Magazine); there were over 40,000 polar bears in 12 herds according to the Canadian National Geographic Society in 2015; and ice growth in the Arctic during November 2017 averaged 30,900 square miles per day according to the National Snow and Ice Data Center. All predictions based on a specific amount of change by a specific date have failed.

Conservation is a good in itself and international treaties are needed but if they are not multilaterally enforced, their net effect is to handicap international trade in the country or countries that abide by them. Bill Gates, once Microsoft's CEO and now philanthropist and venture capitalist, claims there are 12 forms of renewable energy undergoing investigation, none of which currently meet the tests of market viability, but some of which he expects will do so within the next 30 years.[39]

Conceptual confusion, anomalies in the data and the lack of double blind procedures essential to science, prevail. Nonetheless, there is a new concept of "climate liability" that permits one country to sue carbon polluters for crop damages. The Columbia University Sabin Center for Climate Liability's has developed the concept and in 2016, 1,400 cases were prosecuted in domestic courts between democracies such as Argentina and the United States. No successful cases have been brought against China, the world's worst polluter in 2017.[40]

Armaments

The last time the UN General Assembly held a Special Session on Disarmament (1978), a preparatory committee prepared a draft declaration, asking each member state to bracket and initial any clause they disagreed with expecting universal agreement. Instead, every clause in the draft declaration was bracketed by somebody. Vague concepts could be agreed to but a plan of action could not. Getting member states to report military expenditures in a common matrix that overcame different currency evaluation, secrecy, re-search and development proved impossible. No subsequent Special Sessions have been held.

THE KEYS TO WORLD ORDER

Stable Peace is only possible when religious liberty is the reality. Arguably, religious liberty based on the primacy of conscience—the ability to know right from wrong—is the foundation on which law rests.

> The idea that religious liberty is the generating principle of civil, and that civil liberty is the necessary condition of religious liberty, was a discovery reserved for the seventeenth century. Many years before the names of Milton and Taylor, of Baxter and Locke were made illustrious by their partial condemnation of intolerance, there were men among the independent congregations who grasped with vigor and sincerity the principle that it is only by abridging the authority of the states that the liberty of Churches can be assured."[41]

A measure of religious liberty has been slowly achieved and faces many challenges. The Peace of Westphalia (1648) resolved the Thirty Years War with the formula whoever rules, their religion. Maryland was an early experiment in Protestants and Catholics living in one English colony. Religious liberty in every state enabled a Catholic to become President only in 1960; Al Smith, a Catholic, had little chance in 1928. Shiite and Sunni militia rival governments in their military strengths guarantee the continuation of wars in the Middle East, while Israel has over a million Muslims practicing their religion in Israel. Martyrs for religious liberty should be identified and honored, not suicide terrorists. Paul Marshall's *Religious Liberty in the World* (2007) offers 100 specifics for what constitutes religious liberty.

Nongovernmental organizations exist to support and advance many purposes. One of them should be the enforcement of international treaties to which their country has agreed. The Helsinki Accords (1975) provide a starting point. The roles of such groups can be spelled out in the treaty they are helping to enforce along with counterpart organizations. If this is done, such groups could be protected in the protocol accompanying the treaty. This initiative understands that the United States Dept. of State is responsible for overseeing compliance with treaties but not accords and agreements, in the bipartisan, Senate ratification process. In democracies, treaties supersede domestic law. The Department of State includes among its responsibilities enforcing over 200 treaties the Senate has ratified. These treaties are enforceable in domestic courts by an independent judiciary or domestic individuals or organizations that bring lawsuits and win judgments. Treaties between democracies and dictatorships have built in discrepancies concerning compliance and enforcement.

The Democratic Peace Prospect: The Next Forty Years

For the purposes of argument, it is assumed here that there is a separate peace among representative democracies in North America and between the European Union countries. There are no weapons targeted against each other and they enforce treaties between each other. They have all voluntarily joined a Commonwealth of Democracies without a common foreign policy but do share intelligence on terrorists' threats.

Maintaining these separate peaces and continuing cooperation with other representative democracies in every region is the first challenge. The following are considered additional achievable goals in the next 40 years:

1. Extension of the regional peace to Central and South America.
2. Maintenance of and openness to reform of the International Monetary Fund and the World Trade Organization, facilitating the further expansion of Southern Hemispheric trade as well as world trade now responsible for more than half of the world's GNP.
3. Augmentation of genocide detection agencies and development of nonviolent responses at the first eight stages of genocide and acceptance of hard power response if feasible at the ninth stage (extermination). Intervention at the ninth stage would be authorized by the Security Council if possible, the Community of Democracies if not.
4. The acceptance of environmental protection goals, adoption of environmental pollution standards (to which the United States has already made an 80% reduction), and permitting tariffs on imports directly related to compensating for other countries not meeting those standards.
5. Continued celebration of half the world's population fully participating in modern economies, and enforcement of domestic civil rights legislation.
6. Formation of an inter-religious board mandated to track religious discrimination and murder with increased recognition that religious liberty is essential to a democratic peace, combining rejection with sanctions against violators led by the religion of the perpetrators.
7. United States leadership in world politics should be toward a world of democratic states, strengthening world civil society, expanding the role of the National Endowment for Democracy and its four institutes (AFL-CIO, Chamber of Commerce, Democratic and Republican Party Institutes) and civil society organizations participating in the World Movement for Democracy.

8. Endowing a World Order Institute charged with developing nonmilitary strategies of peace designed to change expansionist sects with state power. North Korea, for example, considers itself a "people's republic" and South Korea is in transition to a consolidated representative democracy.
9. Develop a capacity to test self-determination claims, so states can, if they so choose, accept independence and be responsible for their own defense.

The most significant conceptual adjustment required is the recognition that a "Sense of World Community" is slow to develop and cannot be created in the strength needed despite increasing economic interdependence, and thousands of organizations and millions of people acting selflessly, even sacrificially, on behalf of others in other states and cultures. The nation-state has survived as the primary agent in world politics and alone has the needed resources. The statement of obstacles, however, can promote discussion of how they could be overcome.[42] [43]

The benefits to recognizing that there are two regions currently at peace are significant. When recognized, (1) you can put no after the question: Is war inevitable?; (2) the 70 (1945–2015) years of peace replace a millennium of wars between short truces (945–1945), the minimum goals that need to be achieved to make regional peace possible become clear; (3) there is a scholarly argument as to why and an answer: representative democracies enforce treaties between them; (4) a thoughtful lay audience can be proud of this limited achievement of United States diplomacy and its being sustained by Madeline Albright, Condoleezza Rice and Hillary Clinton; (5) peace studies can have a positive focus; (6) as the Chinese proverb states, a journey of 1,000 miles begins with a single step, but it helps if you are pointed in the right direction; and (7) the difficulties of achieving the regional peaces are plain in European history as are the failures of many peace plans and efforts; remaining is the challenge of maintaining and extending the regional peaces in time and place.

There are many reasons to doubt these achievements. They call into question much peace rhetoric but offer confirmation of Gene Sharp and Robert Pickus's claim that "the end of capitalism is not the end of war." On the contrary, all of the thirty countries involved are representative democracies with primarily private, regulated capitalist economies, and agreed rules for monetary exchange with the institutions and understandings that make them "safe for free societies." They debate and quarrel about everything. They are also challenged by terrorist organizations and must use police powers to protect themselves. But there are no weapons targeted against each other.

A survey of other regions that may possibly transition in 40 years to a regional peace in which war is illegitimate is needed here, but it is beyond the scope and expertise of this summary. Suffice it to say, the prospect in Latin America are challenged by drug cartels and US consumption of their product. Cuba supports revolutionary movements throughout the region. Ecuador's authoritarian government represses free speech and makes peaceful change difficult; and Venezuela is on the brink of civil war (2017). Still, stable peace could be achieved in 40 years.

In Africa, rival Jihadist organizations are waging war in 13 Africa countries: Burkina Faso, Central African Republic, Chad, Democratic Republic of the Congo, Guinea, Liberia, Mali, Mauritania, Niger, Nigeria, Republic of South Sudan, Senegal, and Somalia. While there are eight United Nations peacekeeping forces deployed in Africa, their missions have been compromised by the criminal behavior of certain peacekeepers (child rape and looting among the charges). France has proposed to the UN Security Council that armed and disciplined peacekeepers be deployed in francophone African States. Three countries (Burundi, Gambia, and South Africa) are leaving the International Criminal Court and its work in Rwanda is marginal at best. The Organization of African Unity provides a forum for governments to address issues such as religious liberty, the rights of women, governmental corruption and mediation. In Africa a common market is under discussion.

Condoleezza Rice maintains there is an overwhelming preference for representative democracy in Africa and she is supported by a Pew foundation study. Since 2005, the National Endowment for Democracy has provided assistance annually to as many as 1,000 principled, nonviolent and democratic civil society organizations in Africa. But to my knowledge, a comprehensive, nonmilitary strategy of peace is yet to be developed.

A survey of the Middle East does not find anyone developing an alternative to peace through military strength. There is an agreement on a Road Map to Peace in the Middle East (EU, Israel, Palestinian Authority, Russia, and the United States) but no progress. A stable peace requires: recognizing Israel as a predominantly Jewish state; normalizing relations (e.g., printing maps that portray Israel accurately); organizing successful transnational projects (for example, addressing Jordan River water utilization); ending the use of terrorism; and recognizing that the destruction of Israel requires the destruction of the United States.

Syria has deteriorated from a nonviolent attempt to open the Assad regime, to a failed UN mediation, to a multi-sided civil war with outside military intervention (ISIS, Russia, and the United States).

A person without a plausible strategy to change Iran, and aware of that nation's stated intention of destroying both Israel and the United States, is faced with the choice between peace through strength or the possible destruction by military force of Israel and the United States. My prediction is that the EU and North American regional peaces will last until 2045 and beyond. They are precarious. But the European and North American formula is likely to hold. It is possible but not likely, that the embryonic world culture will evolve in the direction of a universal, democratic peace, but only if a powerful nation offers the leadership.

Both Kissinger and the World Without War Council opposed unilateral disarmament in the face of expansionist sects, movements, or states. Robert Pickus in contrast to Kissinger advocated general and complete disarmament as a goal and offered American peace initiative acts which when reciprocated would constitute progress toward that goal while reforming international institutions into treaty enforcement agencies. UN reform has not taken place. Damage limitation is one definition of the primary responsibility of a United States Ambassador to the UN as one former UN Ambassador, Daniel Patrick Moynihan, stated in his *A Dangerous Place*. Missing now is the recognition that nonviolent transitions from various forms of dictatorship are not only possible, but 20 such transitions occurred between 1974 and 2003 (see list in archives at Hoover and Swarthmore) with three significant failures (China, Iran and Syria). Also missing is a nonviolent strategy to gain enforceable agreements between adversary states.

Complete the American Initiatives Project, A New Course for American Foreign Policy. The Prospectus written by Robert Pickus and George Weigel in 1981 identified two Phases of the Project. Phase one policy recommendations submitted to the project are summarized in chapter two. Phase two promised "(we) will continue the process of refining and connecting the initiatives into an integrated foreign policy for the US."[44]

Challenge the Climate of Denial and Develop a Nonmilitary Strategy of Peace

The stated intent of the Islamic Caliphate, Iran and North Korea is to destroy the United States. In a world politics based on 195 nation states with ineffective peacemaking institutions, recognize that Russia is waging a war of aggression in the Ukraine and threatening Latvia, Lithuania and Estonia with nuclear destruction on behalf of a Russian minority and China occupies Tibet, intimidates Taiwan and conducts its engagement in world politics with a growing military presence.

Develop a nonmilitary strategy of peace at the individual, societal, and government levels. In World War I, 67,000 drafted men choose conscientious objector states, while an additional 3,000,000 did not register at all. Individuals can also engage in exchange programs, travel, arrange family visit across lines of division, host a student born in another country, consume less or none of a product of a bellicose country; use the world wide web.

There is a vast array of national, nongovernmental organizations and many international egos. Most European countries have branches in other counties. One step to this kind of engagement is the four branches of the

National Endowment for Democracy: AFL-CIO, US Chamber of Commerce, Democratic Party Institute, and the Republican Party Institute. Many religious, ethnic, sports, gender, race, scientific, environmental organizations join business and labor and have affiliates in other countries.

Governments must deal with personalities, issues and challenges. Diplomats enter a profession with hundreds of years of precedent. Avoiding war while defending the national interest is the first maxim.

Arms control, not disarmament, is the subject under discussion among decision-makers, elected or not. There are eight nuclear powers in 2019, including Israel. The key concept is reciprocation. Leadership by example is also crucial. The initiative concept offers both but requires reciprocation by adversaries and allies alike. The complexity of the concept has been previously discussed in chapter two, as has the aggression of terrorism and intervention to prevent genocide. The complex subjects of the environment, trade, and armaments are the domain of experts, but here it can be clarified that the initiative concept can be applied and does not in itself rely on organized mass violence.

The goal is stated. Some power takes the first step of say 10% of the goal. Other powers will want to inspect thereby opening themselves to similar inspection. Then they will be required to reciprocate to have the initiating power reduce another ten percent. Reducing for three or six months to encourage reciprocation may be part of the calculous. The process can be reversed at any point. One expectation is that negotiations can be resumed at any point.

This is when developed becomes one of a number of options available to decision-makers. The complexity of history, personality, and much else will need to be dealt with at the National Security or other level. If there were a near universal Commonwealth of Democratic States that enforce treaties between them, this would increase the credibility of the policy. In addition to the three problems above, no state can solve alone the problems of genocide or terrorism, which are discussed earlier in this chapter.

These conflicts will not wait until the United States is without sin, but you should also ask compared to what State, with what achievements, based on what ideals. This is not asking for bland self-approval (there is some truth in each charge) when all that is needed is to assert that the United States is a legitimate political community, capable of offering the needed leadership. Defended here is the fact of two regional peaces, among 31 representative democracies, 50 years of world economic growth lifting a billion people out of poverty and increasing global life expectancy from 51 to 69 years (1960–2010). All unprecedented achievements in human history; much left to be done.

There is no successor organization at this time that has accepted the World Without War Council's premises. There are real military threats to the

United States which no one charged with national security responsibility can ignore. Those threats can possibly be met by a developed, nonmilitary, strategy of peace. And they can gain the consensus needed to be implemented by the United States.

NORTH KOREA: TOWARD A NONMILITARY STRATEGY

A nonmilitary strategy of peace is needed for each of the five bellicose dedicated adversaries. This list of suggestions for promoting a reunified Korea is prepared for laymen with the intention of engaging others and challenging those with the expertise to develop and make available a nonmilitary strategy of regime changes. This is illustrated here by programs intended to unify the Korean peninsula under a government safe for free societies. That North Korea is threatening other states with nuclear armed ICBM's reveals much failed diplomacy. What nonmilitary strategy could change that which we consider evil? Will the strategy of reunification avert a crisis and contribute to a stable peace—as the reunification of Germany has done—without appeasement or provocation?

- Begin with study and becoming aware of the history, culture and language of the Korean peninsula. Cho Myoung-gyon, South Korea's Minister of Unification and its chief delegate to the December 2017 inter-Korean talks, has taken the first step. He negotiated with a North Korean counterpart (Ri Son Kwon), the reopening of the military hotline to avoid war by miscalculation and the fielding of combined teams in selected Olympic events. Minister Cho Myoung-gyon set the standard: "The most important spirit of the inter-Korean talks is mutual respect."[45]
- Clarify intention in order to offer suggestions which decision makers at the East Asian Institute (Seoul), or the Ministry of Unification (Seoul) could develop into a coherent strategy of nonviolent regime changes in consultation with North Korea's subjects, South Korean citizens, and offering the support of American nongovernmental organizations in conceiving and implementing a coherent strategy of nonviolent regime changes.
- Evaluate and apply to North Korea the "Pluralizing the Soviet Union" proposals and consult with Yuri Yarim-Agaev[46] and veterans of the Center for Democracy in the USSR (Philip Siegelman, Edward Kuzneter and Michael Bernstam among others) learning "how [our] successful experience could be applied to solving problems with current totalitarian regimes."[47] The Taiwanese democracy promotion institute has expertise also based on experience, including shadow city governments on the mainland.

- We must ask the hard questions. Do you support military brinkmanship, appeasement, accommodation or regime changes leading to reunification? Which is the riskier strategy? Is there a nonviolent means capable of changing the two regimes?
- North Korea claims legitimacy as the last refuge of global "scientific socialism," calls itself a "people's republic," has a command economy with seven year plans and a gulag based on Stalin's, and rejects all citizen rights and protections, such as those specified in the US Bill of Rights. In South Korea the government claims legitimacy as a representative democracy, but it does not allow a fully independent civil society and resists giving women an essential role in a modern economy.[48]
- Not addressed here but vital to the success of the strategy are questions of timing and whether various kinds of reciprocation from North Korea can be induced. Are there people in North Korea able to act like "Tank Man?" and when they do so will they inspire the man in the tank to obey his conscience not do his duty?
- We must enter the public arena. The Hon. Susan A. Shelton, Acting Assistant Secretary of State for East Asian Pacific Affairs, announced the United States is opposed to regime change, July 2017[49] and the National Endowment for Democracy (NED) is charged with promoting democracy that is understood here as requiring regime changes in North and South Korea.
- We should also build on current programs. State the Goal to the Ministry of Unification (Seoul) that regime change in North and South Korea could realistically lead to reunification. Radio Free North Korea exists, is a NED grantee, and should become a regular source of information about the dialogue proposed below. Its maintenance and ability to overcome jamming is essential to this proposal.
- A window into North Korea has been the creation of open markets in which people come to trade and purchase products and exchange information. These markets are important drivers of social change and opening in North Korea as they now provide one of the "few ways to obtain information about the outside world."[50] The markets reveal the failure of the State economy and are the start of an alternative similar to Vietnam's "shift from a centrally planned to market economy [that] has transformed the country from one of the poorest in the world into a lower middle income country. Vietnam is one of the most dynamic emerging countries in the East Asia Region" in 2017.[51]
- Support the NED grantee Daily North Korea whose newspaper is "utilized in country markets to provide the international community with detailed information on the development of private markets in North Korea."[52]
- Support the Defector Empowerment Program. The right to emigrate is basic to making governments responsible to their citizens. South Korea

has more than 30,000 defectors from North Korea who participate in programs funded partially by NED. These programs aim to promote "human rights and democracy" in North Korea; the experience and knowledge of both cultures that these defectors have make them especially valuable resources for such time as "when the country eventually opens up."[53]

Developing New Resources

Clarifying the choices: Rule out war and open discussion of how to achieve regime change considering alternative routes, such as (1) a Constitutional Convention, (2) Reform of existing institutions, (3) a Trusteeship, (4) a Security Council-imposed reunification plan, and (5) Laissez Faire ("let it be"), the world economy is all the inducement needed. South Korea has outperformed its once more prosperous Northern "blood brother." The strength of a unified Korea in the democratic peace framework is manifest and market forces will respond, helping to consolidate the unified democratic transition.

Many organizations in North Korea have received NED grants in the recent past, including: the Center for Korean Women in Politics (CKWP), Citizens Alliance for North Korean Human Rights (NKHR), Now, Action and Unity (NAUH), Network for North Korean Human Rights and Democracy (NKnet), North Korean Development Institute (NARI), North Korean Strategy Center (NKSC), NK Watch, North Korean Writers In Exile, and the Young Defectors Alliance for North Korean Human Rights (YDA).[54] Leaders from these organizations should meet and discuss strategies for associating with like organizations, their members, and individuals in North Korea or in the defector community and propose additional ways to influence the people of North Korea.

The typology of organizations contained in the Swarthmore Peace Collection is a starting point for someone with knowledge of South Korean society to match organizations in other democracies in the region for the purpose of building support through linkages.

Create an open dialogue about a mutually acceptable alternative. All governments have similar structures, a chief executive, a legislative branch, a judiciary. All sign international treaties, consider themselves enforcers of human rights and provide for national security. The first step toward representative democracy is to identify the crucial choices which make the chief executive impeachable, the legislative branch powerful (the power of the purse, for example), or the judiciary independent.[55]

The many structures of government changes needed can be identified and the discussion opened with a list of 12.[56] After a period of public discussion, representatives to a unified Korean constitutional government could be selected. Delegates from municipalities, professional groups (Doctors, lawyers, college teachers) should be invited and empty chairs filled from among North Korean exiles.[57]

Among the questions to address is: Is North Korea's variant of "scientific socialism" prepared to change as China and Vietnam[58] have changed? How would improved data clarify understanding between citizens of the two societies on these ten points: life expectancy, gross national product (GNP), per capita income, volume of world trade, currency exchange rates, imprisonment for nonviolent offenses, the amount of foreign assistance needed, religious liberty, form of representation in government, and free circulation of ideas including in colleges and universities.

Develop quality data.[59] Only "non-sensitive materials are generally made available by governments" and "most data are still banned from public distribution due to national security concerns" with the World Bank's 61 indicator country profiles (2017) missing 57% of the data. Any engagement intended to produce a meaningful discussion of reunification. requires better data, particularly if humanitarian aid and development assistance is to be evaluated. Steps toward better data included insisting on accurate results when, renewing aid with appropriate reciprocation rewarded by renewed aid.

The successful achievement of quality data in all 61 indicators is a functional task that could take generations. There are wide gaps such as political prisoners which Amnesty International estimates as 120,000[60] and the North Korean government claims is zero. Data to base the exchange of the won (North Korean currency) in international trade opens opportunities for achieving quality data and a lever for reciprocation. Specialists are needed with the requisite skills and abilities to extrapolate from questionable sources to reliable if not accurate data. There is leverage here to anticipate reciprocation at least in nonmilitary areas of interdependence with the world economy.

Organizations in South Korea should link with similar organizations in the United States. Linkage can take many forms, from functional (business, labor, and religious groups) to learning how concepts like "representative democracy" and "People's republic" are understood in different cultures. Linkage is not seen as a financial relationship but rather as organizational strengthening, awareness of funding possibilities, becoming self-sufficient, relationship to the media, and staff "keeping up" with changes each is experiencing. The Committee for Human Rights in North Korea could coordinate and enlarge the various forms of linkage now in existence and develop new ones.

Radio Free North Korea should report on Gene Sharp's 198 nonviolent acts and recommend one more: broadcasting a request that everyone stand still, in place, for one minute at a certain time on a symbolic date, for example, the day North Korea first ratified the Covenant on Civil and Political Rights.[61]

Treaties once ratified provide opportunities for "Living the Lie" which means acting as if the treaty was the law of the land by obeying it. The Democratic People's Republic of [North] Korea has signed 101 treaties[62] including the United Nations Charter, the Convention on the Rights of the Child with optional protocol, and the agreement establishing the International Fund for Agricultural Development. People who abide by these agreements risk imprisonment or worse. "Living the lie" succeeded when first KOR and then Solidarity adopted these tactics in Poland. International recognition was/is a partial form of protection when requested. An example of "Living the Lie" is obeying the law on religious liberty by practicing it.

Encourage visits of family members to and from North Korea on religious holidays. Buddhist, Christian, Jehovah Witnesses exist in both Koreas and these visits need not threaten security concerns.[63]

Implement the signed covenant on civil and political rights. Call a conference at the East Asian Institute (South Korea) congratulating North Korea on its ratification of the International Covenant on Civil and Political Rights with the goal of developing proposals for implementing it and offering an integrated strategy for getting from here to there.

Promote religious liberty. The North Korean Constitution guarantees freedom of religion but an outside agency, Open Doors, considers it the worst persecutor of Christians out of 60 countries monitored. Similar Buddhist agencies should be engaged such as the World Fellowship of Buddhist and the Josse Order with 10 million members.[64] Christian fundamentalists over a ten year period negotiated an agreement that opened a University 100 miles from Pyongyang. The content of the courses is closely monitored but there is opportunity to broaden the curriculum beyond economic determinism to conscience, citizenship and the rule of law.

In 2017 there are 328,547 Chinese students studying in the United States, most of them granted visas as a "fixed perk of Communist Chinese culture."[65] Visa Diplomacy is an important contribution to introducing peace to the Korean Peninsula. Transfer 10% of visa applications for study in the US from Chinese elites to "ordinary Chinese citizens" (those with no special family connections) and ask the Chinese government to pressure North Korea to abandon its nuclear program. Failure of China to do so would mean progressive loss of access by China's elite to American educational institutions.[66] China's influence comes in part from the fact that it provides North Korea with most of its food and energy.

Broadcast the message on Radio Free North Korea, including religious services, democratic practices, debates about how to support individuals "living the lie" of obeying treaties North Korea has signed.

Share scientific research. An Iowa farmer[67] has developed hybrids that produce nutritious soybeans with one half the space between rows thus doubling production. There are many other miracle seeds available to a North

Korea open to the world. Designate North Korean Agronomists to attend international conferences on such keys to feeding the North Korean population, rejecting visas of those who only have regime approval unless they could implement the knowledge. The Farm Bureau, land grant colleges with A&M after their name and others and the Agency for International Development have the needed specialized knowledge.

Publicize the workings of the IMF, WTO, and World Bank and the benefits to a unified Korea of fully participating in world trade.

Teach Democracy. Refresh the translations of the American Federation of Labor's Curriculum teaching the understandings that support representative democracy with South Korean advisors as well as Gene Sharp's *From Dictatorship to Democracy*.

South Korea

South Korea has a National Endowment for Democracy promotion institute, the East Asian Institute, that participates in the World Movement for Democracy which could provide a forum to evaluate these and other advisory opinions aware of cultural differences.

Intention Clarifying peace Initiative: Call a special session of the East Asian Institute on a Non-Violent Transition to Democracy focused on North Korea including veterans of the 20 nonviolent transitions toward democracy (1974–2003) as well as those that failed identifying special proposals and intending to offer an integrated strategy.

In the UN among agencies using democratic rhetoric, develop a self-determination plan for a unified Korea. If no progress is made shift the self-determination plan for a unified Korea to the East Asia Institute (Seoul) to be presented to the World Movement for Democracy and then to the Community of Democracies.

Hold a special session of the UN general assembly on the question of self-determination. How could the people of North and South Korea exercise the right of self-determination? The major choices must be made internal to North and South Korea.

What is offered here, is a question: Will these steps gain reciprocation? Can they lead to the goal of a reunified Korea with a government safe for free societies? Who in this country and the world will accept the risks and act to help assure that treaties to which their country has agreed, are actually enforced?

Many will no doubt contest the wisdom of these proposals. Informed dialogue will improve them and hopefully add many others. People, institutions and organizations in North and South Korea must be engaged to make nonviolent regime change possible.

CONCLUSION

Hope resides in the reaffirmation of the institutions and understandings that constitute representative democracy, informed by religious insight and independent judiciaries that enable treaties to be enforced between democratic States. Peace initiative acts that gain reciprocation can break open blocked negotiations, help resolve crises and clarify intentions to pursue constructive goals, if not to achieve a transformation of world politics.[68] Nonviolence has produced success in aiding transitions from dictatorship toward democracy . . . more than twenty 1974–2003 (Poland, Portugal, South Africa, etc.) and failed in China, Iran and Syria. Governments of, by and for the people are in jeopardy everywhere more so than even facing it's perennial challenges, rejecting transitions mandated by elections. In their preservation, and in extending the democratic peace that exists among them, in nonviolent transitions from dictatorships toward democracy, there is realistic hope.

This is an incomplete application of Robert Pickus's and the World Without War Council realistic, sustained and challenging attempt to abolish the institution of war through leadership by the United States, the reciprocation of allies and adversaries alike, leading toward a world order capable of enforcing treaties that would reliably defend free societies. This summary is offered in the belief that the goals can be pursued within the framework of military security strategies and sustainable development that do not give military advantage to adversaries of representative democracy.

NOTES

1. See "Pacifism, Critical," *Oxford Encyclopedia of Peace* (New York: Oxford University Press 2006).

2. "Seven Roads to a World Without War" is available from Hoover and Swarthmore Peace Collection. They are 1) law, 2) general and complete disarmament, 3) world economic development, 4) a sense of world community expressed in human rights promotion, 5) nonviolent means of forcing needed change, 6) affirming moral or ethical roots, and 7) most importantly enforceable agreements.

3. *Winning the War on War*, Joshua Goldstein (New York: Dutton 2011).

4. *Winning the War on War, the Decline of Armed Conflict World Wide*, Joshua S. Goldstein, p. 328 (New York: Dutton 2011). See also Steven Pinker's *The Better Angels of Our Nature: Why Violence Has Declined* (2012).

5. Our world order is based on treaties agreed to by states and so-called "customary law." Custom governs the choice of leadership in international organizations, for example. No Secretary General has ever come from a permanent UN Security Council state. The World Health Organization head is a third world prerogative.

6. Uppsala University Conflict Resolution Program lowers the threshold to 250 deaths per year.

7. See the Fund for Peace's annual Failed State Index.

8. CSpan, 2/12/2017 televised a six-person panel of the American Historical Association entitled "The Summer of Love, San Francisco 1967." Males were considered a class responsible for atomic warfare and a policy of imperialism (sic) toward Vietnam and Native

Americans, females as a class bonded with the environment and were, by giving birth and child rearing, endowed with unconditional love.

9. The "general will" is a concept articulated by Rousseau in contrast to John Locke's contract theory of legitimate governance. It was appropriated, some would say misappropriated, by Adolf Hitler and Leon Trotsky, who destroyed parliamentary bodies, claiming they belonged in the "dustbin of history."

10. See *Journal of Democracy* and John Locke, *Second Treatise of Government*; John Stuart Mill, *On Representative Government*; and Alexis de Tocqueville, *Democracy in America*. The Liberty Fund in Indianapolis publishes a catalogue with an extensive introduction to the subject.

11. *The God That Failed* (1948), reissued 2003 with essays by Andre Gide' (France), Richard Wright (United States), Ignazio Silone (Italy), Stephen Spender (England), Arthur Koestler (Germany), and Louis Fischer, American correspondent.

12. CNN 3/18/2016 report which includes the statement that ISIS "forced Christian women and girls into slavery," the House voted 393–0 supporting the genocide designation but with the realization that the genocide designation "does not legally obligate the US to take any particular action." Unilateral disarmament was advocated in *Speak Truth to Power* and in Acts for Peace's publication of Erich Fromm's "The Case for Unilateral Disarmament." Some advocates of "civilian defense" (Sharp, *Civilian Defense*) including Gene Keyes estimated the casualties as high as 300,000 at the hands of an adversary. Critics have higher estimates given that dictatorships killed more people than died in wars in the 20th Century. See R. J. Rummel, *Death by Government, Genocide and Mass Murder Since 1900* (1997).

13. See Middle East index: "In sum, without change in the Arab world's politics, economics, role of women, press, attitude toward Israel, etc., there will be no peace. Whatever Israel gives, short of disappearing, won't help without such change." Letter to brother Eddie Pickus on World Without War Council Letterhead, 10/16/2000, at Hoover.

14. See Samantha Power, *A Problem From Hell: America and the Age of Genocide* (New York: Basic Books 2013). Power lists the 20th century genocides: Armenia (1915), the Holocaust (1945), Cambodia, Iraq, Bosnia, Rwanda, Srebrenica, Kosovo. R. J. Rummel, *Death by Government* (1997), finds that adding Communist, theocratic and other dictatorships to the total, dictatorships killed more people than died in wars in the 20th century.

15. See Gregory H. Stanton's "The Ten Stages of Genocide," The Genocide Education Project. Eight stages were identified while Stanton was at the Department of State in 1996 and revised in 2013 when he led Genocide Watch. Stanton explained the purpose of his analysis as follows: "By knowing the stages of genocide, citizens are better equipped to identify the warning signs and stop the process from continuing." He further stated: "Genocide is a process that develops in ten stages that are predictable but not inexorable. At each stage, preventive measures can stop it. The process is not linear. Stages may occur simultaneously. Logically, later stages must be preceded by earlier stages. But all stages continue to operate throughout the process." (2016)

16. See report of the International State Crime Initiative, Queen Mary University and "The Cautionary Tale of Samantha Power," *Commentary, February 2017.*

17. "The Accuser, the Case Against Saddam Hussein and the Woman Who Built It," William, Langewiesche, The Atlantic, March 2002.

18. There is a Genocide Intervention Network which offers Carl Wilkens scholarships. Wilkens is credited with being the only American to remain in Rwanda during the genocide. The Network was organized out of Swarthmore College and also STAND was organized at Georgetown (2004). See *"Activism and Darfur, Slowly Driving Policy Change,"* Colin Thomas-Jensen, Juli Spiegel, *Fordham International Law Journal*, Vol. 32, Issue 4, 2007.

19. A United Nations Report of the International Commission on Intervention and State Sovereignty (2005).

20. *American Purpose*, Vol. 7, No. 4, April 1993, pp. 32–34.

21. Zuhdi Jasser, America Islamic Forum for Democracy, argues that toleration and state sponsorship of terrorism are a threat to Islam. He has a 12-step program for reform of Islam that posits the adaptation to Islam of the institutions and understandings of representative democracy as the key.

22. Preamble to the Charter of the United Nations.

23. See Lincoln Bloomfield, *The Power to Keep Peace, Today and in a World Without War* (Berkeley: World Without War Publications 1972) which maintained as the instruments of coercion went up, consent for their use went down.

24. See Janet Mackey (editor), *Terrorism and Self-Determination, a Tragic Marriage We Could Help Decouple* (Chicago: World Without War Publications 1982) Swarthmore Peace Collection.

25. See Robert Pickus and Robert Woito, *To End War* (New York: Harper and Row 1970), pp. 49–66.

26. Robert Pickus ran as a delegate to a world constitutional convention in 1969. His college's president, Robert Maynard Hutchins had prepared with Elizabeth Mann Borgese and others a *Constitution for the World* (1948).

27. See Eric Blantz's, succinct descriptions of the twelve.

28. Community of Democracies, 1998.

29. Compare *Freedom at Issues* data or ask which country's human rights record you would prefer: Costa Rica or Cuba, North or South Korea, East or West Germany, China, or Taiwan.

30. There are different ways in which people are represented in government. The British Parliament, the French Estates General, and the Spanish Cortes are examples. A dictator who claims he or she expresses the "General Will" is not a form of representation.

31. p. 1010, *The Great Ideas, a Syntopicon,* Encyclopedia Britannica, Inc. 1952. Robert Maynard Hutchins was president of the University of Chicago. He engaged the faculty in a Great Ideas program and employed Robert Pickus as a research assistant on the project.

32. This is one of 12 perspectives on global governance Blantz describes, asking you to consider which perspective best represents your view. Henry Kissinger's *World Order* develops this view, rejecting intervention or the right to protect.

33. Leon Trotsky, *Permanent Revolution.*

34. Good Global Governance, Twelve Possibilities, 1995, Eric Blantz.

35. New York Times, August 2017. See also "International Trade" by Esteban Ortiz-Ospina and Max Roser (2017).

36. *Climate Change in 2017*, 22 essays.

37. MIT website, Center for Global Science Change.

38. MIT Center for Global Change Science values the Paris Accords for the "ongoing annual meetings to regularly revisit and ratchet up national climate goals, making them more ambitious over time." See MIT Center for Global Change Science and the US Global Change Research Program. Richard Lindzen, emeritus scientist from MIT, has coined the phrase "climate alarmists." He rejected the Kyoto Accord because "it would increase the cost of electricity for no gain and put signatory states at a competitive disadvantage." He also questions "whether the move from largely private funding to public support has introduced bias into science and public policy informed by science." See also *Climate Change: The Facts*, 2017, edited by Alan Moran.

39. Gates interview, Charlie Rose show, February 2017.

40. See Sabin Center for Climate Liability website, Columbia University.

41. Lord Acton, *The Liberal Interpretation of History*, p. 292.

42. For a succinct starting point, see *US Foreign Policy 1996, Goals, Obstacles, Means to Overcome the Obstacles.* The popular culture worries humans about war with other species (Planet of the Apes), aliens (War of the Worlds) and Satan (Armageddon). There are real threats, worry about them now. You can wait until apes form a baseball team, aliens if they got here from light years away have technology that suggests you are in more trouble than you think and virtue recommends itself in any case but not everybody defines it in the same way.

43. Henry Kissinger, *World Order* (2014); in contrast the World Law Fund's Model World Order Project has now been incorporating into an organization warning against the rise of "fascism" in the United States.

44. American Initiatives Project Prospectus.

45. Quoted in the Seattle Times, 1/10/2018 in an article by Anna Field.

46. See Yarim-Agaev's Wall Street Journal article, 9/24/2015.

47. *Ibid.*

48. Kim Yong Kim became World Bank President in 2012. He was re-elected to a second five-year term in 2017. Kim was born in Korea but grew up in Muscatine, Iowa.

49. See also 101 Things You Can Do in a Crisis updating decision-makers, sources of information, other organizations at work, national and international actors whose engagement may also be needed to develop a nonmilitary conflict resolution arena.

50. NED website.

51. World Bank report, 2017.

52. NED website.

53. *Ibid.*

54. See also *Europa Yearbook*, current edition for a universal listing of nongovernmental organizations in South Korea, participants in the Civil Society whose independence is guaranteed by the Constitution of South Korea. This yearbook in its 57th year and includes a universal listing of international organizations, including summaries of each country's government, recent history, and organizations. The most recent edition (London: Europa Publications, 2016) had 5,024 pages and cost $1,514.96.

55. *Decision at Richmond, June 1788, a Documentary Drama of the Constitutional Ratification Convention in Virginia*, the only ratifying Convention for which there is a transcript, here edited from 660 pages to 174.

56. 1) How is the chief executive chosen? 2) Is there a unicameral or bicameral legislative body? 3) Is there an independent judiciary? 4) Are there independent nongovernmental organizations? 5) Is the right to emigrate respected? 6) Is there a free society? 7) Is the right of the majority to make laws within the limits set by a constitution respected so long as majority rule does not infringe on minority rights? 8) Given the importance of international trade, does the state seek a level playing field or insist on protection via tariffs that it does not reciprocate? 9) Is there an established church or other religious institution and religious liberty for all faiths? Or does the state see itself as the source of religious authority, the source of all moral authority? 10) Is there a human rights tradition which defines a space where the individual, not the state, is sovereign? 11) Is the existing IMF dominating by the 16 wealthiest democratic economies accepted as a fair mechanism to supplement currency exchanges? 12) Are environmental treaties enforced in all states or only in democracies?

57. The Ministry of Unification and the East Asian Institute, Seoul are good places to start to find leadership to organize the dialogue. The exile community includes former government officials.

58. The World Bank Reports (2017). "Vietnam's shift from a centrally planned to a market economy has transformed the country from one of the poorest in the world into a lower middle income country. Vietnam is one of the most dynamic emerging countries in the East Asian Region." A 6.4 % annual growth rate was achieved in the 2000's driven by "resilient domestic demand and export orientated manufacturers."

59. David Hawk, *The Hidden Gulag: The Lives and Voices of Those Who Were "Sent to the Mountains"* (New York: Amnesty International 2014).

60. David Hawk, *The Hidden Gulag: The Lives and Voices of Those Who Were "Sent to the Mountains"* (New York: Amnesty International 2014).

61. This is done for five minutes annually in Turkey on the date Kemal Ataturk died.

62. The treaties North Korea has ratified are readily accessible online.

63. Initiative is used here as an independent act taken outside of negotiations intended to facilitate agreement in negotiations without giving up what Gandhi would define as an experiment with the "truth."

64. President Carter submitted this Covenant to the US Senate for ratification with 52 "understandings" and "reservations" designed to protect existing United States human rights laws from being lessened by an international treaty.

65. This brief is drawn from William McGurn's column "How to Squeeze China," *Wall Street Journal*, 7/11/2017. The formula of a peace initiative is based on that column but is not stated by him.

66. See also Robert Pickus's "Initiatives to End the War in Vietnam."

67. Harry Stine, Bill Eby, Stine Seed Farm, Inc., Adel, Iowa.

68. Immanuel Kant, *On Perpetual Peace* (1795); Francis Doyle (1970); Bruce Russett, *Grasping the Democratic Peace* (1994); Charles Lipset, *Reliable Partners, How Democracies Have Made a Separate Peace* (2005). See also Edith Wynner and Georgia Lloyd, *Searchlight on Peace Plans, Choose Your Road to World Government* (New York: Dutton 1946) for summaries of over 200 peace plans from Pierre Dubois (1306) to Clarence Streit (1939).

Chapter Seven

Other Voices

Comments, Criticisms, and New Ideas

This chapter consists of comments and criticism from key figures in the Peace Community working during the past four decades. Each "Other Voice" is noted, with their comments, along with a response by the author.

Michael Bernstam, Moscow Helsinki Watch Committee, fellow, Hoover Institution:

> I think if various ethnic and other community groups jointly redrew the borders, this would remove a major cause of conflicts. This is especially urgent in Africa where artificial borders spawn perpetual genocides of which one seems to be emerging in the Congo (Kinshasa). Millions of people die. Tens of millions suffer for decades. The problem is a core obstacle of economic growth. One of the costliest phrases in human history is "territorial integrity" as if a given area always an accident of history were a human community. [1]

Response: The Organization of African Unity (replaced in 2002 by African Union) does not have a procedure to process self-determination claims. The Gowan reforms (Nigeria 1970s) were an attempt to supplement tribal identities with the national one after the Ibo's sought to secede into Biafra. "Territorial integrity" is a crucial concept, but implementation could also trigger a war of all against all. Self-determination is an answer but with 57 secessionist movements in the world (Catalonia, South Sudan, & Scotland) and different forms of government, it is unresolved, even conceptually. In lieu of a nonmilitary means, armed people will claim territory until procedures are developed and followed.

Eric Blantz, Good Global Governance program, World Without War Council Inc., University of Chicago, critic of earlier drafts. Allan Blackman, career in Public Health, draft counselor, author of *Face to Face With Your Draft Board*, 63,000 copies sold. Doug Bond, WWW Council Midwest Intern, PhD with R. J. Rummel, University of Hawaii, Correlates of War research project. Rummel discovered more people died at the hands of dictators in the 20th Century than died in war (Democide), Bond worked with Gene Sharp, Program on Nonviolent Sanctions, away in the summer of 2018 on peacemaking mission to Ethiopia and Nigeria and consultant on nonmilitary reunification of the Korean Peninsula.

Warren Crowther, pensioned by the UN after working for eight UN agencies, University of Costa Rica, specialist on Latin America, 60 years of argument, still friends; submitted 25 pages of comments and criticism. Warren wishes to add he has a special interest in "post conflict (post war, post dictatorship, post Communism) transitional justice":

> I am most concerned about the epistemological and ethical ramifications of the transition, and have an ingrained rejection of indirect and direct military intervention where they only add fuel to the fire, including those by consolidated democracies toward other countries, as I have had to deal with these effects during my 50 years working directly for 8 UN agencies in 39 countries. In this regard, I see model proposals, but not of empirical demonstration.[2]

Lucy Dougall:

> I admire your effort to carry on Pick's vision, validate his and the Council's work and present your own take on what needs to be done in today's world. TTP [Turn Toward Peace] and WWWC [World Without War Council] have an impressive list of accomplishments. I realize that Pick's lifelong work was to develop non-violent alternatives to war, which he summarized in the Seven Roads. He claimed he was a pacifist but sometimes both he and you seem to be talking in terms of realpolitik. He was a harsh critic of anti-war activists, choosing the most extreme examples.
>
> My comments, as always, have been that my attraction to WWWC has rested on its commitment to peace by way of non-violence. The founding document, to my mind is AFSC's Speak Truth to Power, A Quaker Search for an Alternative to Violence, offered by Stephen Cary in 1955. I read in Pick's obituary that in the 1950s he called for a pacifist statement that became Speak Truth to Power of which he was co-author. (Pick was one of twelve signers). It states clearly that simultaneous reliance on military force and the assumption that evil can only be met by violence, or at least the threat of violence, are assumptions that cannot be sustained.[3]
>
> You and he make the case that every national government is obligated to protect its citizens by relying on military force even while trying diplomacy. I

believe you do not give enough weight to non-violence. I didn't note any reference to the great American example of Martin Luther King, Jr.'s Montgomery Bus Boycott, the March on Washington, etc. You seem to prefer pointing out the follies and outrages perpetrated by extremists. As a historian, I believe you should refer to more examples. You mention Gene Sharp's three volume work only in footnotes. Although Pick worked with Quakers in AFSC, and was co-author of STTP, you document makes no reference to the work of Quakers for non-violent social change and civil disobedience, for example. You don't give credit to examples in Buddhist and other traditions, such as the Dalai Lama (except for a footnote saying Paul Ekman is working with him now). You don't give credit to Desmond Tutu for his non-violent work in South Africa against apartheid. You don't give credit to Thich Nhath Hanh's response to the Vietnam War first in his workshop in Vietnam giving assistance to both sides in the conflict through his tireless work for non-violence and through his advocacy of it, even to our own Congress. You don't mention the first independent peace group in the USSR founded by Sergei Batovrun. You give unequivocal support to Israel in your statement. Why is there no mention of a two state solution or any view of the opposite sides position? I was strongly drawn to WWWC by Pick's Acts for Peace and the Seven Roads to a World Without War and both Anne Stadler and I and the whole Seattle office worked on many "acts for peace." I wish you good luck.[4]

Response: I'm not sure why the origins of *Speak Truth to Power* (STTP) or the text are at issue here but I do understand the importance of the statement and that the text be accurate. Gene Keyes has also said four paragraphs were left out of the original text, but were added for later editions. I have reprinted the four paragraphs in Gene Keyes "Other Voice" contribution. I will check with Wendy Chmielewski, Curator, Swarthmore Peace Collection.

There is in the Council archives a statement by Pick that he was working through "other minds." You and I have rarely been in a meeting with Pick in which he did not consider himself the dominate voice. I recall, as I am sure you do, his insistence on stating others opinions "as if they were coherent at the time they were speaking." Steve Cary, Robert Gilmore, Bayard Rustin, and others each might claim to be the dominate voice, but let's agree Robert Pickus was "a force to be reckoned with in the deliberations."[5]

In my interpretation, what is at stake is not whether Quakers and other pacifists witness for an impossible ideal; all agree they do and challenge others to live up to that idea. But Robert Pickus and Gene Sharp agreed that pacifists could not expect to influence public policy unless and until they had a nonmilitary strategy of peace adequate to meet the threats the National Security Council said existed at any given time. Robert Pickus could be said to be seeking a seat at the NSC table with 40 years of constituency building speaking for the NGO world and offering a strategy of peace that could realistically meet national security threats that the United States could implement. Gene Sharp developed a strategy of civilian defense—nonviolent resis-

tance to occupation—as his alternative. Robert Pickus (with many colleagues) developed a nonmilitary strategy of American Peace initiative Acts,
albeit within the framework of military deterrence strategy but designed with
step-by-reciprocated-step to replace it.

Robert Pickus, no doubt in consultation with others, is credited in The
Progressive with being the author of the summary of STTP printed in October 1955. The Progressive symposium also included critical responses by
seven people three of whom were in my view devastating: (1) Disarmament
must be multilateral, not unilateral (Norman Thomas); (2) So significant a
change in policy as advocated by STTP requires a new consensus to be
implemented (Dwight Macdonald); and (3) the power of love to transform
dedicated (ideological, theocratic or authoritarian) adversaries is limited. Determined adversaries state their intention daily and must be contained before
any strategy of peace can be implemented (George F. Kennan).

From 1955 to 1961 Pick did act on the Progressive magazine claim that
the possession of the weapons themselves was the source of the problem. It is
clear during the Acts for Peace years, that unilateral disarmament was an
option but not the only one. When choosing between nuclear deterrence and
civilian defense one could plausibly do a cost/benefit analysis and choose the
risks of the latter. There were suggestions in STTP to support the UN, embrace decolonization Gandhi style, etc. but no answer to the question "How
do we get there from here?" So also there was no answer to Kennan's claim
that those ideas were already under consideration but could not be acted on
because you were faced with a determined adversary. Pick said the point of
pacifist witness should not be to give military advantage to an adversary. Is
your claim that only unilateral disarmament by the United State was a decisive enough act that would break the momentum of an arms race and that
Gene Sharp's developed civilian defense the only strategy a pacifist could
embrace?

In 1961, I argue, Pick had an epiphany. In an amazing letter to 10 pacifist
colleagues, including Kale Williams, he articulated the Seven Roads and the
Turn Toward Peace policy framework. To A. J. Muste's astonishment, Pick
rejected unilateral halting of nuclear testing until it was combined with reciprocation as Kennedy did in his Strategy of Peace[6] statement indicated he
would halt on a unilateral basis, but would test on one for one basis if the
Soviet Union tested. Unilateral initiatives to achieve multilateral disarmament became Council doctrine. The TTP policy framework was an invitation
to Just War advocates, national interest diplomacy realist and others to develop and implement an American Strategy of Peace Initiative Acts.

Forgive me if you can, but my empathy goes not with Bayard Rustin's
conscientious objections to World War II but to the soldiers in the landing
craft headed for Omaha beach (1944). I imagine a soldier might have thought
someone should have come up with some strategy of peace better than the

League of Nations, neutrality legislation and keep us out of war isolationism. In the meantime there were 300,000 men, in landing crafts waiting for the front shield to drop under fire as the shore based machine guns blaze away. George Weigel speaks of the "fog of war" which is true enough if you get to the beach but in the meantime there is nothing foggy about it, your life expectancy drops to seconds when they lower the shield. Military discipline, the belief there is no alternative, patriotic obligation, the prayer that God is on your side, all can come to the mind of the soldier. There are costs to not having an adequate and realistic strategy of peace as we do not now when faced with Islamic jihadist, waging a holy war against all other religions and perhaps 99% of Islam. Contain, deter, roll back all military terms, come to mind. They make more sense to me than appeasement, claiming Syria did not have chemical weapons when they did or making fun of the Commander in Chief 24/7.

This is not a criticism of witness for an impossible ideal. It is a criticism of the belief that Robert Pickus failed one of his closest supporters because he came to believe disarmament must be multilateral, unilateral initiatives must be reciprocated, and a consensus must be reached to support a "New Foreign Policy." We leave our successor with three such strategies: (1) civilian defense, (2) democratic peace,[7] and (3) a reinvented American Peace Initiatives strategy. Is there a voice in AFSC land for Civilian Defense as a nonviolent alternative to defense spending?

There is bipartisan support for the National Endowment for Democracy and its programs intended, in my view, to induce regime change and unify the Korean Peninsula under a government, safe for free societies. I have claimed for Robert Pickus and Gene Sharp along with many other people the insights that have created two regional peaces', one in North America, another in Europe. Can you join in toasting these achievements in world politics while recognizing your father, you, and Pick's helped bring it about?

There are unanswered questions: (1) Does a successful counter-terrorism strategy blur the line between legitimate police powers and illegitimate acts of war? (2) Is the coalition to end genocide's support of violence at the ninth stage (mass annihilation) justified? Is there a non-violent alternative to the mass annihilation stage? For that matter, is there a violent solution in a world of sovereign states? (3) Was the Gulf War justified given that it was UN Security Council approved response to a cross border crossing or war of aggression when the failure to act would risk the irrelevance of the UN as the League of Nations became irrelevant? (4) Does the failure to enforce the convention against genocide in Srebrennca, Kosovo and today in Burma, provide motivation for the Islamic Caliphate? (5) Was Kennan's warning prescient in the face of determined adversaries, military containment is a prerequisite of any successful strategy of peace in world politics? And (6) Should we expect mass conversions to pacifism when even the threat of nuclear war did not do it? If mass conversions took place, what strategy of peace would be possible in the face of Islamic Jihadism?

Thank you for the life time of shared steady work. Your publications War/Peace Film Guide, War and Peace Literature, Raising the Curtain & the World Without War Game (with Anne Stadler and others in Seattle) are among your wonderful contributions. Thanks also for wishing me well with this project. I hope it inspires a successor person or organization. In the meantime, my thanks also to Bill and the soldiers in the landing crafts headed for Omaha Beach. They are also my heroes. Last word: "There is no Way to Peace, Peace is the Way," A. J. Muste. "Blessed are the Peacemakers," St. Francis.

Gene Keyes, Committee for Nonviolent Action (1961–1964); originator of the Cahill-Keyes World Map (1975), assistant professor (ret.) world politics; author of "Bucky and Pick: Two Grand Designers of a World Without War: An Essay; Review of Robert Pickus, *To End War* and R. Buckminster Fuller, *Utopia or Oblivion*" (see genekeyes.com). Keyes summarizes Arthur I. Waskow's (1963) proposed model for a triplex peace police (suitable in principle for the Myanmar genocide, 2017–2018):

> Among many proposals over the years for some type of international police force (most of them armed) I will cite Arthur Waskow's model for a triplex peace police written up in 1963. This too is not entirely non-violent except at lower levels, but the plan had a number of sophisticated design features. There would be three police bodies (for Disarmament, Borders, and Special Situations), each controlled by separate Councils, in turn responsive to World Court orders. The court would be acting on data turned up by an inspectorate, a fourth police body, unarmed. The force level authorized for any of the three peace police would be according to a pre-set, time limited, aye-vote ratio in their respective controlling councils. For instance, disarmament treaty violations would be blamed on low-level individuals (such as a factory manager); disarmament police would serve court orders on him to cease and desist not— his government. So far the action would be small and unarmed; but with the greater council consensus in the face of persistent violation, greater increments of police units and weaponry would be authorized. As before, I dissent at the weapons phase. The Special Situations Force could deal with the likes of the Myanmar genocide, 2017–18.[8]

Response: When would a state consent to be policed in these ways?

Gene Keyes, citing classic Bob Pickus from expanded version of 1955 *Progressive* magazine symposium:

> The pamphlet "Speak Truth to Power" was a serious effort to launch a dialogue on nonviolent resistance with foreign policy realists. Among its prime movers was Robert Pickus a "realist" pacifist par excellence. He and Stephen

Cary defended STTP in a symposium published in the October 1955 issue of *The Progressive*. Among the critics were George Kennan, Reinhold Neibuhr, Norman Thomas and Dwight Macdonald. Oddly enough in the original magazine, Pickus and Cary sidestepped an oft-heard criticism, here voiced by Macdonald, that Communist invaders "would not shrink from whatever measures of extermination seemed necessary." But in an expanded reprint version of the symposium, four paragraphs were added, coming to grips with that poser.[9]

As part of the addendum, Pickus and Cary conceded: "This is not to suggest that non-violent resistance could be carried out without suffering. Against a totalitarian opponent it would clearly receive a far sterner test than against one imbued with an ethical tradition of the sacredness of human life. Indeed, the prospect of suffering that would be involved is appalling to contemplate."[10] These are the four paragraphs not in the original STTP but added in expanded reprint version by Pickus and Cary.

Both Thomas and Macdonald complain that the pacifist alternative has no universal application, but is appropriate only to particular situations. Gandhi's successful use of nonviolence, says Macdonald, would not work against the Communists who "would not shrink from whatever measures of extermination seemed necessary."

Keyes responded:

> This position assumes that the same human response that was felt by the British would not be felt by the Communist. Yet our critics argue at another point that Communists will be deterred by a sufficient display of force. They are thus assumed capable of the human response of fear. On what grounds then are other human responses to be excluded? Either we must regard Communists as inhuman and therefore expect them to be unswayed by any human responses, or we must admit the possibility of their reacting to the whole emotional catalogue. We admit the shaping power of an ideology, but we deny that it can eliminate completely the normal human responses that men feel when they confront each other directly. This leads us to reject the idea that non-Communists can arbitrarily select certain responses as being applicable to Communists, and arbitrarily exclude others as not being applicable. Moreover, there is actual precedent to support our point of view. In June 1953, during the East German uprisings, Soviet soldiers did refuse to shoot unarmed demonstrators, and were court-martialed for their insubordination. This is but a straw in the wind, but enough to suggest that the rank and file human beings who make up the armies of every nation can be counted on to have similar responses to human situations. It is not the hardened Communist leadership who would feel the weight of non-violent resistance but the Russian people who comprise the armies.
>
> This is not to suggest that non-violent resistance could be carried out without suffering. Against a totalitarian opponent it would clearly receive a far sterner test than against one imbued with an ethical tradition of the sacredness of human life. Indeed, the prospect of suffering that would be involved is appalling to contemplate. But what other alternative is there? We see no hope

whatever in a violent response, which can neither change our opponents' mind nor crush their ideology. Nor is there any greater hope inherent in the deterrent concept. How can the concept of human dignity, which is the central value we wish to uphold, be advanced by building up our ability to kill and destroy in unprecedented volume? The method we would employ at least offers hope of something positive. It could change our opponent because it appeals to his best and not his worst side. It would preserve our values because it is based square-ly on them. A pacifist is a pacifist because he sees neither a moral nor a practical alternative. A sense of necessity moves him to his radical position. [11]

Response: Does the same rhetoric apply today to racist? White supremacist? Only Black Lives Matter advocates? The Republicans? Islamic Jihadist? All determined adversaries?

Louis Kriesberg, professor emeritus, Peace and Conflict Studies, Syracuse University: "I think it is worth noting that there was widespread interest and considerable support for world government, world federalism, etc. soon after the end of World War II. Popular support can be drawn to it. Many problems are global in nature and therefore need global treatment." [12]

Response: The first use of atomic weapons focused the discussion and helped create the United Nations whose charter states the aim of eliminating "the scourge of war" from world politics.

Kriesberg: "You should give more attention to the alternatives to war some of which contributed to the decline in wars in the 1990s and earlier. One element of that is the growth of peace and conflict resolution thinking and practice." [13]

Response: There is a distinction in the conflict resolution thought between "hard" and "soft" approaches. Pickus offered a strategy of American peace initiative acts as his signature contribution to replace "hard" (i.e., military) approaches. He also supported civilian defense (1955–1961) as a fallback option if negotiations, UN reform, and so on, failed. There is also a demo-cratic peace strategy that seeks to replace hard power with nonmilitary transi-tions to power applicable even to North Korea. Your *Realizing Peace: A Constructive Conflict Resolution Approach* has the right title. Robert Pickus made a significant contribution to nonmilitary conflict resolution detailed in the archived Overview document and within States in his support of repre-sentative government. The urgent need today is to implement constructive conflict resolution approach with determined adversaries ISIS, Iran, and North Korea as well as China and Russia. I offer 20 specific programs in-tended to reunify the Korean Peninsula under a government "safe for free societies." as my contribution to an alternative to war. I hope the Ministry of Unification (South Korea) will develop them and others into a strategy of peace. I rely on several programs financially assisted by the National Endow-ment for Democracy. The intention is to change a determined adversary.

Kriesberg: "You make much of Hillary Clinton's reference to a [basket of] deplorables and minimize the whole tenor of the vulgar, uncivil, lying conduct of President Trump. [It] seems to me that the slip away from democracy is Trump's! Really!"[14]

Response: The accusation of lying has a specific and relevant, bi-partisan instance. After President Obama drew the line in the sand, Obama, John Kerry, and Susan Rice assured the public that the Assad regime had destroyed all their chemical weapons on multiple occasions. President Trump presumably based on classified information, found they had not and attacked the offending facilities with 67 Tomahawk missiles. Which President was lying?

I have argued you need bi-partisan support for any strategy of peace. Hillary Clinton by calling all Republicans racist without naming one elected Republican as a racist excused herself by claiming they speak in "Dog Whistles." This precludes bi-partisan support. President Obama by signing an Accord with Iran avoided the Senate Treaty ratification process. President Trump was elected by a majority of the electoral college and the results certified by all fifty Secretaries of State. President Trump has found, if he did not know it before, that the checks and balances institutionalized in the United States limit executive authority. By not recognizing the President elect, by being part of the violent resistance movement both symbolically and actual, not loyal opposition, by welcoming Michael Brown's father to the convention after the Attorney General Eric Holder found Brown had robbed a convenience store and tried to kill the arresting officer, by encouraging the assassination of the President (Shakespeare in the Park), this is more than "a slip away from democracy." It is a denial of one of the strengths of democracy, the peaceful transfer of power from one party to another. Is this a self-righteous desire for one party rule "by any means necessary" the result of identity, vanity, politics? My statement is All lives matter. Obey the Law, contest arrest in court, not the streets. Domestic violence is an obstacles to a bi-partisan foreign policy as are ad hominem arguments 24/7 against the elected President.

Kriesberg: "And what is it about Cuba? Are people who urge engagement in order to bring about change to be tarred as lovers of dictatorship?"[15]

Response: No, but there is a theory that economic rights are more basic than civil and political rights and if the poor are well fed, that is a form of "virtual" representation. Senator Rubio points out there are many steps that engagement could push for: (1) freeing of the nonviolent, political prisoners, (2) orderly departure procedures, (3) religious liberty, (4) a free press, and (5) steps toward women fully participating in a modern economy.

Kriesberg: "It seems to me that the current slippage away from democracy and the rise of authoritarianism in America and elsewhere in the world, is a worrisome, new development. It is a reason to advocate for your ideas now more than ever. That could help frame your new beginning."[16]

Response: My New Beginnings seeks recognition for two regional peaces, one among EU countries in Europe, the other among Canada, the United States, and Mexico. All of the countries are representative democracies. By my calculation that is 73 years and counting of peace in these two regions. There is bi-partisan support for extending these regional peace to other regions, given that democracies rarely war on each other, in the support for the National Endowment for Democracy (NED). NED has four separate institutes, the Democratic and Republican Party Institutes and the AFL-CIO and US Chamber of Commerce Institutes. There is also a World Movement for Democracy that meets every two years and gathers activists, grantees, and resource people to discuss strategies of support and change. There are also democracy promotion Institutes in Canada, England, Germany, Taiwan and South Korea and a Community of Democracies that acts as a caucus within the UN but could act independently. Transparency International is the European Union's worldwide corruption fighting resource. There is also global civil society institutions like the Catholic, Orthodox, Protestant and National Association of Evangelical which facilitate change outside of government and nineteen million plus member other religious communities. Besides these organizations, there are civic, educational, sports, political, ethnic, and others all listed in the annual Europa Yearbook. There is no end of opportunities to advance a nonmilitary strategy of peace.

Recommended reading by Louis Kriesburg: *Conflict and Collaboration; For Better or Worse,* Co-edited with Catherine Gerard (New York: Routledge, 2018). *Constructive Conflicts: From Escalation to Resolution,* 1998, 5th edition 2017 with Bruce W, Dayton. *Perspectives on Waging Conflicts Constructively. Cases, Concepts and Practice* (Lanham, Rowman & Littlefield, 2017). *Pioneer in Peace and Constructive Conflict Resolutions Studies Series* (Switzerland: Springer, 2016). *Realizing Peace: A Constructive Conflict Approach* (New York: Oxford University Press, 2015). Also recommended: Gene Sharp, *Waging Nonviolent Struggle: 20th Century Practice and 21st Century Potential* (2005).

Walter Naegle, former member of the Executive Committee of the New York Region of the AFSC, partner of the late Bayard Rustin:

Is War Inevitable? Based on human history, it would appear that war is inevitable. Conflict certainly is and whether a conflict escalates into warfare can depend on a variety of factors including but not limited to, the nature and type of threat perceived by the parties at odds. Is the threat seen as existential or one that can only impact on a country's interest abroad. Is this a threat to an ally or to property controlled by a power, but not part of its defined borders? Another factor is the balance (or imbalance) of military power between the parties involved? The form(s) of government of the parties involved can also play a role. It is often said that democracies do not war against each other, and while this has been true up to now, it is not impossible to imagine, particularly in a time when some states seem to be moving away from the liberal democratic model that has been in place for the last 70 years.

Replace war with arbitration and mediation? At the same time, wars between nation-states can be ended if countries agree to arbitration and mediation. My hope is that nations which are both democratic and militarily powerful will pressure parties at odds to work towards diplomatic solutions through an international body. However, given the track record of the United Nations and what appears to be a trend toward isolationism, my hopes are not high.

Obstacles to ending war by 2050 . . . Several come to mind.

- The growing militarization of some smaller countries and their interest in becoming nuclear powers in an attempt to "level the playing field" with large, more powerful nations. North Korea is a current example of this tendency.
- The increasing gap in wealth between the "have" and the "have nots" and the eroding of hope among individuals for improving their lot in life. While I believe that revolutions spring from hope rather than despair, I also see where despair can lead to acts of desperation and terrorism by individuals or small groups.
- The emergence of a retreat from the commitment to the idea of a world community with shared interests. Expanding nationalist sentiments incorporating notions of homogeneity and resistance to immigration and diverse communities, whether religious or ethnic. Such ideas can lead to the demonization of "the other," and assigning blame for problems that have little, if anything, to do with superficial human differences. In such a climate, forced displacement of minority groups and even attempts at genocide can erupt.
- A rise in authoritarian ideology and the suppression of popular grassroots movement towards democratization.
- A movement towards expanding military budgets at the expense of human needs.

A. J. Muste, perhaps the best-known US pacifist, once said "There is no way to peace, peace is the way," an idea consistent with Gandhi's citing the necessity of the compatibility of means and ends. If individuals and/or countries desire peace, they must promote ideas, behavior and strategies that will reach that end. Wars generally come about because of three factors: 1) human needs are not being met within a society and the society responds with civil unrest or aggression against another society it holds responsible for problems it thinks can be solved through the seizing of assets—natural resources, property, or finances; 2) A person or groups of people in a "strongman" regime that sees aggression against an outward "foe" as a way to deflect attention from its failures at home and/or to unite its base behind it. 3) An extreme ideology sometimes religious, sometimes political, sees its mission as spreading its beliefs using violence as its means. These are not mutually exclusive. Democracies tend to provide a means for addressing both 1) and 2) through elections, civil society, a free press, and allocation of power through branches of government. The result being that as has been frequently cited, democracies do not tend to wage war against each other. To avoid war and/or civil unrest, societies are wise to address the basic needs of their populations (jobs, healthcare, education, shelter) and to guard against gross class inequality. At the same time to be a "democracy that is worthy of the name" (to paraphrase Pick in his reference to the US peace movement), power should be shared and not concentrated in the hands of the wealthy few. It is worth noting here that in its 2018 report, Freedom House saw a "slow decline in political rights and civil liberties in the United States for the past seven years . . . in 2017, however, the deterioration accelerated. The United States lost three points on the 100-point scale used by Freedom in the World' the organization's annual publication. Freedom House was an organization often cited as reliable by Pick, and often seen as suspect by the left.

Recent events seem to point to a US administration that is less friendly toward our longtime democratic allies, and more admiring of authoritarian regimes, while questioning basic democratic safeguards at home such as a free press, the right of peaceful assembly. and due process in enforcing our laws. A large cutback in health and human services, combined with robust funding of the military and the somewhat bizarre proposal of a large military parade in our capital, seems to indicate that we are moving in the wrong direction if it is peace and prosperity we seek.

Addressing #3, radical religious or political ideologies, is more troubling for the pacifist. Pacifisms and nonviolence have always relied on appealing to the humanity and reason of an opponent, usually in a face-to-face situation (example the anti-colonial struggles in India, the US civil rights movement). In a world where face-to-face combat is diminishing, appeals to reason must be made through diplomacy. However, if a country is faced with an adversary that is not a recognized government but rather a radical fringe group willing to die for its cause and use violent means to achieve its ends there seems to be little choice but to resist it violently. One hopes that this would be done strategically with minimal civilian casualties and without destroying the infrastructure necessary for the society to return to functioning as it had prior to the conflict. Large civilian casualties and needless destruction will only drive people into the radical camp. But does a recognition that violence may sometimes be necessary mean that we must support a return to a global arms race, massive military buildups (during a time when cyber wars seem to the weapon of choice for the most powerful countries), and unilateral provocative threats? I don't think so. If there is to be war, it should be done cooperatively with allies who share our values and will share the cost both financially and in terms of human life and suffering. For democracies, war should always be a last resort, not a first response. [17]

Response: Arbitration, mediation, enhanced conflict resolutions skills wonderful; and when they fail, and the conflict is about mutual incompatibilities as with ISIS, Iran and North Korea, and Russia and China, there may still be alternatives to war or surrender similar to those proposed to produce regime change unifying the Korean Peninsula. How much military is enough? Not our department or skill set. Can the five mutual incompatibilities be gotten to disarm? No they are dedicated adversaries. Could the Bayard Rustin Fund develop four more nonmilitary strategies of change to be implemented within the framework of deterrence strategy? In this world, there is really no other way to work on it. Do you consider the programs in South Korea aimed at North Korea blanks? Thank you for stating that ISIS is a problem. But the period from denial to war is the period we want to broaden, even make it permanent.

Augustin Nicolescu: Only EU member countries enjoy Positive Peace. Augustin was a WWWC-M intern, received his BA from McGill and an MA from the European University Center for Peace Studies in Austria. In 2018 he is the co-director of the Herbert C. Kelman workshop in Vienna; He is currently at work on the crisis management initiative to support the development of mediation policies. He delivers trainings on conflict transformation, dialogue, and conflict sensitivity in Europe and Central Asia:

> Two cases are suggested as being regions of peace—the European Union and North America under the North American Free Trade agreement. To what extent this is accurate and whether these cases can help us in establishing further regions of peace and ending wars and violent conflict is worth examining.

How to Define a "Region of Peace" and What Are Possible Criteria?

> It should go beyond simply being a geographic area where there have not been violent interstate or intrastate conflicts lately; there needs to be some formal arrangement in place, a structure enabling the peaceful resolution of conflicts within and among member states.
>
> It should have a positive impact in terms of peace, democracy, human rights beyond its borders, military interventions, whether collectively or by individual member states should be undertaken in accordance to international law and humanitarian principles.
>
> Finally, a peace region should probably also require a kind of peace beyond the mere absence of war. That is, a significant level of positive peace within the region, with strong relationships between states and citizens across the region; low level of social violence and economic disparity, high rates of education and health, and other social and cultural indicators of quality of life; an effective mechanism and a political culture geared towards resolving disputes and preventing violence.
>
> Looking at the European Union today, it remains undoubtedly an extraordinary achievement, a testament to the vision for a peaceful continent in the aftermath of two devastating World Wars. The countries of today's European Union have not been in internal and colonial conflicts as well as the Cold War, which divided the continent for over four decades. Taking the Treaty of Maas-

tricht in 1993 as the start of the modern European Union, however, the risk of war or even of a more limited violent conflict between member states has been and remains close to zero, and member states have largely known peace for these past 35 years.

The EU certainly satisfies the criteria for formalized structure. Today, the EU encompasses 28 members (pre-Brexit) with further states at various stages of gaining membership. The EU has well-established government structures, including an executive body led by national leaders, a parliament, and processes for further monetary integration (the Euro) and border management (the Schengen zone), although these face their own mounting challenges. For better or worse, a common European military force remains a distinct possibility, spurred in recent times by an increasingly unpredictable US foreign and defense policy.

The EU is the recipient of the 2012 Nobel Peace Prize (which places it in at times dubious company) "for over six decades [having] contributed to the advancement of peace and reconciliation, democracy and human rights in Europe." The Good Friday Agreement would not have been possible without the EU as a framework and the open border between Northern Ireland and the Republic of Ireland. Further enlargement across the Western Balkans, will over the coming decades bring the parts of the former Yugoslav republic back together rendering less relevant the border's greatest failures in modern times. The EU is a strong carrot for states which aspire to join its ranks, and the EU attempt to also extend its soft power to the wider European neighborhood; the EU has its own diplomatic corps in the European External Action Service and engages on numerous issues related to peace across the globe. It is the largest funder for humanitarian and development aid and focuses on human rights and peace mediation efforts. Forging a common foreign and security policy remains a challenge, and member states are not bound by the EU consensus and individual EU member states have engaged in or supported military action of dubious legitimacy in the eyes of international law, most notably the invasion of Iraq in 2004.

Positive peace is a high standard, requiring constructive relationships, structures which address the needs of all in an equitable manner, and the ability to constructively resolve conflicts. On a relational and cultural level, the EU has developed extensive mechanisms for fostering exchanges between their citizens—such as the education-oriented Erasmus and Grundtvig programs, resulting in the emergence of an "Erasmus" generation and experience and ties to others across the European Union. However, fostering and nurturing a sense of common European identity remains a challenge.

EU Cohesion Funds pour into low-income sub-national regions and into new member states during and after the accession process. The funds go towards infrastructure, and human and productive capital. The results have been significant and measurable, with poorer newer states joining the EU seeing rapid and significant growths in GDP. But not all is well, and discontent is rife among many constituencies who see "Brussels" as a group of distant technocrats who interfere too much in local affairs. National politicians are often quick to play off this sentiment and to point the blame toward the EU institutions for domestic difficulties. A driving factor is that if disparity between member EU states has been reduced, intra-state disparities have been on the rise—a global phenomenon. In the face of the economic crisis, austerity policies have dominated, leading to growing resentment in states which have been forced to accept devastating budget cuts on a national level. Germany has for decades pursued policies preventing wage growth, itself a form of austerity. The discontent brought on by austerity measures was one of the driving forces behind Brexit and throughout Europe this discontent has fed ultra-nationalist and xenophobic sentiments. Far right parties, once thought to have been relegated to the dustbin of history, have been resurgent and further emboldened by the arrival of large numbers of refugees from outside the European continent.

The arrival of refugees from outside of Europe compounds the challenge, with a few countries facing the challenge of accommodating the influx, while others seek to avoid any contribution to the resettlement of refugees. This is despite having often been the source of significant numbers of refugees and political asylum seekers in the past, and still sources of economic migrants would be any easier for European states were the EU not to exist.

The greatest challenge for the EU will be to address the internal disparities within its member states and guarantee the economic and social cohesion sought by the endeavor of European integration. If it can succeed in doing so, while further promoting a European identity that can exist alongside national and regional identities, the EU can continue to strengthen the positive peace it has been instrumental in establishing across the continent.

Positive peace it is not, but war is not likely between the US, Canada or Mexico. NAFTA is quite a different creature than the European Union. Although the populations of the two regions are similar, and they have similar GDPs, the differences are quite evident. While the EU currently has 28 member, NAFTA has three-Mexico, the United States of America, and Canada one of which is vastly more powerful than the others, and one which is significantly poorer than the others. NAFTA is a trade agreement only, not even a customs union, with far less integration than the others. NAFTA is a trade agreement only and very limited supra-national structures. NAFTA has a small secretariat and a Free Trade Commission, neither of which has been particularly effective. NAFTA does not address cultural or political issues.

So how does the area NAFTA covers measure up as a peace region? One measure mentioned is whether there is peace in the region and whether the institutions (NAFTA in this case) is the source or at least contributes to that peace. There has never been a war between the US and Canada since the latter's independence. The last between these two countries, took place a few decades later following the annexation of Texas, and by the end of which Mexico had ceded half of its territory to the US. The US would intervene militarily into Mexico several times during its revolution, including John J. Pushing's pursuit of Francisco "Pancho" Villa, and the last incursion of US Forces into Mexico in 1919. During the 75 years since that time and NAFTA coming into force, there were no military engagements between these three countries. Since WWI, Canada and the US have developed deep ties in common defense, the depth of which can be seen in the joint North American Aerospace Defence [US spelling Defense] Command (NORAD). But it does not have any relation to NAFTA, and it does not invoke Mexico in any way. There is no common defense agreement between the US and Mexico which is not a member of NATO either) despite current close cooperation around border and custom controls, especially drug and migration issues. The legacy of the past conflicts between the two countries, largely forgotten in the US, has left deep marks on the collective psyche south of the border, and particularly on Mexico's military. An alternative explanation for the enduring (negative) peace between the three country blocs is that neighbors of super powers find it in their interest to avoid the risk of any kind of military confrontation with the super power.

In the case of NAFTA then, there is a limited structure for cooperation, focused entirely on trade and not reaching the level of customs union. The absence of violent conflict predates the agreement, and an alternative explanation for this can be found in the dominance of the US in this quadrant of the globe.

If the EU struggles to develop its Common Foreign and Security Policy, there is no correlate for the North American region under NAFTA or otherwise. Canadian foreign policy, while largely aligned with that of the US especially on issues of Human Rights, democracy, and free markets, has diverged on key issues, and prominently so in the case of the second Iraq war and since. Canada remains strongly committed to multilateralism, even while the US continues to depart from the multilateral institutions it was once the architect of. The well documented shift in US foreign decision making away from the State Department and increasingly handed to military advisors in the White House and the Defense Department, which can be traced back at least to the early years of the Clinton Administration, has continued to accelerate and has reached new extremes under the Trump administration. The long-term strategic engagement of diplomacy has increasingly become short term tactical engagement on a military level. Priorities such as human rights and democracy have fallen to the wayside as a result of this short-term military to military approach, undermining the credibility of the US on the world stage. Even free trade seems to be on the out. The Trans Pacific Partnership, a trade pact which was designed to be a counterweight to the rapidly growing influence of China was abandoned. The China-led Regional Comprehensive Economic Partnership with many of the same countries is going ahead without the US.

What of positive peace? With very developed economies, and a pre-existing free trade agreement, a big change in the economies of Canada and the US could not have been expected. There have been positive impacts, and a net positive result for the economies of all three countries—export-oriented jobs pay more than jobs which moved to lower-waged Mexico, and manufacturing jobs received a big boost. But whereas new EU member states received large transfers of structural funds, and experience dramatic rises in their economic productivity as they joined the EU, neither has been the case with Mexico.

As is the case in the EU, wage stagnation and increases in income inequality (though not closely related to NAFTA) have fed anti-NAFTA sentiments. More worryingly, attitudes among the population of the countries have soured, especially between the US and Mexico. Mexicans see America as imperialist and under the current Trump administration attitudes which were previously 66% favorable to the US are now nearly 66% unfavorable. Attitudes of Canadians, who have long had a largely positive view of the United States, have also changed significantly in recent times. Over 60% now view the US negatively, a dramatic 12 point shift from a decade ago. Canadians favor peacekeeping operations and oppose military operations. They are also less likely to cross the border, where Canadians have been at times arbitrarily denied entry, meaning there is less exchange between people. Much, although not all of these attitudinal shifts have to do with the Trump administration and its policies. What is clear is that there has never been a coherent effort to address the past and foster improved relations between citizens of each country, or to foster a common North American identity. There is no Erasmus-style program for North America (Spring break in Tijuana doesn't count). Even as Brexit looms over the EU, the reality is that the US may still beat it with a rapid exit from NAFTA. Is war likely between the three NAFTA countries? Far from it but positive peace it is not, and it isn't NAFTA which keeps the (negative) peace.

Twenty-Two Regional Organizations, Their Importance

Regional organizations have a significant role to play in addressing conflicts and are highlighted in the UN Charter. Though they vary greatly in their structures, purposes, and capacities, some two dozen regional organizations span the globe. Many of these regional and sub-regional organizations have an economic focus as their point of origin, but many of those have found that there is a need to address violent and political conflicts within and among their members. Despite significant variations in capabilities, organizations from all regions of the world have developed structures and policies for mediating conflicts. The OSCE is one of the regional organizations with the most developed mediation and mediation support, capabilities, yet has struggled with increasing conflicts among participating states, mostly in the post-Soviet space, the biggest challenge being Eastern Ukraine. In the end, international organizations are only as effective as their participating states allow them to be and regional organizations seeking to address conflict and encourage peace are quite different from peace regions where sustainable peace has been achieved.

Western Europe dealt with its own dictators on the Iberian Peninsula and in Greece well into the 1970s, delaying the integration of those countries. The iron curtain long divided the continent. There have been violent independence movements (in the Basque country and Northern Ireland), as well as colonial wars in North Africa, Sub-Sahara Africa, and Asia. The Algerian war of independence took place well after France, the driving force for European integration, had begun the process, and during a time when the European Economic Community (ECC) was formed. Yet unlike in centuries past, European countries did not seek to use these conflicts to undermine each other. And the progress has been significant. Despite mounting challenges, it remains inconceivable for EU states to go to war with each other.

Territorial disputes between Balkan states remain, even between EU member states Slovenia and Croatia. It has been recently arbitrated, and although Croatia still refuses to implement the ruling, the risk of violence remains very low. The territorial disputes among non-EU Balkan states will pose a greater challenge still, but the carrot of accession to the EU remains a powerful motivator to find solutions. This is even the case in success stories, such as Poland which has seen its per-capita GDP more than double in the past 20 years, accelerating since the 2004 accession, and largely avoided entering into a recession.[18]

Response: Despite the negative peace onus on North America's claim, your essay confirms the point that there are two regional peaces' in the world, one achieved through the on-going process of political integration (the EU countries), the other through the preponderance of power. Why does not the Uppsala University faculty recognized the Regional peace in Europe? Perhaps they take it for granted.

In a world of 195 sovereign states, territorial claims are important. The EU as you say, addresses them and finds enforcement of judicial decisions difficult. There is no constituency in the United States for forgetting the Alamo, or for remembering the 19th Century slogan was "54 Forty or Fight." Territorial claims challenge all truces, and are open to infinite regress. A formula for self-determination is difficult to find. My claim is that the two peaces' are based on the fact that all thirty-one countries are representative democracies. Sixty percent of the Mexican population may claim they are victims of [capitalist?] imperialism, but they have a trade surplus and the only thing worse than capitalism, is no foreign capital to fuel development. Perhaps 11 to 35 million illegal immigrants express revenge, but these are law enforcement not the organized mass violence of war questions. No weapons are targeted on each other. In the meantime, Russia is on the prowl, occupies the Crimea, arms troops in the Ukraine, threatens nuclear war in Estonia, Latvia, and Lithuania and Islamic Jihadists threaten both regional peaces. If NATO's budget is the issue, Trump like Bush and Obama before him, insist perhaps less politely that Germany et al. pay their dues.

There are many open questions. Is there a "positive peace" formula, without which no peace in your view? Each element of such a formula is open to question. There is no "dust bin of history" in a representative democracy. You can rightly argue, that I think territorial claims among the 31 are non-negotiable, are in the "dustbin of history." Since the phrase is Trotsky's and originates in the Bolshevik armies driving the elected Social Revolutionaries out of the Duma (Parliament), my argument is doubly vulnerable.

The Norwegian peace researcher, Johan Galtung and others argue, the structure of European and United States' society are "structurally violent." Violence to overthrow them becomes "defensive." There are economic redistribution opportunities in representatives democracies, but is there a positive peace formula other than "progressive"?

Can one of these peaces be extended to other regions in 40 years? Yes, say I through transitions to representative democracy building on existing institutions in Latin America and Africa. Do you see promise in the political integration model, which the Council first thought possible sustained by a sense of world community. In the meantime, Kennan's warning that you first need to contain and deter expansionist sects or there will be no peace applies in my judgment to Islamic Jihadist among others. The EU and the North

Atlantic trio need democratic allies in other regions such as Taiwan, Japan, South Korea, Indonesia, Nigeria, South Africa, Ghana, Tunisia, Costa Rica.

If you will, let me replace "negative" peace, with minimum conditions for peace as reformulated in the "Seven Roads to a World Without War" document. Minimum peace requires representative governments ("safe for free societies") with religious liberty, private enterprise economies, monetary exchange agreements, trade dispute resolution institutions, and most importantly, treaties between states that are enforceable in domestic courts. They enjoy free speech and the free circulation of ideas. There are vibrant civil societies that insist that their governments abide by treaties to which their governments have agreed. There are no weapons targeted against each other. All of Gene Sharp's 198 nonviolent means are available to protest or claim justice is denied. And I need to add that they accept the results of elections, securing the transfer of power from one party or party coalition to the next.

Peace Research Questions: In 2015 there were 59 significant secessionist movements, for example in Kurdistan, Catalonia, Quebec, and Scotland. The Fund for Peace publishes an annual "Failed State index." The tribal map of Africa supports or undermines the map of Nation States. Mass violence has resulted in Biafra, the Democratic Republic of the Congo, Rwanda and the Sudan. Should the UN Trusteeship Council be revived, or the Organization of Africa Union, or the Community of Democracies take up the task of developing a judicial forum for testing self-determination claims?[19]

If the industrial Revolution was the predominant change in Europe from 1750 to 1950, is the digital revolution likely to "write the history . . . of the twenty first [century]"?[20]

According to Drum, artificial intelligence harnessed with quantum computing will in 20 years enable robots to do everything better than humans from open heart surgery to flipping burgers. Drum foresees that the consequence will fulfill the mad scientists dream, climate change will become a predictive science, the study of politics will become a science and, perhaps wars will be fought in space, killing replaceable robots. Who is programming their conscience? Still digitalization like other technological innovations will change many things but not the decision-making institutions or the perceptions of divinity or truth.

If tribes, not nation states, replace the source of political identity, the power of sub-national identities will "remain a powerful force everywhere."[21] According to Amy Chua "In recent years, it has begun to tear at the fabric of liberal democracies in the developed world and even at the postwar liberal international order. To truly understand today's world and where it is headed, one must acknowledge the power of tribalism.

Noah Pickus, Duke University, is the son of Robert Pickus. He worked closely with staff in Project South Africa and on citizenship programs for immigrants, authoring *True Faith and Allegiance* (2005). These are excerpts from his eulogy.

> Robert Pickus (1923–2016), who devoted his life to developing non-violent alternatives to war, died on Friday in St. Helena, CA. He was 92. War, he argued, could come about by building arms, and by not building arms. The task, therefore was to build legal and political alternatives to war. "In the shadow of Hiroshima," he wrote in his 1968 preface to a reprint of Albert Camus' Neither Victims Nor Executioners, "we had in America a clear goal and a moral commitment to sustain it. That goal was to end war. The moral commitment was the refusal to legitimate murder." "The problem of a paci-fist," he told an anti-war rally in 1965, "is not just to condemn violence, but to work out a way to counter the other side's violence. While criticizing military escalation, he held anti-war activists responsible for focusing exclusively on America's faults. I believe if those of us in this room were to stand before a mirror, we would see an obstacle to disarmament," he told a gathering of NGO leaders in 1978. [22] [23]

Holt Ruffin, Council colleague 1970–2004, Stanford University, BA 1966 (history), member, Honors Program in Social Thought and Institutions, Princeton University MPA 1975, Woodrow Wilson School of Public and International Affairs. See Chapter 8, "A Regional Director's Memoir and a New Beginning in the Center for Civil Society International."

Philip Siegelman, Professor Emeritus of Political Science, San Francisco State University 1966–1992, department chair; founder of Center for Sino-American Studies. From 1953 to 1966, instructor to professor, Department of Interdisciplinary Studies, Humanities Program, University of Minnesota. Visiting professor and research fellow, University of California (Berkeley) intermittently from 1970 on. Book review editor, American Political Science Review from 1970 to 1976. Cofounder books for Israel, cochair, seminars on Zionist Thought, executive secretary board member of Scientists for Sakharov, Orlov and Sharansky (SOS) 1982–1990. Founding member and Board of Center for Democracy in the USSR. Founder of California Association of Scholars, board member of National Association of Scholars. Ford Foundation fellow, China Program, Harvard University. Visiting fellow, School for Advanced International Studies. Siegelman wants to make clear that "What follows are excerpts from informal correspondence rather than carefully considered didactic exposition."

The Essence of the Conceptual Problem

Siegelman: "My instant guess is that your correspondents have no difficulty with the belief that 'this country has determined adversaries.' Am I right, the stumbling block is that said hardly anyone has a realistic non-military strategy to conduct and resolve the conflict with an adversary."[24]

Response: Yes that is the essence of the problem. Pickus from the *Speak Truth to Power* summary until 1961 accepted unilateral disarmament to break with the arms race to nuclear annihilation combined that nonmilitary strategy of peace with advocacy of developing the UN into an effective institution capable of enforcing treaties. Civilian defense was offered as a nonmilitary defense strategy should Kennan prove accurate, that the United States not only had determined adversaries but they were expansionist. There is plenty of denial that there is any determined adversary and significant agreement that Pogo got it right: "We have met the enemy, and he is us."

Siegelman:

> How do you define war? A significant part of my uneasiness with the discovery about the absence of war in the North Atlantic Region of the world centers around the key word "war." In the contemporary world, as I understand it, that noun has been virtually pummeled to death—as is well known. We have assimilated it to wars against drugs, poverty . . . sexual discrimination, etc. At this moment, we are increasingly conscious of cyber warfare which can completely circumvent the most dominant use of the term, which once, invariably, assumed violent encounters between enemies. Now, cyber warfare can be engaged in between non-military institutions that exist in politically friendly countries. Do you include secret arrangements that might be made for mounting violent encounters between armed nations?[25]

Response: The Council defined war as "organized, mass violence." Mass was defined as "large scale" by Robert Pickus and more precisely added with 1,000 or more casualties a year. Uppsala University peace and conflict studies departments publishes an annual listing of wars and lowers the threshold to 250 casualties a year. The Council definition includes violent inter-state conflict, wars of aggression, civil wars & revolutionary wars which pass the threshold from police to armies but would exclude the conflict in Northern Ireland which did not cross the threshold. This restricted usage of the noun war, raises the question of whether war is inevitable but answers it "no" and focuses the work on making it illegitimate by developing and advocating realistic alternatives to organized mass violence which fulfill and replace wars legitimate functions. Gang violence in Chicago approaches the casualty threshold, undermines confidence that representative democracy is functioning, but is at this time a police matter. Jesse Jackson has on occasion called for the National Guard and there could then be a war between the National Guard and the estimated 70 gangs if they could unite.

Siegelman: "Democracies have engaged in many wars, 1945 to the present Korea, Vietnam, Afghanistan, the Gulf War, Iraq . . . In brief, it seems that your diagnosis of the behavior of many of the 31 states have been at 'peace' needs some kind of recalculation. For example is war by proxy a synonym for war?"[26]

Response: Democratic peace theorists do not claim that democracies do not go to war, they acknowledge that they do. They claim that democracies do not war on each other and offer statistical proof (Michael Doyle) and an explanation why (Charles Lipson).

Siegelman:

> Your theory is useless. Your finding about the 31 North Atlantic States is not unique. There are no such equivalent clusters of states anywhere else in the world. To apply this finding to the possibility that it is a demonstration of useful predictability about ending war is useless. In my judgment, you offer nothing resembling conclusive evidence, to support a theory about how to end war. Nor do you offer anything resembling recommendations to other investigators about how to test or enlarge the credibility of your views. This is a slangy way of saying your views have no scientific standing.[27]

Response: My claim agreed to by critics is that there have been no wars since 1945 between the 31 Democracies in the North Atlantic Region. 1945 is disputed as a start date, but Finland was a democracy that fought for geopolitical reasons in the Axis side. There are troubling counter examples, the Union blockade of the South brought war close with England, the parliaments of England and Germany voted overwhelmingly for their state's World War I budgets. If you equate science with predictability, political science becomes a contradiction in terms. If individuals have free will, they can know right from wrong, if they live "under the ordinance of time" change becomes the one reality. Do all 20 monotheistic religions teach such things? I am trying to show what is possible. But your claim that the North Atlantic states are unique is my point, they are all representative democracies and they do not target weapons against each other. There are also democracies within every culture, Costa Rica, Chile, Ghana, Nigeria, and South Africa, Tunisia is in transition,[28] Indonesia, India, Israel with a million plus Muslim minority, Taiwan, Japan, and South Korea, among others. The way world politics has been played for a millennium, you need allies.

Siegelman:

> Disarmament. Arms Build-ups lead to the abuse of power, if not war. I've made no mention of the traditional pacifist embrace of disarmament. Part of the argument has usually cited arms buildups as part of a scarcely visible cycle of hostility and inevitable, eventual explosion. Of the 31 states you cite, the US has the largest military budget, more aircraft carriers and nuclear submarines, etc. Of course, we are at peace with Holland and England, etc. But the explosive appearance of Trump VIVIDLY [Caps in the original] demonstrates that stock piles when not used, are seductive invitations to the abuse of power and are always incisively present even in the absence of overt violence.[29]

Response: The Council view as expressed succinctly by Pickus and Weigel is stated in Advises and Cautions to Peace Leaders. The first six are (1) Ask the right questions, with How should America engage in contests for power and to what ends, set against what standards? (2) developing alternatives to war, (3) pursue minimalist goals, (4) consider contexts, then issues, and (5) ignoring an adversary's power makes war more not less likely. I assume Pick and the other pacifist lions are toasting each other with ambrosia in Valhalla, but quarreling about whether these advises and cautions should be reformulated given the "explosive appearance of Trump."

I was an Air Force Information Officer when John F. Kennedy was President and deterrence doctrine as presented to the public was the means to prevent war. Deterrence would succeed as a defense, it was argued, if enough forces survived a first strike to retaliate and inflict unacceptable damage on the aggressor. "Unacceptable" damage was defined by Robert McNamara, Kennedy's Secretary of Defense, as killing 50 million people. Deterrence to be effective also required that the triad (B-52s, ICBMs, and SLBM) be on hair-trigger alert, a third of the B-52s in the air all the time and the crews psychologically prepared to retaliate before the 30 minute early warning is up.

The doubts about whether or not Robert Pickus remained a pacifist reduce themselves to two questions: Do you mean unilateral disarmament or multilateral disarmament? And second, is the United States capable of offering leadership toward general and complete disarmament without nationalizing private corporations or, what comes close to the same thing, imposing 400,000 regulations for which they must keep meticulous records to avoid legal liabilities.

The Council embraced general and complete disarmament (multi-lateral, 1961–2016); Pickus said in *Speak Truth to Power* that the weapons of war were themselves an obstacle, perhaps the overriding one, and acted on that judgment in Acts for Peace. He also advocated an international order capable of enforcing treaties and, if that order failed to develop or proved faulty then civilian based, nonviolent defense could be available in the worst case scenarios. But it would have to be prepared for; it has not. Does less military power by the United States make it more or less "seductive to the abuse of power" or to the US's determined adversaries? In either case, as Dwight Macdonald put it in 1955, "Pacifists are relying on arms. even as they claim they are for disarmament," and as Pickus said, "coming in second in an arms race is possibly the worst possible course of action," meaning you lose the moral clarity of your advocacy, and do not credibly or militarily deter war.

The open question is whether the Council is a betrayal of *Speak Truth to Power* or a developer of it, replacing nonviolent civilian defense which has a small constituency even in pacifist circles. With a peace initiative strategy that required reciprocation to get to disarmament from here.

George Weigel:

> In looking back over some of the Pick materials that Noah assembled on that Duke based Web site, I was powerfully struck by how much of the impulse that eventually led to the WWWC [World Without War Council] and JMF [James Madison Foundation] came from the WW II and immediate post-war periods. That that experience, and the moral seriousness it begot, are largely forgotten today tells us something, I expect, about the sad state of "work for peace" in the early 21st Century—that, and the staying power of both the "god that failed" and Gramiscian politics. But I keep soldiering on at the National Endowment for Democracy board, even though that work is getting harder and harder both to conceive and execute. It's getting harder to conceive because it's clear that there are certain cultural pre-requisites for success and sustain democratic transitions. It's getting harder to execute because of our being banned from work in Egypt, China, Russia and other authoritarian states.[30]

Selected Works by George Weigel: *Tranquillitas Ordinas: The Current Failure and Future Promise of Catholic Thought on War and Peace* (New York: Oxford University Press 1987). *Witness to Hope: The Biography of Pope John Paul II* (New York: Harper Collins 1999); *The End and the Beginning: Pope John II—The Victory of Freedom, the Last Years, the Legacy* (New York: Doubleday 2010); *Lessons in Hope: My Unexpected Life With St. John Paul II* (New York: Basic Books 2017); *The Final Revolution: The Resistance Church & the Collapse of Communism* (New York: Oxford University Press 1992); "Pope Francis is Playing Realpolitik" (Washington: Foreign Affairs 2/2018); "Through a Glass Darkly: Ten Principles for the Renewal of Moral Debate About Foreign Policy" (First Things, August 2010); "Democracy and Its Discontents," Ethics and Public Policy Center, William E. Simon, Annual Lecture, (March 2018).

Response: If Germany made it anybody can. Drip by drip water wears away stone, but in time?

NOTES

1. Bernstam, Michael. Informal conversation, 2018. Reprinted with permission.
2. Crowther, Warren. Informal conversation, 2018. Reprinted with permission.
3. The copy of *Speak Truth to Power*, which I have among my papers, has a crucial typo in section VII, An Affirmation. The short line which should state, "The politics of time and the politics of eternity, substitutes 'enmity' for 'eternity.'" I trust the correction will be made.
4. Dougall, Lucy. Informal conversation, 2018. Reprinted with permission.
5. See Chapter 4.
6. June 6, 1963.
7. Gene Sharp's *From Dictatorship to Democracy* is a major contribution to this. See also my Extending the Democratic Peace and the list of 20 nonviolent transitions (1974–2003) with the caution "toward" inserted.
8. Keyes, Gene. Informal conversation, 2018. Reprinted with permission.

9. Keyes, Gene. Informal conversation, 2018. Reprinted with permission.

10. From Gene Keyes, "Heavy Casualties and Nonviolent Defense" (1991) http://www.genekeyes.com/ Heavy Casualties.

11. Keyes, Gene. Informal conversation, 2018. Reprinted with permission.

12. Kriesberg, Louis. Informal conversation, 2018. Reprinted with permission.

13. Kriesberg, Louis. Informal conversation, 2018. Reprinted with permission.

14. Kriesberg, Louis. Informal conversation, 2018. Reprinted with permission.

15. Kriesberg, Louis. Informal conversation, 2018. Reprinted with permission.

16. Kriesberg, Louis. Informal conversation, 2018. Reprinted with permission.

17. Naegle, Walter. Informal conversation, 2018. Reprinted with permission.

18. Nicolescu, Augustin. Informal conversation, 2018. Reprinted with permission.

19. The Council's contribution to resolving this problem is Janet Mackey (Ed.), *Terrorism and Self-Determination: A Tragic Marriage We Could Help Decouple*.(1986). For a current discussion of Separatism see Tanisha M. Fazal's "Why Rising Separatism Might Lead to More Conflict," *Foreign Affairs*, July/August 2018.

20. See Devin Drum, "Tech World: Welcome to the Digital Revolution," *Foreign Affairs*, July/August 2018.

21. Amy Chua, "Tribal World, Group Identity is All," *Foreign Affairs*, July/August 2018.

22. San Francisco Chronicle, 1/28/2016. See also "Political Integrity and Its Critics, Liberation."

23. Pickus, Noah. 2016.

24. Siegelman, Philip. Informal conversation, 2018. Reprinted with permission.

25. Siegelman, Philip. Informal conversation, 2018. Reprinted with permission.

26. Siegelman, Philip. Informal conversation, 2018. Reprinted with permission.

27. Siegelman, Philip. Informal conversation, 2018. Reprinted with permission.

28. See Archives for 20 nonviolent transitions from dictatorships towards democracy between 1974 and 2003.

29. Siegelman, Philip. Informal conversation, 2018. Reprinted with permission.

30. Weigel, George. Informal conversation, 2018. Reprinted with permission.

Chapter Eight

A Regional Director's Memoir and a New Beginning in the Center for Civil Society International

by Holt Ruffin

The model of the World Without War Council (WWWC) was fundamentally flawed. At root, I think Bob Pickus ("Pick") aspired to leadership of a peace movement transformed from an unwavering opponent of the use of American military power into a creative advocate of efforts aimed at building the international structures of peace. A peace movement, "worthy of the name," as Pick put it, would bring moral and political pressures to bear on the US government *and* our adversaries alike—to adopt measures that would strengthen international law, build transnational peacekeeping forces, devise more effective methods for preventing the outbreak of wars, reduce national military establishments, enlarge instruments for international arbitration, mediation and conciliation, and so on.

After some years working for the WWWC, beginning in 1970 in Berkeley and continuing fourteen years later in Seattle, I came to the conclusion that the American peace movement was not capable of being reformed. Most certainly it was never going to come around to the views of the World Without War Council. American grassroots peace movements historically had done little more than express a loud but simple pro or con position on a single issue: for example, no to the Mexican-American War (1846–1848); no to the Philippine-American War (1899–1902); yes to the Neutrality Acts of the 1930s; no to the Vietnam War (1955–1975); and yes to the nuclear freeze movement of the 1980s. Much more difficult to imagine was a grassroots movement that would articulate support for the complex elements of a long-term campaign to end war by building alternative institutions.

123

The proper emphasis of the WWWC, I came to think, should have been on assembling a global cadre of leaders—scholars, diplomats, business figures, senior military officials, clergy, refugee and relief workers, others— connected through something like an international think tank whose central mission would be to (a) foster research and discussion on possible architectures of global peace and (b) promote clear policy initiatives to that end.

The World Without War Council should also have striven to be an international movement, with chapters in several nations and regions, for example, the Soviet Union, China, South Asia, and Africa. Each chapter's mission would have been to educate local publics about regional threats to peace and promote national and multilateral actions to reduce these threats. In this way, an international World Without War Council would have forsaken fruitless campaigns of "peace education" based only on an American (or Western) perspective and instead become an organizing force for ideas and policies to deter threats of mass, organized violence worldwide, near-term and long-term. The Rwanda massacres of 1994 are an extreme example of the consequences of a void of international mechanisms available to protect endangered populations from genocide and mass violence—even when the weapons used were as simple as machetes.

THE CENTRAL PROBLEM FACING ANY EFFORTS TO END WAR

In today's world, organized around the nation-state, military forces can be instruments of defense or of aggression. Since history provides many examples of the latter, it is irresponsible for the leaders of any nation to neglect this threat and fail to maintain some kind of deterrent against violent aggression from outside. This is the central conundrum that all people concerned with eradicating the scourge of war face: no major power will eliminate its military forces unless others do the same or until alternative methods of preventing aggression and ensuring national security exist.

In the first years of the twentieth century, diplomats and international lawyers thought the solution was to bind nations in a thick web of bilateral and multilateral treaties that would prevent acts of aggression from occurring among them. World War I broke out before any such web could be woven.

In the years following World War I, some believed that the manifest horrors of that conflict had produced such a revulsion against war that it was unlikely to occur again. All that was needed was a treaty signed by most nations that formally outlawed the phenomenon. The Kellogg-Briand Pact, signed by approximately 60 nations in 1928–1929, renounced the use of war for resolving "disputes or conflicts of whatever nature or of whatever origin." The lack of enforcement mechanisms and the various acts of aggression that would occur in the decade that followed—including by signatories Italy,

Germany, and Japan—led some to mock the pact as "peace by incantation." In fact, modern scholars have argued that the Kellogg-Briand Pact was more than simple moral posturing; it was a signal achievement that informed the development of the Nuremberg Principles, the Tokyo Tribunal, and the UN Charter, and even contributed to a reduction in the frequency of interstate wars in the decades following its enactment.[1]

THE CONTRIBUTION OF BOB PICKUS AND THE WORLD WITHOUT WAR COUNCIL

Fast forward to the early sixties and the period when Acts for Peace and Turn Toward Peace, later to be renamed the World without War Council, were founded by Bob Pickus and a small group of supporters in Berkeley, CA. The US was now a military superpower in an age of nuclear weapons, a founder and leader of NATO, and proponent of the doctrine of mutual assured destruction as a strategy for peace with the Soviet Union. The Vietnam War was heating up and would soon convulse American society. Long gone were the isolationism of political leaders like Robert La Follette and movements like America First. Vietnam would spawn new movements in the name of "peace," led by organizations such as Students for a Democratic Society (SDS) or Vietnam Veterans Against the War (VVAW). Whereas antiwar organizations of the interwar years had been nationalist and isolationist, the antiwar forces of the Vietnam War era were anti-militarist and anti-American. At public demonstrations they routinely referred to police officers as "pigs" or US government leaders as "fascists." They scorned the notion that communist power and ideology represented a threat to the US. In criticizing the flaws of American policy, both foreign and domestic, they routinely suggested the US was morally equivalent to the Soviet Union, or even Hitler's Germany.

Against this corrosive view of the US the WWWC offered a more balanced, accurate, and fundamentally hopeful perspective. It was one in which America's democratic values and political institutions, despite our flawed history, might still offer the world some useful references in efforts to bring an end to war between nations. Recognizing the threat that armed totalitarian states like the Soviet Union and the People's Republic of China posed to free societies, the Council also affirmed that the problem of interstate war must be solved by changes in the policies of multiple military powers, not just the US, but the process could begin with the US if Americans would show leadership, pursue "the seven roads to a world without war," and deploy a series of diplomatic and military "initiatives" aimed at changing the thinking and policies of our adversaries, the international system could in a reasonable amount of time eliminate the phenomenon of mass, organized violence known as war.[2]

THE PROBLEM OF A "FORMED PUBLIC WILL," THE GRASSROOTS FOCUS, AND THE AMERICAN PEACE MOVEMENT

To encounter the WWWC in December 1970, as I first did, in the midst of the Vietnam miasma, was both a shock and an inspiration. There was no other voice like it in radically chic Berkeley. The uniqueness of the WWWC lay in the balance with which it advocated in favor of its goal and in its fundamentally positive view of the role of the US In all of its literature, especially *To End War*, the Council made clear that its goal was to end the institution of war, not just American participation in wars. The Council's message had great integrity and consistency and, as a result, it appealed to many people for whom otherwise words such as "activism," or "peace action," or "grassroots" set off alarm bells.

But the Council was a small organization with very limited resources, aspiring to accomplish very large social change. These facts alone were not a reason to dismiss it. Many great social and political movements have grown from slender roots. Sometimes one lonely author and a single publication have catalyzed great change: for example, Harriet Beecher Stowe's *Uncle Tom's Cabin* or Rachel Carson's *Silent Spring*. Other times, exceptionally gifted organizers have built great movements from just a handful of people—sometimes with dire consequences, sometimes with propitious. China's Communist Party was founded clandestinely in 1921 on a tourist boat on a lake in southeast coastal China. Only 12 people attended this first "party congress," among them one Mao Zedong. In the latter half of the twentieth century, a charismatic Atlanta preacher named Martin Luther King, Jr., achieved great social and political reforms in US race relations using the tools of nonviolent action and democratic institutions.

So its small size alone was not a real limitation on the World Without War Council. More important was the vision and strategy the organization had for its own growth. Were the considerable energy and persuasive powers of its founder harnessed to a plan of action that was workable? To whom was the Council's message addressed? Was it to thoughtful citizens seeking to engage in "intelligent peace activity" at the local level, as *To End War* stated? Or was it to foreign policy elites, professionals in government, the military, the media and academia—people whose experience and professional positions put them in the category of "influentials"?

What about the publications of the WWWC? Did they carry weight with the elites involved in foreign affairs? Or were Council materials persuasive only for the general public, people who felt compelled to "do something" about the problem of war but were relatively uninformed and would use a resource like *To End War* as a starting point?

At first blush I was impressed with the range of Council publications and especially with the considerable research that had gone into *To End War*. As authors Pickus and Woito wrote, these materials contained "a body of thought that gives rational sustenance to such a goal" for policy professional and citizen activist alike.[3] Over time, however, I came to question the realism of the WWWC emphasis on "the crucial role of the American citizen."[4] How many well-meaning Americans, with jobs and families and other claims on their time, would follow the annotations in *To End War* and choose a set of dense texts in international relations to study at home in order to become "intelligent peace activists?" Very few. It would have been far more useful, I came to think, for WWWC to make foreign policy elites its primary audience and constituency. With close ties to respected scholars in universities and think tanks, to experienced diplomats and military officers, the Council might have become a catalyst and organizer of innovative proposals in the various sub-fields of peace and conflict studies. It could have helped to disseminate to the general public some of the better ideas within elite policy circles. And it might have developed a reputation as an organization that had answers to the problem of war rather than one that sometimes seemed only to have questions.

There was an additional problem with the grassroots focus of the WWWC. When Pickus and Woito wrote about the need for a "formed public will" to underlie American acts for peace, the American citizenry were not exactly a *tabula rasa*. A "formed public will" already existed, shaped by a US antiwar movement often led by hard-left activists in political parties, universities, churches, and pacifist organizations. Articles published in magazines such as the *Nation, Progressive, Mother Jones, Harper's Weekly, Ramparts, In Our Time, Bulletin of Atomic Scientists*, and *Liberation*—as well as the more mainstream press—gave regular intellectual nourishment to this movement and defined its ideas. The "antiwar" perspective of the US peace movement that resulted was very different from the one advocated by WWWC. It was described well by Pickus and Woito as follows:

> the central thrust of this position is withdrawal of American power from world affairs. It demonstrates little interest in international institutions. In sum, it usually leads to the gradual replacement of a commitment to peace with a priority for domestic change and/or support for a variety of internal (e.g., black, drug, youth) or third world revolutionary perspectives.[5]

The avatars for this view were many and seemed to be everywhere: On the airwaves of NPR, in the lecture halls of colleges and universities, in documentaries and feature films from Hollywood, and on the editorial and letters pages of local newspapers. Howard Zinn, whose *A People's History of the United States* sold in the millions and was a required text in many US history classes across the country, was a chief avatar. So was MIT scholar Noam Chomsky, a relentless critic of the Vietnam War, the Cold War, US policy in the Middle East, missile defense (SDI), water boarding of prisoners, and virtually every other aspect of US foreign policy. Journalists such as I. F. Stone and Seymour Hersh, in their own ways had great influence in shaping public opinion, and their views on war/peace issues complemented those of Zinn and Chomsky.

In short, the American peace movement already had a "formed public will" about conflict and foreign affairs, but it pointed in a substantially different direction from the ideas of the WWWC. Its view was that responsibility for war and aggression in the international system lay primarily with the US A corollary of this "blame America first" view was that when antiwar organizations in the US "spoke truth to power"—an inspired expression now become a cliché—it was to American power alone that they usually spoke.

The usual demands followed: for the US to scale down its role as a world power, to reduce the size of its military, to stop funding any ongoing military interventions, and to rely on an unreliable UN or an ephemeral "multilateralism" as the solution to conflict in the international system. This was the dominant and often the only point of view heard at countless public meetings where citizens discussed war/peace issues in cities around the country. A perspective such as that of the World Without War Council was rarely encountered, and if encountered, was often misconstrued.[6]

SEATTLE: A CASE STUDY IN THE FAILURE OF THE WWWC COMMUNITY PEACE EDUCATION MODEL

I moved to Seattle in September 1984 to become executive director of the WWWC, which was losing key staff. The organization was in very poor financial shape and teetering on the verge of closing. For at least 15 years the Seattle WWWC had been an active, vibrant force that reached many Seattleites and had capable leaders who were well-known and respected in the community. The organization had seen its best days, however, during the Vietnam War years and in the late seventies during the nuclear freeze movement. Its executive director in the latter period had been Steve Boyd, a former UW student body president. He put on many programs in the community that gained the organization wide recognition. Steve had even persuaded the mayor of Seattle one year to designate a certain day as a "World Without War" day.

But for all of the visibility and recognition the Seattle WWWC had achieved, the organization in 1984 had no ongoing community educational programs. At the same time, Seattle abounded in organizations focused on the wars in Central America and especially on stopping US funding for the anti-Sandinista insurgency known as the *contras* in Nicaragua, as well as cutting off support for the government of El Salvador, which was fighting a Marxist insurgency known as the FMLN.[7] I decided to make Central America a focus of the Seattle WWWC. We would offer programs that modeled WWWC values and demonstrated what we meant by truly antiwar educational programs.[8]

A problem that became clear to me at this time was that virtually all public discussions of the conflicts in Central America relied on sources of information that were preponderantly from the left, usually *only* from the left-and sometimes only the *radical* left. To improve the quality of the public debate, it seemed that an annotated directory of *all* organizations in the US that were concerned with Latin American affairs might be useful. So with the help of a talented volunteer named Richard Tada, we researched and published such a directory. Many of the organizations described in it published newsletters, sold books and other literature, or offered a speakers' bureau. Some sponsored trips to the region for small groups of people. Politically, they spanned the political spectrum from right to left. Our *Directory of US Organizations Working on Latin America* was so good that Congressman John Miller from the First District of Washington State recommended it to other members of Congress and entered some laudatory remarks about the publication into the Congressional Record.

Among many activities the Seattle WWWC carried out connected with Central America, one was a large and well-attended conference that brought experts to Seattle from USC and the RAND Institute. We also sponsored talks by individuals who were from the region. One was a representative of the Sandinista government, another was a former Sandinista named Arturo Cruz, who had been the revolutionary government's first ambassador to the US and also president of the nation's central bank. Cruz had broken with the Sandinistas as their authoritarian and crypto-communist tendencies had emerged. (More on the Cruz visit below.)

Finally, another issue that was related to the wars in Central America was "sanctuary," an issue again very much in the news today. The University Baptist Church in Seattle had declared itself a "sanctuary church" and had a Central American family living in the church under its hyper-publicized "protection." There were other centers of sanctuary activity in the city. The city council had declared Seattle a "city of refuge" and created a Central America Commission, with a budget and part-time staff. Among the functions of the staff was to brief delegations of Seattleites—sometimes jokingly

referred to as "sandalistas"- who were traveling to Central America to show
solidarity with the revolutionary government of Nicaragua.[9]

At some point in late 1985 I met a Seattleite named Mitch Hughes who
was firmly opposed to the city declaring itself a sanctuary city. In January
1986 Mitch pulled together a leadership group (which included Ron Bemis, a
WWWC Board member, and myself) and submitted an initiative (to be
known as Initiative 30) for the November 1986 ballot. The initiative asked
Seattle voters:

> Shall Seattle enact an ordinance rescinding "City of Refuge" Resolution
> 27402; dissolving the Citizens' Commission on Central America; and direct-
> ing the Mayor, City Council, and City Officials to cooperate in enforcement of
> immigration laws, among other matters?

Mitch and his team worked hard on this campaign. They did not have large
numbers of volunteers or much money. However, even in very liberal Seattle, the left had gone too far with their City of Refuge Resolution. In particular, Seattleites of all political leanings disagreed with the city instructing
police and other authorities not to help enforce federal immigration laws.
Getting enough signatures to put the initiative on the ballot turned out to be
fairly easy. As November neared, the anti-sanctuary campaign gained momentum. Governor Richard Lamm of Colorado, a Democrat, came to Seattle
in late October to campaign for the measure and tape some radio messages.
On Election Day in November 1986, Initiative 30 passed with 77,325 votes
for and 64,308 against.

What did Initiative 30 reveal? In brief, it showed that Seattle was really
two cities. One city was unquestionably liberal, but liberal in a way that was
respectful of differences in political views and accepted the outcome of elections.

The other Seattle was more radical, and intolerant of the democratic process. It included Mayor Charles Royer who immediately after the election
results were announced declared that the voters had been confused by the
language of Initiative 30. According to Royer, many of the voters who voted
"yes" for the initiative ignored the plain meaning of the text, which included
words such as "rescinding" and "dissolving," and thought they were *affirming* the existing City of Refuge status. This was flim-flam, but it was typical
of the contempt the Seattle hard left felt for opponents of their views.

In this Seattle, political figures who diverged from ultra-left orthodoxy
might not even be allowed to speak. Case in point: Arturo Cruz, a former
Sandinista leader who had turned opponent of the regime and had briefly
campaigned for president against Daniel Ortega, came to speak at the University of Washington in 1985. He was almost prevented from doing so by a
mob. The group CISPES (Committee in Support of the People of El Salva-

dor) organized a "die-in" during his talk. In this form of political theater, large numbers of students came up on the stage, dressed as Central American peasants, and pretended to die in heaps in front of the speaker. It was as if to say to Cruz, "You are responsible for the killing of so many innocents in your country!" Much rowdiness, taunts and other forms of interruption accompanied the "die-in," to the point that I had to threaten to stop the event if they continued.

But by that point the eloquent Cruz had said enough to persuade many students that they wanted to hear more; *they* intervened and told the disruptive radicals to shut up. This worked. The lecture hall quieted down and stayed quiet as Cruz completed his remarks. In this way the event was saved. But it was a limited save. After all the disrespect shown to this wise man and Nicaraguan patriot, Cruz shortened his remarks considerably and took no questions. He had been insulted and probably felt disgusted. Although order had been restored in the lecture hall, there was still a noisy demonstration going on outside. The campus police showed us to a little-used exit by what seemed like a secret passageway and we were able to leave the building unnoticed.

I had learned a lesson. Over the course of the several years in which the Seattle WWWC ran programs on Central America, it became clear that there was little or no interest on the part of the "antiwar" community of Seattle in learning about Nicaragua or El Salvador from a non-Sandinista or non-FMLN point of view. The Arias plan was largely ignored. Opportunities for meetings with independent Nicaraguan leaders who came to Seattle from time to time, such as independent labor official Alvin Guthrie,[10] were of little interest. It was impossible to get a reasonably sized group together to hear Enrique Bolaños when he came to Seattle. A cotton grower and prominent figure in Nicaragua business circles before the Sandinista revolution, Bolaños headed his nation's equivalent of our Chamber of Commerce. He was an intelligent, courteous person, fluent in English, who might have become president of Nicaragua in more peaceful and democratic times. The fact that the antiwar Seattle left would have no interest in hearing him could have been predicted by two words in his biography: business leader.

Over time, the WWWC accumulated a list of contacts for Nicaragua who were politically independent. Some still lived in the country; others had emigrated. Among the latter, one of the most interesting was Humberto Belli, author of *Breaking Faith: The Sandinista Revolution and Its Impact on Freedom and the Christian Faith in Nicaragua* (Good News Publishing, 1985). Belli came to Seattle in 1986 sponsored by the WWWC and was hosted for an overflow talk at the home of John and Helen Szablya, themselves 1956 refugees from communist Hungary.

When it was appropriate, we offered Seattleites planning "solidarity" travel to Nicaragua help in educating themselves about a complex situation.

If the Seattle traveler was interested in taking some aid or relief to Nicaragua, we offered contacts who knew organizations and projects that would welcome such support and had reputations for honesty and integrity. If the Seattle traveler was going on more of a look-and-see trip, our network of contacts could be counted on to have information and perspectives that would never have been offered through pro-Sandinista networks. It was a rare person who took us up on such offers.

THE FINAL STRAW: *THE SEATTLE TIMES* "EXPOSES" CADRES OF SUN MYUNG MOON AND THE UNIFICATION CHURCH, INCLUDING MYSELF

Over a period of roughly four years, the WWWC under my leadership had organized numerous events focused on Central America. We had published op-ed pieces in the local newspapers and written letters to the editor. We had appeared on TV shows and in numerous debates. Always our message had been the same: opportunities existed for peace-concerned Americans interested in Nicaragua to speak out for nonviolence and to give support to those working for negotiated and inclusive approaches to political conflict. Seattle-ites traveling to Nicaragua could meet with leadership figures, organizations, and projects that were core elements of civil society in that country. These needed to be recognized and assisted, not ignored and isolated. Our interest was to build support for civil society in Nicaragua, to help find a nonviolent way out of the conflict. We always encouraged learning about the Arias plan and giving support to its provisions. Many times we were mischaracterized as "contra supporters," or "anticommunists," or sometimes, "wolves in sheep's clothing."

Yet I had no idea as to the lengths that the left in Seattle would go to attack their critics . . . until one Sunday afternoon in February 1989 when I was returning from a cross country ski trip in the northern Cascades. It was a cold, sunny day, with patches of snow on the ground. Our group stopped in a café in Wenatchee for a bite to eat and I noticed a stack of copies of the weekend edition of *The Seattle Times*. On the front cover was a large photo of the Rev. Sun Myung Moon, head of the Unification Church. A long article surrounded the photo and continued on the back pages. The headline alluded to something sinister—perhaps a conspiracy—involving a religious sect led by this self-declared Korean messiah who was famous for carrying out mass marriage ceremonies between Unification Church members he had picked out for each other.

The Unification Church was strange, for sure. But I never thought of it as a serious danger to American society. "Moonies," as they were nicknamed, never advocated terrorism or violence as a means of social change—in contrast to some of the Muslim extremists of our day. The practice of arranged marriages was of course alien to most Americans; but it was not so uncommon in other parts of the world. Nor was it odd that Rev. Moon, a survivor of a North Korean labor camp, had strongly anti-communist views.

But this article went far beyond "revealing" well-known facts. This was sensationalist journalism aiming to stigmatize a group of people in the Seattle area because of their religious beliefs or political views. Wasn't it opposition to such intolerance that was the basis of our Constitution's First Amendment? Six local people featured importantly in the article as nonmember operatives for the church and they were named. I was one of them. Among other things, it was alleged that I had been flown back to Washington, DC by the church in order to participate in national trainings of some kind. This was a total lie. The author of the article was a reporter named Walter Hatch, whom I had never met and who never tried to interview me about the allegations in the article.

I was stunned. Yes, I had known about the Unification Church for years. I was friendly with some of the church members in the Seattle area and one even worked at the WWWC offices for a brief time as an assistant to me. But that was it. I was not a member of the church myself, and had never expressed support for its practices or its leader. Contrary to Hatch's assertions, I had never accepted offers of free travel back to Washington, DC. I had never organized a WWWC program together with the church or co-sponsored a program with it.

I called a Board of Directors meeting to discuss how the WWWC should respond to *The Seattle Times'* hatchet job (pun intended). The board had two attorneys on it at the time and I was hopeful that they would advise suing the *Times*. In fact there turned out to be no appetite on the board to take the fight to *The Seattle Times*. One Seattle attorney, not associated with the WWWC, did call me in the days that followed, offering to sue the *Times* for us at a discounted rate. But the advance payment required to get started was still high and I was loathe to spend that much money on what many people were telling me was sure to be a losing case—so difficult were the laws on slander or defamation in Washington State. So I decided not to sue *The Seattle Times*. In retrospect, I think this was a poor decision that I regret to this day. The newspaper's arrogance and irresponsibility should have been challenged, even if this might have meant delivering pizzas or driving a cab to help finance the lawsuit.

Instead I had a meeting with the managing editor of the *Times* in the days that followed and he agreed to print a pitifully small correction on page 2. It was a ridiculous remedy.

About a week later there was a small squib in either the *Times* or Seattle's other daily newspaper, *The Seattle Post-Intelligencer*—I don't remember which. It reported that a large warehouse located in Seattle and belonging to the Unification Church had caught fire and burned to the ground overnight. The value of the building was estimated in excess of one million dollars. The cause of the fire was being investigated.

The results of that investigation were never reported but I was certain it was arson. Fear and hatred were the intended fruits of that *Seattle Times* Sunday smear job. For Walter Hatch and his allies in Seattle—this city that saw itself as a national paragon of tolerance and civic-mindedness—the torching of the Unification Church warehouse was probably a welcome piece of collateral damage. The newspaper printed no letters to the editor in subsequent days lamenting the loss or connecting it to the earlier weekend edition hit job on the church.

DEFEAT AND RENEWAL

The February 1989 *Seattle Times* Unification Church article marked a turning point for me. I felt defeated. The power of the antiwar hard left in Seattle had proved too great. After years of "community peace education" ostensibly carried out by the WWWC of Greater Seattle, the city seemed completely under the spell of myriad "peace" organizations and their radical perspectives. President Reagan's UN Ambassador Jeanne Kirkpatrick had described these collectively as the "blame America first crowd."[11] Pickus and Woito had described them simply as favoring the "withdrawal of American power from world affairs." Whatever they were called, I wanted to have no more to do with them. I did not want to continue running an organization with a name that sounded like it belonged to the mainstream antiwar movement. I also did not want to continue organizing public education programs on war/peace issues for a public that felt no need to be educated and already had highly formed opinions on issues of US foreign and military policy.

One of my keener disappointments had been to see so little evidence of the "Council voice" in the Seattle environment, where the WWWC had been laboring for more than 15 years. Marx had written about "the long march through the institutions." This incident convinced me that the mainstream antiwar movement had long ago completed its long march through the institutions of the Puget Sound region. They owned the high ground. Theirs was "the formed public will" about which Pickus and Woito had written. I saw little hope for an organization with the perspective of the WWWC ever changing this, even with a much bigger budget, the best programs, and best leadership, I began thinking of a different organizational name and a different mission for the ex-WWWC.

THE ALTERNATIVE: A CENTER FOR CIVIL SOCIETY
INTERNATIONAL

In March 1985 Mikhail Gorbachev became General Secretary of the Communist Party of the Soviet Union, initiating changes that would lead to the demise of the Soviet Union. In the months that followed, Gorbachev gave signs of being a significantly different Communist leader. He spoke repeatedly of *glasnost, perestroika,* and *uskoreniye* (*openness, restructuring,* and *acceleration*). In a short period of time, many signs emerged that Soviet society was changing "from below." Newspapers started publishing articles routinely that would have been unthinkable two or three years back. Demonstrations began occurring in Moscow and other cities without being brutally suppressed by the police. In the Baltic republics, Ukraine and other parts of the Soviet Union, nationalist movements came alive and began calling publicly for independence. Political opponents of Gorbachev, such as Boris Yeltsin, even began demanding an end to the monopoly status of the Communist Party of the Soviet Union.

I started to travel to the Soviet Union and Eastern Europe—my first trip to the USSR in July 1986 was sponsored by Seattle Action for Soviet Jewry (SASJ)—and quickly learned two things: (a) there was a great deal more social ferment and independent citizen activity there than I had imagined; and (b) the opportunities for travel, contacts and communications between citizens of the West and citizens of the "East" were also much greater than imagined. A pioneer in these contacts was SASJ, formed in 1974 by Judy Lash Balint, and later associated with the Union of Councils for Soviet Jewry. By promoting travel by Americans to the USSR and visits to the homes of "refuseniks"—and security forces did not always allow access to these homes—Soviet Jewry activists like Balint did a great deal to give hope to these persecuted individuals while also educating Americans about Soviet anti-Semitism and systematic violations of the Helsinki Accords, signed in 1975. Ultimately, it is not an exaggeration to say that sustained campaigns for adherence to the Accords by civil society organizations such as the UCSJ were one of the factors in the dissolution of the Soviet Union and the collapse of communism in Europe.

As the Soviet Union became more open, contacts between citizens in the West and elements of civil society in Russia and the other Soviet republics, as well as Eastern Europe, grew rapidly. These contacts might be with groups formed to monitor compliance with the Helsinki Accords, such as Charter 77 in Czechoslovakia or the Moscow Helsinki Group. Or, they might be with burgeoning national independence movements such as Sajudis in Lithuania. Memorial, in Russia, was an interesting organization that was formed to preserve information about the victims of Stalin's repressions—before thousands of still-living relatives of these victims passed away. In its early years,

Memorial received important technical and other assistance through a Seattleite named Richard Greene as well as the Henry M. Jackson Foundation.

At the same time as these "cause-oriented" contacts between citizens East and West were growing, the "citizen diplomacy" movement was also gathering force. Seattle was one of the US cities where it was most dynamic and this owed greatly to the Seattle-Tashkent sister city relationship established in the mid-seventies. By the mid-eighties the two cities were annually having extensive exchanges[12] between a widely diverse group of residents: for example, painters, musicians, physicians, quilters, chefs, mountain climbers, TV broadcasters, drug store owners, and so on.

There was great enthusiasm for these exchanges. For one, they reflected the penchant for activism of Americans and their belief in the power of mobilized citizens to solve social and political problems. American exchange participants often expressed the view that they were lowering international tensions by offsetting the belligerence they saw in their own government.

The participants in such exchanges usually learned a good deal about the countries they were visiting, and this too satisfied many Americans' interest in "experiential learning." There were sometimes interesting wrinkles, however, when American exchange participants were not only "goodwill ambassadors" but passionate critics of US foreign policy. They saw their exchange activities as an extension of their peace activism, or as what one scholar termed "political pilgrimages": journeys to show solidarity with the citizens of countries, such as the Soviet Union, that were seen as victims of American militarism and hostile policies.

Thus it came as a surprise to many Western peace activists—alarmed by the election of Ronald Reagan as president in 1980 and the subsequent crisis over the deployment of intermediate range nuclear missiles in Europe—to learn that human rights activists in Russia and other parts of the Soviet bloc had little interest in supporting demonstrations for a "nuclear freeze" like those that swept Western Europe. The West European freeze campaign leaders had assumed that leaders of the various Helsinki monitoring groups in the Soviet bloc—well-known figures such as Vaclav Havel and Jiri Dienstbier of Czechoslovakia, or Zbigniew Romaszewski of Poland—would be eager to sign on to the freeze campaign.

The reasons this was not the case were brilliantly explained in an essay written by Havel and published as a pamphlet in 1985 by Charta 77. Titled *The Anatomy of a Reticence: Eastern European Dissidents and the Peace Movement in the West*, the essay explained that, for citizens of East European countries, the threat of a nuclear attack by the West was a distant and somewhat hypothetical concern; whereas the nightmare of living in a repressive communist state was a day-to-day reality. Liberating themselves from such a situation was the first priority of the East European and Soviet "captive nations." If they could do this peacefully and reduce international tensions at the same time, all the better. But independence, respect for human rights, and the end of communist rule were their priorities. To Poles of all political leanings, for example, it made little sense to engage in antiwar campaigns with the West that sought to freeze levels of nuclear weapons while also freezing the political status quo imposed by the Soviet Union. Getting out from under Moscow's thumb was Poland's deepest wish. For similar reasons, Havel and his fellow dissidents in Czechoslovakia asked the leaders of Western peace movements to endorse Charta 77's freedom-and-peace agenda by demanding Soviet compliance with all provisions of the Helsinki Accords, including respect for the sovereignty of historically independent nations.

I found these developments very exciting. In the first place, they were occurring in spite of all the restrictions on free speech, travel, and association that Soviet bloc governments routinely imposed on their citizens. Second, although explicit commitments to nonviolence were not a major element in appeals of the human rights activists, the hallmarks of nonviolent campaigns were obvious:

- A commitment to dialogue and reason, and a rejection of the language of uncompromising militancy and threats;
- A focus not on seizing political power, but on the fulfillment of a clear and limited set of agreed commitments (i.e., the provisions of the Final Act of the Helsinki Accords); and
- An ethical and humane vision underlying all civic and political action. In another seminal essay, *The Power of the Powerless*, Vaclav Havel showed how lies and propaganda were central to totalitarian rule and its longevity. To his fellow citizens, accustomed to decades of hearing false communist dogma in all spheres of life—none of which they believed—Havel wrote that only by "living in truth" could the insidious power of totalitarianism be defeated.[13]

As I reflected on all the amazing events of the late eighties, I started to discern the outlines of a new mission and new identity for the Seattle World Without War Council. At the front was the then-novel concept of civil society. It was not the same as peace, but it seemed related to peace. If the elements of civil society could be strengthened worldwide, would this not also improve the prospects of lasting peace between nations? Would not nations that showed tolerance for political diversity domestically also be less aggressive and more negotiable internationally? The concept of civil society seemed less utopian, but it had this advantage: it made international peace look more achievable. This, too, was a plus.

As for the precise meaning of civil society, it had to be admitted that the term could be used in different ways by different people, and it contained some ambiguities or contradictions. For example, if a religious faith denied the equality of women in the workplace, should it be considered a protected institution of civil society? The concept can provoke such thorny questions. As far as I was concerned, however, it was enough to see civil society principally as the realm of free and independent voluntary organizations: business and professional associations, clubs, self-help groups, religious institutions (where there is separation of church and state), trade unions and guilds, political parties, advocacy organizations, publishers, social media, and so on. Viewed in these terms:

• Civil society was an essential feature of a modern state, a crucial arena for the interplay between governmental, commercial, and nongovernmental sectors. If the nations of the world subscribed to the importance of having robust civil societies—and the great majority at least gave lip service to this—then the world was that much closer to replacing war and violence as a means of conflict with dialogue, debate, and negotiation.
• Healthy and legally protected civil society offered a space within which even deep national conflicts, such as between different religious traditions or ethnic groups, could be contained and channeled without descending into civil war. It could be argued that the strength of civil society in Chile, for example, significantly eased the nonviolent transition from military dictatorship under General Pinochet back to democracy.
• Civil society was separate from the state and needed to be protected from capture by the state, as had occurred in totalitarian systems. In this sense, to talk about civil society was to acknowledge the need for limits on state power. Since the military was always an organ of the state, limits on the power of the state also implied limits on the power of the military—and a corresponding enhancement of the principle of civilian rule.

Besides these considerations, I also thought, how understandable the notion of civil society was to activist Americans interested in international affairs. When delegations of American citizen diplomats met with their counterparts overseas, if the discussion turned to questions of civil society in their respective countries, everybody immediately knew what was being discussed.

Finally, if one believed as I did, that nations with a democratic culture and system of government were less likely to go to war with each other than those that had authoritarian or dictatorial systems . . . then the promotion of independent and free civil societies globally, inasmuch as these are foundational aspects of democratic cultures, became an obvious strategy for those concerned to end war. In other words, I thought there were numerous convergences between the ideas of the WWWC and those of a new organization based on the concept of advancing civil society worldwide. So, having applied to the Secretary of State of Washington State for authorization to change our name, we received from Secretary Ralph Munro a Certificate of

Amendment that authorized that change. On June 25, 1992, World Without War Council of Greater Seattle became Center for Civil Society International (CCSI).

CENTER FOR CIVIL SOCIETY INTERNATIONAL: A NEW IDENTITY FOR THE NINETIES

From the very first day of operating with the new name, it seemed that a burden had been lifted. No longer was there a question of our embattled relationship with other "peace" organizations, some of which routinely accused us of being clandestine government operatives. No longer were we arranging public education programs for audiences that were not really interested in learning but just wanted a public opportunity to vent about the evils of US foreign policy.

To begin, we decided we would be an information service for those interested in the growth of civil societies worldwide, and we would begin by producing resources for those interested in the transforming countries of the former Soviet bloc. Our audience would not be limited to the Seattle area but would be national and international.

Our first projects were to develop publications about independent social organizations in Poland and Russia that we had learned about from attending conferences in each country. After attending a human rights conference in Krakow in 1988, where we met activists in the youth organization *Wolnosc i Pokoj* ("Freedom and Peace"), we came home and published a collection of the writings by principal members of this grassroots organization that campaigned for environmental causes as well as the right of conscientious objectors to military service to perform alternative civilian service.

Following this, we began publishing information on so-called *neformaly*, independent grassroots organizations that had popped up throughout Russia in the late eighties. The University of Washington Press saw one of these publications and asked if we would like to co-publish an expanded paperback edition with them. We said we would and two successful editions of *The Post-Soviet Handbook: A Guide to Grassroots Organizations and Internet Resources* followed in 1994 and 1996. Also in the late nineties we published a similar directory focused on the five former Soviet republics in Central Asia. Its title was *Civil Society in Central Asia*.

The Internet was developing rapidly in the mid-nineties and it soon became clear that we needed to put all the data that had gone into our print publications onto a website, accessible for anybody with a computer. We did this with a generous grant from the Eurasia Foundation. In a separate project, during the mid-nineties we participated in four annual conferences in Russia that were sponsored by USAID and intended to introduce Russian journalists to the potential for online journalism. These conferences, whose chief organizer was Seattle journalist Alan Boyle, were highly successful and reinforced for me the growing power of the World Wide Web.

As the nineties came to a close, CCSI had established a reputation as a rich source of information about civil society in the former Soviet bloc nations, as well as opportunities for exchanges, scholarships, and jobs in the nonprofit sector related to these countries. Our website contained descriptions of hundreds of independent organizations in countries from Estonia to Uzbekistan. We operated an active listserv that had about 900 subscribers, many of them young people looking for opportunities to work in the nonprofit sector in the FSU (former Soviet Union). In short, CCSI had established a successful model for engaging with one large region of the world that could possibly be applied to other regions, for example, the Middle East, China and North Korea, possibly parts of Africa.

Unfortunately, the long term viability of this work required levels of annual funding in excess of what we were able to achieve. We either had to develop an organizational model that involved selling some of our information services—everything on our website was free—or find some foundation or similar institution that would be prepared to subsidize us indefinitely. We were never able to accomplish either of these goals, so in 2003–2004, we had to close the offices of CCSI, only 11 years after its inception.

With a little more luck, we might have been able to stay open and expand our work. I believe there is still a role for an organization like Center for Civil Society International that tracks and collects information on the central elements of civil society and the challenges they face in various countries—especially but not only in "closed" or authoritarian societies. If a website were created for such a purpose, it would need to be curated and moderated to prevent some of the problems that sites like Facebook have had with false accounts and imposters. The Internet today suffers from too much information that is neither organized well nor very reliable. If a new CCSI website could provide this service, somehow insuring the accuracy and integrity of its information, it might be a useful resource for the continued strengthening of civil society worldwide.

NOTES

1. Oona A. Hathaway and Scott J. Shapiro,*The Internationalists: How a Radical Plan to Outlaw War Remade the World* (New York: Simon and Schuster 2017).

2. See Chapter 14, "A Context for Work to End War," in Robert Pickus and Robert Woito, *To End War* (New York: Harper & Row 1970), pp. 223–239.

3. Pickus and Woito, *To End War,* p. 238.

4. Pickus and Woito, *To End War,* p. xv.

5. Pickus and Woito, *To End War,* p. 215.

6. Guenter Lewy, *Peace and Revolution: The Moral Crisis of American Pacifism* (Grand Rapids, MI: Eerdmans 1988). Most Americans know little about the organizations that are at the core of the American peace movement. This important study revealed the degree to which the anti–Vietnam War movement had brought historically pacifist groups such as the American Friends Service Committee (AFSC) and War Resisters League (WRL) together with nonpacifist organizations that were essentially Marxist. In these coalitions the Marxist point of view tended to prevail and compromised the principled witness of Quaker, Mennonite and other pacifist sects.

7. FMLN = Frente Farabundo Martí para la Liberación Nacional. Around this time, I had picked up a neighborhood newspaper in Seattle's University District that contained a directory of "movement" organizations working on Central American issues. I was astonished to find that they numbered 38!

8. As events developed in Nicaragua over the next three-four years, Oscar Arias, a former president of Costa Rica, would emerge as a champion of a peace accord that eventually would be the basis for an end to hostilities. In Seattle, most antiwar organizations simply echoed the Sandinista line on issues, only seeking to discredit President Reagan's policies. The WWWC worked to develop a better understanding of the Arias Plan and what it called for.

9. Paul Hollander. *Political Pilgrims* (Oxford University Press 1981) is the classic account of the numerous Western intellectuals and opinion leaders who traveled to communist nations such as the USSR, the People's Republic of China, and Cuba and found them to be models of good governance and social justice.

10. Guthrie also happened to be from the Miskito minority group in northeast Nicaragua, so he was a good source of information on two issues: Sandinista labor relations and treatment of minorities. We managed to get Guthrie on some radio shows and even achieved a meeting with Mayor Royer. But the mayor gave Guthrie very little time and showed minimal interest in hearing about Sandinista attacks on the Miskitos or independent labor. At the end of the meeting Royer would not allow a photo to be taken of him together with Guthrie!

11. In a *Commentary* magazine article that received wide attention at the time, Kirkpatrick wrote: "For these reasons and more, a posture of continuous self-abasement and apology vis-à-vis the Third World is neither morally necessary nor politically appropriate. No more is it necessary or appropriate to support vocal enemies of the United States because they invoke the rhetoric of popular liberation. It is not even necessary or appropriate for our leaders to forswear unilaterally the use of military force to counter military force. Liberal idealism need not be identical with masochism, and need not be incompatible with the defense of freedom and the national interest."

From Jeanne J. Kirkpatrick, "Dictatorships and Double Standards," *Commentary*, Vol. 68, No. 5, November 1979, pp. 34–45. See also her book by the same title (Simon and Schuster, 1982).

12. The term "exchanges" is a bit of a misnomer because it suggests a balance in the numbers going each way. In fact, considerably more Seattleites made the trip to Tashkent than vice-versa. As a senior executive at The Seattle Post-Intelligencer once put it, "These 'exchanges' are a six-lane highway in one direction, but a cowpath in the other." However, in 1990 Seattle hosted the Goodwill Games and in this instance literally hundreds of Russians (and some other Soviet nationalities, too) came to Seattle for about a month of programs featuring sports, the arts, and many other areas of common activity, including discussions of human rights.

13. In addition, many post-communist East European civil society activists exhibited a strong aversion to utopian schemes of any sort. They had had enough of grandiose, strident communist rhetoric to last them a lifetime. No more celebrations, please, of "the vanguard role of the revolutionary masses," for example. They were content to have achieved the freedom, as they put it, just "to live normal lives."

BIBLIOGRAPHY

Belli, H. (1985). *Breaking faith: The Sandinista Revolution and its impact on freedom and the Christian faith in Nicaragua.* Wheaton, IL: Good News Publishing.

Hathaway, O. A. and Shapiro, S. J. (2018). *The internationalists: How a radical plan to outlaw war remade the world.* New York: Simon and Schuster.

Havel, V. (1985). *The anatomy of a reticence: Eastern European dissidents and the peace movement in the West (voices from Czechoslovakia).* Stockholm: The Charter 77 Foundation.

Havel, V. and Keane, J. (1985). *The power of the powerless: Citizens against the state in Central Europe.* New York and Oxford: Routledge.

Hollander, P. (1983). *Political pilgrims: Travels of western intellectuals to the Soviet Union, China and Cuba, 1928–1978.* New York: HarperCollins.

Kirkpatrick, J. J. (1979 November). Dictatorships and double standards. *Commentary.*

———. (1982). *Dictatorships and double standards: Rationalism and reason in politics.* New York: Simon and Schuster.

Lewy, G. (1988). *Peace and revolution: The moral crisis of American pacifism.* Grand Rapids, MI: Wm. B. Eerdmans.

Pickus, R. and Woito, R. (1970). *To end war.* Revised Edition. New York: Harper & Row.

Ruffin, M. H., McCarter, J., and Upjohn, R. (1986). *The post-Soviet handbook: A guide to grassroots organizations and internet resources.* Seattle, WA: University of Washington Press.

Ruffin, M. H. and Waugh, D. (1999). *Civil society in Central Asia.* Seattle, WA: University of Washington Press.

Tada, R. (1989). *Directory of US organizations working on Latin America.* Seattle, WA: World Without War Council.

Zinn, H. (2015). *A people's history of the United States.* New York: Harper Perennial.

Chapter Nine

World Order Studies

There are twenty million member mono-theistic religions to guide us and millions of divinely inspired individuals. The resilient institutions and understandings supporting representative democracy have been affirmed here as essential to national conflict resolution, religious liberty, and determining the United States' engagement in world politics. Although some dispute whether the Presidential submitted budget and house appropriation committee decide the level of military spending, those disputes are not addressed here. The question that needs to be addressed is "How should America engage in contests for power and to what ends, set against what standards?" Robert Pickus's claim that "even paranoid people have at least one real enemy" is confirmed here with five dedicated adversaries identified. If a county breaks all protocol and arrests your diplomatic corps, becomes a theocracy, and calls you "the great Satan" that ends the discussion of adversarial relationships but not the question of what strategy of peace you want your country to adopt. There are five determined adversaries identified here: Islamic Jihadists, Iran, North Korea, Russia, and China. Your strategy of peace may deny this but if so, your strategy of peace will be criticized here. Only North Korea is addressed. Denial, leads to appeasement, appeasement to war and thus is a fatal flaw for any strategy of peace.

Robert Pickus and his colleagues contributed to the first three strategies of peace introduced below. None of these strategies featured in Presidential politics 2016–2020, although they were intended to become the dominant form of engagement by the United States in world politics. Despite all the consensus building, there is no consensus.

This chapter is intended to clarify what is your preferred strategy of peace in this changed and changing arena of world politics to help build a new consensus to sustain the United States' engagement. I have ordered the debate by having Robert Pickus introduce it with a 1992 statement apropos of the present (2019). Each of the contenders should be asked six questions with answers cited in various sources. Everyone is encouraged to go to the source to capture the full intent of the spokesperson or submit an additional strategy of peace and ask it the same six questions. This chapter is intended to teach "how possibly" people have reached different understandings and have adopted alternative strategies of peace. That dialogue, difficult even in teaching institutions in 2020, is needed. The presentation of complex ideas in these brief summaries will inspire you to develop your own or rework one of the inadequate strategies of peace that follow.

STRATEGIES OF PEACE

Illustrated here are three distinct nonmilitary strategies of peace, which advocate, develop and seek to implement realistic nonmilitary alternatives to war or surrender, along with six military-based strategies of peace that acknowledge national interest rivals and promote arms control over disarmament, among other ideas

1. Traditional Pacifist, for example *Speak Truth to Power* (1955), A. J. Muste, Robert Pickus (1955–1961), STTP Summary.
2. Just War Coalition that seeks the cooperation of pacifists and diplomats who see war as a last resort, to develop a realistic nonmilitary strategy of peace, for example the Catholic Church, Robert Pickus (1961–2016), Turn Toward Peace, World Without War Council canon: A Non-Military Strategy Of United States Peace Initiatives Acts, *Turn Toward Peace Policy Framework*, "Seven Roads to a World Without War," and *To End War*.
3. Democratic Peace Strategy—Michael Doyle, Charles Lipson, R. J. Rummel—democracies rarely war on each other. Extend in time the two existing regional peaces and nurture transitions to democracy by nonviolent means in other countries. The peace formula is representative democracies, private enterprise economies, agreed to rules of monetary exchange, trade dispute resolution institutions, religious liberty, enforce Treaties between them in domestic courts, and accept Sharp's 198 nonviolent means to protest or claim justice is denied.
4. State–Centered Realism—World Order among 195 Sovereign Nation States, Henry Kissinger, Architect.
5. Liberal Internationalist Strategy of Peace—Presidents Woodrow Wilson, Franklin Delano Roosevelt, John F. Kennedy, and Brian Urquhart, Madeline Albright, and Hillary Clinton.

6. Conservative Strategy of Peace—Presidents Herbert Hoover, Dwight David Eisenhower, Richard Nixon, George HW Bush, George Bush, and Condoleezza Rice.
7. Global Environmentalist Strategy of Peace with Climate Liabilities—Bernie Sanders, Jill Stein, Amory Lovins, and Lester Brown.
8. The God that Failed Strategy of Peace, Reborn—Marxism, Leninism, Maoism combined with national interest diplomacy; Vladimir Putin transformed by enterprise zones, trade, and expansionist foreign policy.
9. Other Worldly Strategy of Peace—After Armageddon, Rapture; Bible, and other holy descriptions of the end time.

We will ask each of these nine strategies these six questions: (1) Goals: What Goals do you seek in world politics? (2) Obstacles: What Obstacles do you expect to encounter? (3) Direction: What is the direction of your foreign policy? (4) Objectives: What are the most important, immediate objectives? (5) Getting there: How do you get there from here? (6) Domestic/Global: What is the mix between domestic and global priorities?

War, the Central Problem of the 21st Century by Robert Pickus (1992):

> The goal of a world without war does not require a world without political conflict, nor a world of perfect justice, but a world which resolves large scale political conflict by means other than war. Advancing toward that goal, in ways which serve the well–being of our own society requires progress on each of the seven roads to peace. These seven roads provide a framework for realistic work toward a visionary goal: an end to war.
>
> The tides of human yearning for peace regularly rise and fall. This 1992 version of the World Without War Council's defining document comes at an ebb tide. The waves of fear engendered by Soviet power and the nuclear arms race have abated. Isolationist sentiment is rising on both sides of the political spectrum. Ironically, now that the long term work needed to make progress toward a world without war is possible as it has seldom been before, few are still engaged in pursuing that goal. Many "peace" groups continue to focus their work on opposition to American military power. Most other world affairs groups do not believe an end to war is a feasible goal.
>
> But the problem of war, now eclipsed by domestic problems, will soon return to the center of the political arena. Familiar pro and contra arguments about a current war will then again dominate public discussion. The present rare opportunity to work constructively on the single problem that most blights the human future will be lost.
>
> It is not simply the destructiveness of war that gives it primacy to any thoughtful agenda for human progress. It is because war, its structures and beliefs, occupies the ground needed for such progress. Whether seen in the broadest value, or the most specific economic terms, war and preparation for war stand as a primary obstacle to a more free, just and humane world.

In the conviction then that a primary focus on the problem of war is still required, WWWC summarizes here its answer to the question: what is required if we are to move toward a world without war? No previous answers have been adequate, so you will be right to approach this answer skeptically. But it is a clear answer. Does it make sense to you? What would you substitute?

Nonmilitary Strategies of Peace

Traditional Pacifist Strategy of Peace

Classic Source: George Fox, John Woolman, Jane Addams.

Modern Source: A. J. Muste, Robert Pickus from 1955–1961, Walter Naegle.

Text: *Speak Truth to Power* (STTP), Summary by Robert Pickus, 1955.

Goal: Convert to pacifism one person at a time through witness: accept the millennium goals of the UN.

Obstacle: The weapons themselves create a mirror image effect, each side stimulating and reinforcing the other. As Robert Pickus said in his summary of STTP: "'It is [not] possible in the Twentieth Century for military power to be applied rationally, and a constructive program for peace carried on simultaneously with a program for military preparedness. . . .' Our military commitment—in its nature an open ended rather than a limited endeavor—renders us economically, politically, psychologically, and spiritually unable to give effect to the policies that so many agree are necessary if peace is to be won."

Policy Direction: "There is no way to peace, peace is the way" is a pacifist slogan referred to in silent meetings waiting on divine inspiration. Robert Pickus, in the Progressive symposium in 1955, states: STTP "presents a reasoned case for the unqualified rejection of reliance on military power; not in the future after world law and agreement on universal disarmament are achieved but now."

Objectives: Unilateral disarmament by one superpower, thereby breaking the momentum of arms competition. International mediation, conflict resolution and transition to state by state political order. Develop world law, with a sense of world community. A fundamental attack on domestic and world poverty. An end to colonialism and an assertion of the sovereign equality of states. Preparation and training for civilian resistance to occupation by an armed, expansionist sect with state power, as developed by Gene Sharp. A policy of "national defense without armaments." Transfer of financial resources from military speeding to meet human needs. We do not act on the constructive goals stated in these objectives because of a "Twentieth Century commitment to organized mass violence." Teach children not to be aggressive: Teeter totters, not competitive sports.

Getting there: Unilateral disarmament followed by international peace-keeping backed up by nonviolent, civilian defense.

Domestic versus global: Every nation-state, each state and province in the United States and Canada must make its own way to a just, pacifist society. Individual witness toward universal goals is required.

Just War Coalition

Goal: A disarmed world under law, safe for free societies.

Obstacles: My nation right or wrong, but my nation; inter-state rivalry, desire to stay ahead in an arms race, whether your intent is to deter or to wage war, preparation for war, bureaucratic and military commitment, the recognition that to deter, you must be prepared to use, reinforcement of implacable enemy images, belief that war is inevitable, and the absence of a nonmilitary conflict resolution institution or understandings.

Policy Direction: Seek policies for our country "not based upon the threat of war or organization for war and not based upon willingness to surrender freedom or democratic values."

Objectives: Disarmament of all nations, which cannot alone solve the problem without world law. World law requires a strengthened sense of world community, through promotion of human rights and achieved by support for just demands for social, political and economic change. Planning for an international peacetime economy and reduction of political tension in crisis areas. Accelerating world economic development efforts. Developing socially organized nonviolent means for defending freedom and producing needed change. Affirming root universal values beyond national interest diplomacy.

Getting there: By seeking to apply "thou shalt not kill" to world politics. By developing alternatives to the organized use of mass violence. Developing diplomatic strategies which rule out organized mass violence. Wise diplomacy which recognizes national interest while aiming to achieve world community. By accelerating the decolonization of the world or attempts to control just not influence other nations. By assuring that the slogan "never again" is realized in preventing genocide. By redeveloping a Strategy of American Peace Initiative Acts.

Domestic/Global Mix: Improve America's Competence in World Affairs. Focus on pre–collegiate education. Engage non–governmental organizations (business, labor, religious, ethnic, in work for a world without war). Build functional relations among NGOs based on training, division of labor, fund-raising, and media. Engage global civil society.

Democratic Peace Strategy

Classic Source: Kant, *Perpetual Peace* (1796).

Modern Application: Michael Doyle (1971), "Democracies Do Not War on Each Other."

Texts: Steven W. Hook, *Democratic Peace in Theory and Practice* (pro and contra anthology); Bruce Russett, *Grasping the Democratic Peace* (1993); Robert Woito, *Extending the Democratic Peace* (2003); and Charles Lipson, *Reliable Partners, How Democracies Have Made a Separate Peace* (2005).

Goal: A preponderance of states governed by representative democracies which enforce treaties between them in domestic courts; transitions toward democracies in theocratic, ideological and military dictatorships.

Obstacles: Dictatorships of various kinds (Communist, theological, military). Nonrecognition that there are two regional peaces in which there have been no wars (defined as organized mass violence with 1,000 casualties a year), the European one, a product of a political integration strategy, the North American one attributed to the preponderance of power of the United States over its Canadian and Mexican neighbors.

Policy Direction: The democratic peace formula is peace equals representative democracies, predominantly private enterprise economies, monetary exchange agreements, trade dispute resolution institutions, secure copyrights and patents, no weapons targeted on each other, and treaties signed by governments enforced in domestic courts with vibrant civil societies insisting that governments abide by treaties they have signed.

Objectives: Annual assessments of civil and political rights. Inter-religious conclaves to refine the definition of religious liberty. Reciprocal lowering of trade barriers, states encouraging to produce those products for the domestic and global markets in which they have a comparative advantage. Maintenance of the International Monetary Fund exchange rates based of the value of the 16 largest representative democracies currency, use the community of democracies and regional bodies as caucuses within the UN Support and expand the National Endowment for Democracy and the World Movement for Democracy. Consider Genocide a global problem, intervene if feasible at the 8th stage (mass annihilation) assuming international bodies have tried and failed to stop a progression at earlier stages. Seek Trusteeship Council reinvention with 10 year trusteeships for failed stakes. Create self-determination processes for states with significant global civil society organizations such as the largest religious institution in the country. Use and develop renewable energy source, enforce as supplements to fossil fuels. Impose import tax on imports from states which do not meet the same environmental standards.

Getting there: Maintain consolidated democracies in which there is no alternative route to governmental legitimacy, support, and defend democracies in every region, nurture societies in transition and support the Community of Democracies.

Domestic/Global: Lower tariff barriers if reciprocated, reduce fossil fuel pollution to 1990 level and tax imports from countries that do not reach 1990 levels. Reevaluate every year.

Military-Based Strategies of Peace

World Order between 195 Sovereign Nation States

Classic Sources: Thucydides, *The History*; Niccolò Machiavelli, *The Prince*.
Practitioners: Metternich, Bismarck, and Henry Kissinger.

Goal: Minimization of inevitable organized mass violence as states adjust their ever changing power relationships to each other.

Obstacles: Failed states, secessionist and irredentist movements, cross border aggressions, civil wars abided by outside forces, terrorism, international bodies that do not enforce treaties that they sign, wars by proxy, secrecy (but diplomacy cannot be conducted without it), and internal and interstate conflict vulnerabilities of each state.

Policy Direction: National Interest diplomacy, benefit domestic constituencies to keep them involved and supportive

Objectives: Arms Control, not disarmament. Downplay human rights, they can get you into wars, comparative advantaged trade not human rights promotion in a state's self-interest. Recognize spheres of influence. International law is not enforceable but treaties provide self-serving breathing space, truces, posturing. Environmental treaties that are universally enforceable, would provide a level playing field; those that are not universally enforced, support national interest diplomacy and punish those who abide by them. Non-intervention in the domestic affairs of sovereign states. Trade that supports 50% of domestic jobs beneficial, tariffs (taxes) provide an open season on obtaining benefits for your prime constituency; Wisconsin dairy farmers (3rd in world behind France and Germany) pay under NAFTA over 200% in tariff fees, billions in cost of goods sold when environmental regulations is to the third decimal point. Defensive arms considered when offensive (deterrent) arms reduced Technological innovation, cyberspace spying, bluffing make minimum violence an elusive terms, which can provide leverage.

Getting there: Claim widespread support in every country. "Never fear to negotiate; but never negotiate out of fear" (John F. Kennedy). Increase the competence in world affairs of your citizens from basic knowledge, to language skills, awareness that lessons from history have different applications as circumstances change. Measure power carefully, use it when necessary for survival.

Domestic/Global: Obtain bipartisan support and constituents for national interest diplomacy. Recommended Reading: Henry Kissinger, *World Order* (New York: Penguin 2015).

Liberal Internationalist Strategy of Peace

Classic Source: Woodrow Wilson and Jean Monnet.

Modern Expression: John F. Kennedy, Madeline Albright, Hillary Clinton, John Kerry, and Susan Rice.

Goal: Nation State cooperation through international institutions to achieve security and prosperity. ". . . liberals argue that a world order with more liberal democratic capitalists states will be more peaceful, prosperous and respect human rights. . . . It is not inevitable that history will end with the triumph of liberalism but it is inevitable that a decent world order will be liberal."

Obstacles: Illiberalism, autocracy, nationalism, protectionism, sphere of influence, territorial revisionism, Brexit, and President Donald Trump.

Policy Direction: National sovereignty respected, engage in maintaining international institutions, reforming them into effective resources in dealing with environmental, terrorists, aggression, and other global jeopardies.

Objectives: Free and fair trade. Encourage state, city, corporations, and individual reductions of fossil fuel jeopardies. Stop nuclear proliferation. Respond militarily, proportionately, to Syria's "egregious violation of international accords." Continue the Bush, Obama policies toward Russia with invitations to participate and constraints against the use of force in the near abroad with military assistance to the Ukraine. Support France's leadership on enforcing International, Environmental Accords. Support the UN when it reinforces liberal values, critically engage when it does not. H. Strengthen the intelligence gathering, police/FBI early warning and interdiction policies. Reject genocide (Burma), mass slaughter (Rwanda) and failed states in Africa (Somalia, the Democratic Republic of the Congo) but put no United States soldiers or people in harm's way.

Getting there: "Despite what the backers of Trump and Brexit promise, actually effecting a real withdrawal from these long standing commitments will be difficult to accomplish. . . . Over the decades, the activities and interests of countless actors—corporations, civil groups, and governmental bureaucracies—have become intricately entangled in these institutions."

Domestic/Global: "The liberal democracies have survived and flourished in the face of far greater challenges—the great depression, the Axis powers, and the international communist movement. . . . Above all the case for liberalism rests on a simple truth: the solutions to today's problems are more liberal democracy and more liberal order."

Military-Based Strategies of Peace

Conservative Strategy of Peace

Classic: Edmund Burke and Herbert Hoover.

Modern Advocates: Governor John Kasich; Senators Mario Rubio, Ted Cruz, and Rand Paul.

Goal: Reclaim American leadership by cooperating with allies, engaging in "open minded civility, mutual respect and compromise" meeting military, terrorist, and other threats from determined adversaries (Islamic Jihadists, Iran, North Korea) and national interest rivals Russia and China.

Obstacles: Trade losses from technological innovations, trade agreements not adjusted to change, war against "overblown" terrorism and adapting to the rise of China.

Policy Direction: Restoring bipartisan consensus to US foreign policy.

Objectives: Maintain China/United States codependency on trade, lending, and environmental protection. Negotiate exit from Afghanistan with all parties to the conflict. Balance budget has been done before, it must be done again. Engage, not retreat, but with allies. Negotiate with trading partners an end to "government subsidies, dumping and unfair trade" including unfree labor and cyberspace intellectual property theft, contain nuclear weapons proliferation, accidental use provisions and step by step approach to denuclearization within the framework of military deterrence. Peaceful regime change in North Korea. Streamline the World Trade Organization's dispute resolution process and insisting on "full reciprocity in market access." Militarily deter China and "make it clear that there will be a significant price to pay for any attack on US assets in space and expand our regional allies' missile and air defense capabilities."

Getting there: "The United States needs a national security doctrine around which a consensus can be built—both between the Democratic and the Republican Parties and with those who share our interests and values overseas. As we continue the search for that, we should work together to secure our economic future, reimagine and strengthen our defenses and alliances, and focus on prime challenges to our national interests. Rather than pulling back and going it alone, America must cooperate and lead."

Domestic/Global: Rebuild a consensus in domestic politics through civility and acceptance that each party offers legitimate opposition whose policy preference can be debated with agreed to compromised outcomes: in global politics renew alliances and counter threats.

Global Environmentalism Strategy of Peace with Climate Liabilities

Classic Source: Thomas Malthus.

Modern Application: Lester Brown and Amory Lovins.

Public Policy Advocates: Gill Stein, Bernie Sanders, Green Party, and Beyond Borders.

Goal: Global transitions to renewable energy economies with legal liabilities for those who persist in using fossil fuels.

Obstacles: Wars for limited fossil fuels; twelve possible renewables, none of which meet market viability according to Bill Gates, inconvenient truths, multiply, and science speculative (to many variables, no control group experiments).

Policy Direction: "Emergency Green New Deal to turn the tide on Climate Change."

Objectives: (From Jill Stein's 2016 Platform) Full income and benefits to workers in fossil fuel industries as they transition to alternative work. Create 20 million new jobs by transitioning to 100% clean renewable energy by 2030. Energy democracy based on public, community and worker ownership of our energy system. Build a nationwide smart electricity grid that can pool and store power from a diversity of renewable energy sources. End fossil fuel subsidies; impose a greenhouse gas fuel tax to charge polluters for the damage they have created. Enact stronger environmental justice laws and measures to ensure that low–income and communities of color are not disproportionally impacted. Guarantee tuition-free, world class public education from preschool through university. Abolish student debt. Stand up for human rights abuses worldwide to hold countries accountable for LGBTQIA discrimination. Base foreign policy on diplomacy, international law, human rights, and nonviolent support for democratic movements around the world. Cut military spending by at least 50% and restore the National Guard as the central component of our defense. Democratize monetary policy to bring about public control of the money supply and credit creation. Bring the United States into comportment with UN's Declaration of the Rights of Indigenous Peoples. Replace NAFTA and other corporate free trade agreements . . . enact fair trade laws.

Getting there: Global Reciprocation and Enforcement of Ban on Fossil fuels by 2030; expanding law suits against all users of fossil fuels.

Domestic/Global Change: Leadership by Example, reciprocation expected, not required.

Strategy of Peace of the God that Failed

Classic Source: Karl Marx, N. Lenin, and Mao Tse Tung.

Modern Application: Plekanov Gramsci.

Goal: Apply science to world politics; the scientific labor theory of value enables the world to determine accurately the price of everything by the cost of labor that went into it.

Obstacles: Nation states with market economies that are governed by the middle class, enhance hegemony of a ruling class, appropriate wealth and natural resources, and destroy the environment with inhuman consequences.

Policy Direction: Impose hundreds of thousands of regulations so the distinction between nationalization and private ownership is undermined.

Nationalize all public utilities and other entities with public ownership of natural monopolies.

Objectives: Only economic rights are meaningful; the right to food, for example. Civil and political rights obfuscate this harsh reality. Prevent terrorism by ending discrimination against Muslim countries, make Israel abide by majority rule on UN resolutions. Make universal climate liabilities where every nation, state, municipality or corporation can be held criminally liable proportionately for the damage their pollution has caused. End genocide by eliminating hate speech from mass communication media and by the Security Council, Nationalized Industry States, Community of Democracies, or regional institution intervening at the ninth stage (mass annihilation) of genocide. Achieve more equitable distribution of resources by taxing 100% of income over the poverty line plus $50,000. Redistribute wealth in every country thus eliminating a cause of war. Maintain Costa Rica's mediation and conflict resolution roles, complement it on its no army approach to national defense and its near 100% transitions to a renewable energy economy. End nuclear proliferation by requesting each country reduce by 10% and then reduce another 10% when other nuclear powers have reduced 10%. Recognize transitional justice is an alternative to massive cultural bias as portrayed in Hollywood movies, network television, and popular culture. Peace yes, NATO no; no western intervention in Syria or the Ukraine.

Getting there: Defense of all existing scientific socialist state, working class revolutions in capitalist states, removal or de-legitimization of theocracies, adaptations of the law of combined development, one platform for the bourgeoisie, another for the proletariat. Only in coalition with the leading anti-imperialist states can domestic peace and justice organizations prevail. Seeks to apply antimilitarism formulas to the United States while leaving unchallenged all other determined adversaries.

Domestic/Global Mix: Challenging domestic institutions and policies considered the most effective.

After Armageddon, Rapture Strategy of Peace

Classic Source: Revelations, many different biblical texts.

Goal: Be Tranquil, the End is Nigh, Each human life is of infinite worth, life eternal awaits the faithful.

Obstacles: Satanic Evil, Humankind's sinful nature, seven deadly sins (pride, greed, lust, envy, gluttony, wrath, and sloth).

Policy Direction: Equality of Opportunity. Broaden and Secure Religious Liberty. Study the end Times Signs. Each person an Apostle, each meeting an opportunity. Seek or maintain separations of Church and State.

Objectives: Maintain national security, one gun keeps another in its holster. Open Borders to Evangelize. Universal Bible distribution, translated into every language. Strengthen broadcast capability, radio and television, internet. Obey secular law, render onto Caesar the things that are Caesars, and onto God, the things that are God's. The body is a temple, do not put acid or other drugs into your brain.

Getting there: Live in imitation of Jesus. Ask for forgiveness of sins. Do good works. Respect other monotheistic religions. Accept the "Golden Rule," "Do onto others as you would have them do onto you." Obey the Ten Commandments.

Domestic versus global: Accept Mission. Seek voluntary conversions. Feed the hungry. Heal the sick.

In addition to these nine strategies of peace, there is a tenth. The national interest of China, Russia, Iran, and no doubt others can be expected to be expressed in their unique strategy of peace. As they emerge, we must ask the same six questions. Unless we develop a successful strategy of peace, these states' national interests will likely settle contested issues by any means possible.

SUMMARY OPINION: ALL THESE STRATEGIES OF PEACE HAVE FLAWS

Traditional Pacifist

> Strength: Moral commitment to reject preparation for war as well as the use of organized mass violence clear and unambiguous.
>
> Possible Flaw: Even in the pacifist world, next to no one has been trained at the national, state or municipal levels in what civilian defense entrails. Without demonstration, confidence with remain NATO 29–Civilian Defense 0.

Pickus/Council Canon

> Strength: Faces determine adversaries, states conditions essential to a world without war.
>
> Possible Flaw: The American Peace Initiatives strategy was never completed into a strategy that could be implemented. Memo to initiative writers not followed; no strategy developed.

Democratic Peace

> Strength: Two regional peaces by different routes among 31 representative democracies, 73 years and counting (unprecedented).
>
> Possible Flaw: Deeply rooted cultural differences and violent resistance to change, no consensus supporting violent (or nonviolent) interventions to enforce even the genocide convention in a world of sovereign states makes any time frame for success highly speculative.

World Order Among 195 Sovereign States

Strength: The fallback position, unless the above three find a way to both confront determined advisories and find a nonmilitary means to engage them in contests for power.

Possible Flaws: Wars will occur between truces, now with nuclear and other weapons of mass destruction.

Liberal Internationalist

Strengths: Reserve of political acumen, influence among secular opinion shapers, limited success of the United Nations in avoiding nuclear war between ideological, nationally opposed superpowers; creation of arena's in which violent intentions are clarified.

Possible Flaws: Do not enforce genocide convention, or routinely enforce accords, treaties, agreements between liberal democracies and religious, ideological, or military dictatorships.

Conservative Strategy of Peace

Strength: Faces determined adversaries.

Possible Flaws: Terrorism considered a police matter and genocide not addressed, trade that accounts for over 50% of jobs in the United States makes tariff reductions crucial, selective environmental regulations enforcement doubles the impact on those same jobs.

Global Environmentalism With Climate Liabilities

Strength: A world in which all species survive (slugs, polar bears, homo sapiens, and other species survive with specific day by day steps to get there from here).

Possible Flaws: No renewable energy means to defend against fossil fuel armed determined adversaries; the inconvenient truth is the predicted dooms rely on speculation data not science and the resulting playing field is anything but level; the states playing are sharply different in what treaties they enforce.

The God That Failed, Reborn

Strengths: The Memorial to the Victims of Communism failed, 500 million victims and still counting, Vladimir Putin added 14 attempts in 2017–2018.

Possible Flaws: 20th Century failures of the state to efficiently and expertly produce food, goods, commodities. Even Kim Jong Un is chauffeured in a Mercedes Benz.

After Armageddon, Rapture

Strengths: Biblical Basis.

Possible Flaw: Ambiguous signs, no definite date.

The Strategies of Peace described here have flaws even with enhanced conflict resolution techniques and "transitional justice" skills added. It is difficult to imagine even Robert Pickus finding the common threads in this dialogue although "putting the field together" and the "Turn Toward Peace
Policy Framework" are, to me, amazing precedents. Have anarchist and
world law advocates ever worked together, before or since? But do pause for
a moment and acknowledge that your own strategy of peace is inadequate,
needs development and that you must persuade others to form a new consensus to implement. You must, in the strategies offered here, find a means of
gaining the reciprocation of current determined adversaries. Also ask your-
self—with the Hippocratic Oath, First Do No Harm—whose national interest
your current posture serves if your strategy of peace is flawed?
    But is war the doom that deserves focus or the contending doom of
climate change? Nuclear war (and conventional war that escalates to nuclear)
and climate change among alarmists portends doom. Neither nuclear war nor
climate change can be worked on piecemeal because each has legitimate
functions that are difficult to replace—security and economic development
driven by fossil fuels. Arguably renewable energies have not, after 50 years
of research, subsidized production, and hope replaced fossil fuels. To avoid
the impending doom, achievements must be accomplished that are universal,
leadership must be reciprocated, the results if they involved the coercion of
law, enforceable. Otherwise, there will be no net gain.
    Lacking in the climate change debate is a recognition that solutions to
climate change are as complicated as avoiding nuclear war, perhaps more so:
(1) There are a discrete number of actors (8 nuclear powers, 195 polluting
States); (2) The presence of weapons may provide a false since of security,
but no alternative gained a constituency throughout the cold war; renewables
have been advocated, researched but after 50 years of research and development, none yet compete with fossil fuels in costs; (3) the fossil fuel driven
economy has produced an increase in world life expectancy from near 50 in
1950 to nearly 70 in 2010; (4) the megatons of damage essential to a doomsday scenario could be calculated and vividly portrayed with nuclear weapons; while the metaphor of an all-encompassing greenhouse in the sky, does
not cast a shadow; (5) in the climate change doomsday scenario the cost of
avoidance is in the trillions, maybe 16 plus or minus two with at best uncer-
tain results; (6) all states must denuclearize together just as all states must
become renewable-only energy states at the same time, or risk being intimidated and conquered by a nuclear hold out or a fossil fuel driven, military
rival; and (7) with nuclear war, the detection of violators is imaginable; with
climate change the potential violators are everywhere.

The sober truth may be that the climate will change as it has for 400,000 years. Adjustments to change are necessary as is conservation of resources, but the best computer models are incapable of accurate protections. The many variables of climate change interact with one another. The end time of 2030 leaves unanswered questions—how measured, at what rate, probability of dissipation, lack of correlation between heat increase, and the accumulation of greenhouse gases. The possibility of adopting universal law, enforcing it down to the residence level, punishing violators, promises a Leviathan State to save us with no limit on its powers.

The world has become increasingly interdependent as world trade has dramatically increased with over 50% of all occupations tied to trade. Technological innovation continues to challenge most occupations. But the knot that remains to be cut is whether enforceable treaties that are mutually acceptable and not in the state's self-interest can be adopted and enforced.

It is possible that a commonwealth of democratic states that enforces treaties between them will supply the missing enforcement capability. Respect for religious liberty is one pillar of this order, as is the regional peace formula, previously stated. You have been offered ten others and will no doubt craft your own. Leadership by one country is required but success requires universal reciprocation.

The hope offered here is that recognition will lead you to develop a nonmilitary strategy of peace capable of addressing and changing determined adversaries as we, ourselves change. The concept of a Commonwealth would be strengthened by the maintenance of representative democracy where it exists now, clarity about what is required to maintain it such as acceptance of defeat in an election when certified by all 50 Secretaries of State, and the addition of members through nonviolent transitions toward democracy.

The obstacles to abolishing nuclear weapons are similar to those blocking climate change—no functional replacement as effective, the absence of enforceable treaties that apply to all and the likelihood that the country that first succeeds, will be intimidated by its fossil fueled adversaries.

Without war or surrender, these are ultimately the challenge any strategy of peace must face and surmount.

Appendix

List of Key Documents in the Archives

Documents related to Robert Pickus's life's work are archived in perpetuity in several locations. The Hoover Institution houses the major proportion of documents for the following organizations: Acts for Peace, Turn Toward Peace West Coast Regional Office, Northern California Regional Office of the World Without War Council and the World Without War Council, National Office as well as the James Madison Foundation. The Seattle regional office's papers are at the University of Washington Library, Seattle and the Hoover Institution. The Midwest office papers are archived at the Swarthmore Peace Collection as are the records of the American Friends Service Committee, and Turn Toward Peace National Office. Lowell Livezey, a Swarthmore graduate, has given his papers to the Swarthmore Peace Collection. George Weigel's records are at the Library of Congress. Access to the documents should be requested from each archive.

SELECT DOCUMENTS ARCHIVED

1. Woito, R. (2003). At stake in world politics. Hoover, Swarthmore.
2. Pickus, R. (1952). War and peace selection. In R. M. Hutchins & M. J. Adler (Eds.), *Great ideas II: A syntopicon of great books of the Western world*. Chicago: W. Benton.
3. Pickus, R. (1955, October). Summary of *Speak truth to power. The Progressive*.
4. Cary, S. (1955). *Speak truth to power*. Chairman of Working Group, American Friends Service Committee. Hoover, Swarthmore.

5. Woito, R. (1982). Definition of world politics that makes ending war a meaningful goal. In *To end war: A new approach to international conflict*. Hoover, Swarthmore.
6. Pickus, R., et al. (1961). Turn Toward Peace policy framework. Hoover, Swarthmore.
7. Pickus, R. (1961, 1992). Seven roads to a World Without War. Hoover, Swarthmore.

PREPARATION

8. Pickus, R. (1961). Self-survey: But what can I do? Staff. Hoover, Swarthmore.
9. Woito, R. (1971). This I can do: Twenty-five careers in world affairs. Hoover, Swarthmore.
10. Inspirational Quotes, compiled by Lucy Dougall, drawn selectively from her book *War and peace in literature*, Hoover, Swarthmore.
11. Blackman, A. (2011). Conscience and war. Hoover, Swarthmore.
12. Woito, R. (1981). 101 things you can do in a crisis. Hoover, Swarthmore.
13. Pickus, R. and Weigel, G. (1988). Typology of world affairs organizations. Hoover, Swarthmore.

CHANGING DETERMINED ADVERSARIES AS WE CHANGE OURSELVES

14. Pickus, R. (1965). Preface. In A. Camus, *Neither victims nor executioners* (D. MacDonald, Trans.). Hoover, Swarthmore. Original published in 1947.
15. Pickus, R. (1978). Obstacles to disarmament [speech]. NGO gathering at the U.N. Special Session on Disarmament. Hoover, Swarthmore.
16. Pickus, R. and Weigel, G. (1988). Advices and cautions to leaders of NGOs that would work for peace. Hoover, Swarthmore.
17. Minert, S. (1982). Evaluating a particular organization. Hoover, Swarthmore.
18. Pollack, M. (1982). Improving American competence in world affairs. Hoover, Swarthmore.

MEANS

19. Sharp, G. 198 non-violent acts. Hoover, Swarthmore.
20. Pickus, R. and Weigel, G. (1983). International human rights quotient: An organizational assessment tool. Hoover, Swarthmore.

21. Woito, R. (1967). Criteria to distinguish true from false Vietnam peace proposals. Hoover, Swarthmore.
22. Pickus, R. (1967). American initiatives to end the war in Vietnam. Hoover, Swarthmore.
23. Pickus, R. (1970). Context for work to end war. Hoover, Swarthmore.
24. Pickus, R. and Weigel, G. (1981). American initiatives project prospectus and memo to initiative writers. Hoover, Swarthmore.
25. Woito, R. (2003). Consolidated, transitional and thwarted democracies, plus dictatorships and twenty non-violent transitions toward democracy, 1974–2003. Hoover, Swarthmore.

COUNCIL INTENT, THE ACHIEVEMENT OF OTHERS

26. United Institute of Peace, 1984.
27. National Endowment for Democracy, 1984, Washington.
28. World Movement for Democracy, 1999, Washington.
29. Pickus, R. and Woito, R. (1996). Foreign policy perspectives. Hoover, Swarthmore.
30. The World Trade Organization, Geneva.
31. International Monetary Fund, Washington.
32. International Atomic Energy Agency
33. United Nations, New York.

FUTURE

34. Democracy roundtable discussion with Carl Gershman, president, NED, 1990. (1991). Hoover, Swarthmore.
35. Blantz, E. (1996). Twelve perspectives on global governance. Hoover, Swarthmore.

WORLD WITHOUT WAR PUBLICATIONS

• Egerer, K., Goodman, M., and Mary, T. (1991). Assembling the mosaic, a guide to greater Chicago world affairs organizations.
• Bloomfield, L. (1970). *The power to keep peace*.
• Camus, A. (1946). *Neither victims nor executioners*.
• Nuttall, G. (1971). *Christian pacifism in history*.
• Woito, R. (2003). *Extending the democratic peace*.
• Clark, G. and Sohn, L. (1983). Introduction. In *World peace through world law*.
• Blackman, A. (1967). *Face to face with your draft board*.

- Gandhi, M. K. (1972). *All men are brothers*. All quotes dated by Tim Zimmer.
- Mahadevan, T. K. (1971). *Gandhi, his relevance for our times*.
- Mahadevan, T. K. (1975). *The year of the phoenix*.
- Woito, R. (1967). *To end war: An annotated bibliography and literature list*.
- Pickus, R. and Woito, R. (1968). *To end war: An introduction to ideas, organizations, work that can help*.
- Pickus, R. and Woito, R. (1970). *To end war: An introduction to the ideas, books, organizations, and work that can help*. Harper & Row.
- Woito, R. (1982). *To end war, a new approach to international conflict*.
- Woito, R. (Ed.). (1967). Vietnam peace proposals.
- Stadler, A. (1972). The World Without War game. World Without War Council Seattle, 1972.
- Dougall, L. (1982). War and peace in literature: An annotated listing of 354 literary works.
- Dougall, L. (1980). *War/peace film guide, 1st Edition*. Dowling, J. (1980). *War/peace film guide, 2nd Edition*.
- Pollack, M. (1993). World affairs organizations in Northern California.
- Reidy, G. and Weigel, G. (1982). Washington's window on the world, a directory of world affairs organizations and institutions in Washington state.

SELECTED BOOKS BY STAFF

- Ruffin, M. H. (1994). *The post-Soviet handbook: A guide to grassroots organizations and internet resources*. Seattle: University of Washington Press.
- Weigel, G. (1987). *Tranquilltas ordinas: The current failure and future promises of Catholic thought on war and peace*. New York: Oxford University Press.
- Weigel, G. (1992). *The final revolution*. New York: Oxford University Press.
- Weigel, G. (1999). *Witness to hope*. Harpercollins.
- Uniform Reporting of Military Expenditures, Joseph Slovinka in consultation with Daniel Gallick, U.S. Arms Control & Disarmament Agency. (1985). Chicago: World With War Publications.

Bibliography

Acton, L. (1870). *The liberal interpretation of history.*

American Friends Service Committee, Working Party led by Steve Cary. (1955). *Speak truth to power: A Quaker search for an alternative to violence; a study of international conflict.* American Friends Service Committee.

Applebaum, A. (2017). *Red famine: Stalin's war on Ukraine.* New York: Doubleday.

Barber, B. (1984). *Strong democracy: Participatory politics for a new age.* Berkeley: University of California Press.

Baron, S. (1963). *Plekanov: The father of Russian Marxism.* Stanford: Stanford University.

Bernstam, M. and Rabushka, A. (2006). *From predation to prosperity: How to move from socialism to markets.* Washington, DC: Hoover Institution.

Bloomfield, L. (1972). *The power to keep peace, today and in a World Without War.* Berkeley: World Without War Publication.

Book of Mormon, Ama.

Brown, M., Lynn-Jones, S., and Miller, S. (Eds.). (1996). *Debating the democratic peace.* Boston: MIT Press.

Dallaire, R. (2004). *Shake hands with the devil: The failure of humanity in Rwanda.* Toronto: Random House Canada.

Dougall, L. (1982). *War and peace in literature.* Chicago: World Without War Publications.

Dove, T. (Ed.). (1970). *The law and political protest: A handbook of your rights under the law.* Berkeley: World Without War Publications.

Doyle, M. (1970). *Doyle's law: Liberal democracies do not war on each other.*

Fisher, L. (1950). *The life of Mahatma Gandhi.* New York: Harper & Row.

Freud, S. (1929). *Civilization and its discontents.* Internationaler Psychoanalytischer Verlag Wien.

Fussell, P. (1975). *The Great War and modern memory.* New York: Oxford University Press.

Gandhi, M. K. (1972). *All men are brothers.* Chicago: World Without War Publications.

———. (1940). *An autobiography: The story of my experiments with truth.* (Originally published 1927, 1929). Boston: Beacon Press.

Gershman, C. (1991). *Democracy transcendent: A discussion of universal democratic values.* Chicago: World Without War Publications.

Gide, A., et al. (1948). *The god that failed: Why six great writers rejected communism.* London: Hamilton.

Goldstein, J. (2011). *Winning the war on war: The decline of armed conflict worldwide.* New York: Dutton.

Hathaway, O. and Shapiro, S. J. (2017). *The internationalist: How a radical plan to outlaw war remade the world.* New York: Simon and Schuster.

Hawk, D. (2014). *The hidden gulag. The lives and voices of those who were "sent to the mountains."* New York: Amnesty International.

Hill, K. (1991). *The Soviet Union on the brink: An inside look at Christianity and glasnost.* Portland, OR: Multnomah Press.

Hollander, P. (1981). *Political pilgrims: Travels of Western intellectuals to the Soviet Union, China, and Cuba, 1928–1978.* New York: Oxford University Press.

Hook, S. W. (2010). *Democratic peace in theory and practice.* Kent, OH: The Kent State University Press.

Hutchins, R. M., et al. (1948). *A constitution for the world.*

Kahn, H. (1961). *On thermonuclear war.* Princeton, NJ: Princeton University Press.

Kissinger, H. (2015). *World order.* New York: Penguin.

Kriesberg, L. (2015). *Realizing peace: A constructive conflict approach.* New York: Oxford University Press.

Kriesburg, L. and Dayton, B. W. (2017). *Perspectives on waging conflict constructively: Cases, concepts, and practice.* Lanham, MD: Rowman & Littlefield.

Lewy, G. (1988). *Peace & revolution: The moral crisis of American pacifism.* Grand Rapids, MI: William B. Eerdmans Publishing Company.

Lipson, C. (2003). *Reliable partners: How democracies have made a separate peace.* Princeton, NJ: Princeton University Press.

Locke, J. (1689). *Second treatise of government.*

MacDonald, H. (2016) *The war on cops: How the new attack on law and order makes everyone less safe.* New York: Encounter Books.

Mackey, J. (Ed.). (1982). *Terrorism and self-determination: A tragic marriage we could help decouple.* Chicago: World Without War Publications.

Marx, K. (1880, 1892). *Socialism: Utopian or scientific.*

Mill, J. S. (1861). *On representative government.*

Mill, J. S. and Harriett. (1859). *On liberty.*

Moran, A. (Ed.). (2017). *Climate change: The facts.* Woodsville, NH: Stockade Books.

Morgenthau, H. J. (1978). *Politics among nations: The struggle for power and peace.* New York: Knopf.

Muravchik, J. (2002, 2003, 2019). *Heaven on Earth: The rise, fall, and afterlife of socialism.* New York: Encounter Books.

Pickus, R. (1991). Chapter 9. In K. Jensen and W. S. Thompson (Eds.), *New approaches to peace.* Washington: United States Institute of Peace.

———. (1969). Preface. In A. Camus, *Neither victims nor executioners.* Berkeley: World Without War Publications.

———. (1952). War and peace. In R. M. Hutchins and M. J. Adler (Eds.), *Great ideas II: A syntopicon of great books of the Western world.* Chicago: W. Benton.

Pickus, R. and Woito, R. (1970). *To end war: An introduction: Ideas, organizations, work that can help.* New York: Harper and Row.

Pinker, S. (2012). *The better angels of our nature: Why violence has declined.* New York: Penguin Group.

Powell, C. (2009). *American power and interventions from Vietnam to Iraq.* Lanham, MD: Rowman & Littlefield.

Power, S. (2002). *A problem from hell: America and the age of genocide.* New York: Basic Books.

Rice, C. (2017). *Democracy: Stories from the long road to freedom.* New York: Grand Central Publishing

Ruffin, H. (1999). *Civil society in Central Asia.* Seattle: University of Washington Press.

———. (1994, 1996). *The post-Soviet handbook: A guide to grassroots organizations and internet resources.* Seattle: University of Washington Press.

Rummel, R. J. (1997). *Death by government: Genocide and mass murder since 1900.* Abingdon, UK: Routledge.

Russett, B. (1994). *Grasping the democratic peace.* Princeton, NJ: Princeton University Press.

Sharp, G. (1994). *Dictatorship to democracy.* Massachusetts: Albert Einstein Institution.

———. (2005) *Waging nonviolent struggle: 20th century practice and 21st century potential.* Manchester, NH: Extending Horizons Books.

Stoner, K. and McFaul, M. (Eds.). (2013). *Transitions to democracy: A comparative perspective.* Baltimore, MD: Johns Hopkins Press.

Snyder, T. (2010). *Bloodlands.* New York: Basic Books.

Swanson, D. (2016). *A global security system: An alternative to war.* Charlottesville, VA: World Beyond War.

Tate, M. and Jones, M. D. (2014). *Democratic peace theory.*

Tatro, M. (Ed.). (1991). *Assembling the mosaic: A guide to the world affairs field in Chicago.* Chicago: World Without War Publications.

Thucydides. (ca. 411 BC). *The history.*

Trotsky, L. (1930). *Permanent revolution.*

Waltz, K. (1942). *Man, the state, and war: A theoretical analysis.*

Weigel, G. (1987–1995). *American purpose.*

———. (1989). *Tranquillitas ordnis: The current failure and future promise of American Catholic thought on war and peace.* New York: Oxford University Press.

———. (2010). *Witness to hope.* New York: Oxford University Press.

Wilson, E. (1959). *To the Finland station.*

Woito, R. (2003). *Extending the democratic peace.* Chicago: World Without War Publications.

———. (1982). *To end war: A new approach to international conflict.* New York: Pilgrim Press.

Wright, Q. (1942). *A study of war.* Chicago: The University of Chicago Press.

Index

About the Author

Robert Woito was born in the Midwest, raised in Iowa, and graduated from Grinnell College in 1960. He spent three years in the United States Air Force, was honorably discharged, and received a PhD in history in 1975 from UC Berkeley. He worked for the World Without War Council, both in the national office in Berkeley (1964–1973) and in Chicago (1974–2006), leading the Council's Midwest office (1982–2006). He edited *Vietnam Peace Proposals* (1967), coauthored *To End War* (1970), and edited the *International Human Rights Kit* (1975). In addition, he was published in the *Wilson Quarterly* "Between the Wars" (1985), edited the modern Classics of Peace series (1975), and wrote *Extending the Democratic Peace* (2003). He contributed "Pacifism, Critical" to Oxford University Press's Encyclopedia of Peace (2019), edited by Nigel Young. He also conducted the Peace Intern program in Chicago with more than fifty distinguished graduates, many of whom became world affairs professionals with other organizations including Gene Sharp's program on Nonviolent Sanctions at Harvard, the Stinson Center, and the Department of Defense. Wes Kriebel, retired Foreign Service Officer, lent realism to the program.

www.ingramcontent.com/pod-product-compliance
Lightning Source LLC
Chambersburg PA
CBHW022318280326

41932CB00010B/1150